# COUNTER-ATTACK!

## Also by Peter Hanson

The Joy of Stress

Stress for Success

# Peter G. Hanson M.D.

# COUNTER-ATTACK!

## The JOY OF STRESS Action Plan for Gaining Control of Your Life and Health

Stoddart

First published in 1993 by
Stoddart Publishing Co. Limited
34 Lesmill Road
Toronto, Canada
M3B 2T6
(416) 445-3333

**Canadian Cataloguing in Publication Data**
Hanson, Peter G. (Peter George), 1947-
Counterattack! The Joy of Stress action plan for
gaining control of your life and health

Includes index.
ISBN 0-7737-2708-6

1. Diet. 2. Cookery. 3. Stress (Psychology).
I. Title.

RM219.H3 1993 641.5'63 C93-093153-X

Printed and bound in the United States of America

NOTE: The information contained in this book is presented as a guide.
For specific medical problems, consult your physician

*Stoddart Publishing gratefully acknowledges the support of the Canada Council, the
Ontario Ministry of Culture, Tourism, and Recreation, Ontario Arts Council, and Ontario
Publishing Centre in the development of writing and publishing in Canada.*

*To my wife, Sharilyn, who has had to do double parenting duty during my many road trips, and who continues to be my best adviser and partner. Without her support and counsel, I never would have been able to find the time to write this book. I am indebted to her pluck in moving to Colorado, and for creating such a good home life for our three children, Kimberley, Trevor, and Kelly.*

# Contents

# Acknowledgments

Book writing is lonely, but no book is written alone. I am indebted to Matie Molinaro, my agent, for introducing me to Jack Stoddart, Don Bastian, Angel Guerra, and the rest of the team at Stoddart Publishing. I am also grateful to my editor, Anne Holloway, and copy editor Maryan Gibson, for their speed, efficiency, and advice in polishing my manuscript. Back at the ranch, Allan Benson and his partner Brenda Palmer have been of inestimable help in setting up my office, and in setting up a fantastic team. My office manager, Laura Willard, has successfully juggled the urgent demands of our publishing deadline with our patient scheduling, and has gone more than the extra mile in the process. Our entire office staff, Marian, Ann, Tracie, and Heather, has exhibited great patience and assistance in looking after our patients, while finding time to run photocopy errands, print out my computer diskettes, and man the fax lines. I am also indebted to my patients, many of whom have reviewed selected passages from the manuscript, and given me good advice about its content.

I am particularly indebted to Pat Bowlen, the owner of the Denver Broncos football club, for having confidence in my medical abilities. His decision to bring his ailing quarterback to me for an acupuncture treatment was indeed going against the grain of traditional mindsets. I am also indebted to John Elway for telling the public that his throwing arm was rescued by my treatment. His comments have given new hope to thousands of pain sufferers of all ages, and have elevated the perception of medical acupuncture by both the public and by my fellow doctors.

I am also grateful to Porter Memorial Hospital for encouraging me to come to Denver, and for helping me establish my Peak Performance Center in their new wing. John Gardner, their Head Marketing Guy (as it says on his cards), has been of great help in defining marketing strategies, and in sending me out to visit the MacDougall clinic in California for a week. I have also been helped by our hospital librarian, Robin Waters, who has fed me regular batches of journal articles and book searches. Joelle Elliston has been a terrific teacher, and has contributed her expertise and experience in crafting many of the recipes included in this book.

I have also been fortunate to meet some of the brightest minds in the new wave of vegetarian work. Peter Burwash of the PBI Tennis corporation, was the first to introduce me to the wisdom of vegetarianism. John MacDougall was a gracious host at his program at St. Helena's Hospital, and he and his staff were superb teachers and role models for healthy eating. John Robbins and I enjoyed working together in Maui, and in sharing our insights between speeches. Michael Clapper, M.D., has also been of great help to other doctors in educating them about the connection between diet and disease, and I have greatly enjoyed sharing ideas with him.

I am also grateful to my parents, George and Donna, who continue to lead active healthy lives. and who have been most anxious to try the new recipes included in this book. While they made delicious meals for my sister Penny and me during our childhood, they are proving to be remarkably flexible in trying new foods. It is my ambition to reach sixty-five and be able to show them both my old-age security card during a game of golf.

To others too numerous to mention here, I extend my warmest thanks. I think of you every time I sit down to type.

# Introduction

When I first came up with the title *Counterattack!*, I was thinking of the checkout counter at drug and grocery stores, and of the food counter at a dinner or restaurant. For make no mistake about it, there is a battle waged at the counter every time we shop or dine. The weapons are the products we are putting into our bodies. Victory lies in choosing the right ones, those that make us strong, resilient, and healthy. Defeat comes when we choose the wrong products, those that make us fall asleep on the job and stay awake all night and, as an added insult, shorten both the quality and quantity of our lives with diseases.

The nature of this battle at the counter is not of a traditional Napoleonic confrontation, where both sides could clearly see their enemy on opposite sides of the field before they engaged. This modern battle is much more along the lines of a chronic guerrilla confrontation, where the enemy is disguised and dangers lurk in even the most innocent of scenes. It is the purpose of this book to help illuminate the shadows, reveal the plots and the subterfuge, and empower the reader to recognize friend from foe.

To begin with, I expose the prevention myth, and the reasons health-care costs are threatening every democracy in the Western world. We will see why it is pointless to throw more money at old mindsets, and why the only hope lies in a reformed and informed consumer. Once the reader realizes the extent to which he or she has been duped by the "system," he or she will become outraged and compelled to make some changes in buying habits. In the same way that an entire system of government can be changed by a single vote, the system of health care can be changed by a single consumer, armed with the right information and taught how to change old habit patterns.

Chapter 2 reveals the extent to which we are slaves to the images formed on the right sides of our brains. In some cases, these images are born of our own experiences, but most of the time these images are contrived for us by modern advertising and marketing campaigns. This institutionalized form of brainwashing is well disguised, not as blatant but just as effective as Orwell's "Big Brother." It leads the public into collective bad lifestyle habits, and these can be reversed only by the active participation of individuals. Once the plot is exposed, the solutions are remarkably simple, and quickly become a part of one's new lifestyle.

In chapters 3 and 4, the reader will learn everything about food he or she should have been taught in school. The values of vegetarianism and the dangers of a high-fat diet are revealed, and the reasons behind each food choice explained. In Chapter 5, the question of obesity, our number-one affliction in North America, is discussed. The reader will be able to see through the fog of diet scams and select a foolproof plan to eat more and weigh less.

In Chapter 6, "hazards lying in ambush" are revealed. Just like the fabled Trojan Horse, enemies often come in friendly disguises. By the same token, consumable products we may have thought to be bad for us can turn out to be harmless, even beneficial. Sometimes the answers lie in the fine print on the label, but often the truths are not even listed. In Chapter 7, the impact of modern stresses on our lifestyle is discussed. It is not the stress that gives us trouble, but rather the poor choices we make in the face of it. While the contrasts are often comic, the results of good choices have most important consequences for us all.

In Chapter 8, we will see the value of exercise. Once part of our ancestors' daily job descriptions and lifestyles, the advance of technology has cleverly faded exercise out of our lives. Now we need to think about how our bodies should move, and how to practise "safe sports."

In Chapter 9, the netherworld of alternative medicine is brought under the microscope. In an age when our so called traditional medicine is dehumanizing the nature of the medical encounter, and when 60% of our lavish health-care budget is spent in the last six weeks of patients' lives, we need to open our eyes to some alternatives. Our medical schools give us only four options for patients: drugs, injections, surgery, and if these fail, the admonition to "just put up with it." From the menu of alternative solutions, cOme a few more options. At the same time, the reader will be able to spot charletan treatments, as well, from both traditional and alternative practitioners.

In the final chapter, the reader will find some of the best recipes around. Some come from our heart disease reversal program at Porter Hospital in Denver, and others from the alpine cuisine of the hotel and spa at Telluride, Colorado. The reader will easily be able to create tasty meals and healthy snacks that fill the stomach and fit the budget.

In the end, as in the beginning, the battle at the counter all comes down to the individual's power of choice. To reach victory, the reader has only to use this book as a guide through the mine field of consumer foods. Our lives will be enriched in matters of energy, humor, performance, and relationships once we wake up to the simple threats around us and begin our counterattack.

> DR. PETER G. HANSON M.D.
> July 25, 1993
> *Denver*

1

# An Ounce of Prevention

W E ARE LIVING in an age of transition, in which we see the old values and habits of our parents becoming outmoded, and the individual's sense of control being overtaken by events. A generation ago, it only took one wage earner to support the family, pay the mortgage, and send the kids to university. Futurists in our parents' era envisioned that life by the turn of the twenty-first century would be a wonder of leisure, with people working a mere twenty-hour week, and filling up their four-day weekends with sports and hobbies. This utopian picture has been dashed by reality. As the millennium comes to a close, it is clear that something is wrong. The miracles of laborsaving technology have come to fruition as predicted, but the lot of the mortals who use it has not lived up to expectations.

Instead of feeling in charge of our lives, we see that the average home is beyond the budget of the single-income family. Instead of fewer people working shorter hours, we have doubled the work force to include women. At the same time, the increasing taxes we all pay have forced many into working extra hours, or taking on extra jobs in a "moonlighting" economy. A whole generation of school kids comes home to an empty house, and sits down to watch an average of five hours of bloodshed, drug abuse, and irresponsible sex on television every night (and that's just the ads). Absent parents cross the country on business, or work the night shift, but even all this frenetic effort does not guarantee job security. Now that satellites and computer technology can bounce messages around the globe as easily as down the hall, we see our manufacturing jobs being exported to third-world countries, where wages are a small fraction of ours. Even if our jobs are not exported, our company could be merged or streamlined, and our jobs made redundant. The individual is becoming a mere pawn, and a frightened one at that.

On the health-care front, our expectations are also being dashed. A few short years ago, the medical staff of the World Health Organization wiped out the first infectious disease in history, as the last smallpox case was isolated in Somalia. Headlines speculated that this was the beginning of a new trend: diseases would be systematically wiped out by our modern medical miracles. Instead, we now have new diseases like the killer AIDS, and old diseases like TB making a deadly comeback with new drug-resistant strains. A hundred years after Pasteur and Lister demonstrated the dangers of bacteria, we read headlines of children dying from contaminated hamburgers served in fast-food chains. Not a day goes by that the media don't frighten us with tales of impending doom.

Against this background of health threats comes a gaggle of sham artists, all espousing their own specious "cure," most no better than the snake oil sold by hucksters a century ago. Even the medical "establishment" is not without its bad press. We read of doctors who overprescribe, surgeons who overoperate, and patients who overconsume medical services. In the meantime, we are fed lies and half-truths by special-interest food lobbies and are duped by drug companies that want us to reach for their products every time we are feeling out of sorts. Big Government has not protected us, and in fact has squandered our children's future standard of living in order to buy our votes. Big Medicine has not protected us, in spite of skyrocketing costs. Big Food Business reports escalating profits while making products that contribute to poor health and environmental degradation.

Instead of feeling secure and at ease, our supposed "leisure generation" is feeling frightened and frustrated by a lack of control over the most essential aspects of life.

## "I'm Mad as Hell, and I'm Not Going to Take It Anymore"

Politicians and the media are treating us like the three little pigs, trying to protect us from the mythical wolf at the door. In the meantime, no one is noticing the real threat: that our houses are being attacked by termites. If we continue to focus all our media and government resources on the wrong enemy, we are doomed to predictable failure. Our enemy today is not an outbreak of stress, nor is it a crisis in health care. Our *real* enemy is incompetence in the choices we are making in our daily lifestyles. My mission in writing this book is to provide the means and the information to reverse this pattern and relocate control where it belongs — with the individual.

Most people are intelligent, but they are being denied critical information. Most people are motivated, but they are being misled by powerful special-interest groups. Most people are determined to survive, but they are being denied the tools to change lifestyle habits. It's high time we put an end to this nonsense and simplify the fight for our lives. *Counterattack!* was written to expose the myths and reveal the hidden dangers we face, and to empower the individual to fight back.

In this book, I reveal the hidden dangers that lurk in ambush, either in the fine print on food labels, or in supposedly "healthy" foods that come with no labels at all. The reader will be shocked to see the simplicity of the imagery that manipulates our habits of consumption, and the ease with which these can be exploited by special-interest groups for their own gains. The reader will also be delighted to find out that once this multibillion-dollar advertising scheme is exposed, the informed individual can fight back as effectively as David against Goliath.

It's not as if there is anything to be gained by ignoring these subversive threats to our well-being. Not only do they jeopardize our health and our longevity, they threaten our performance on the job. In a time when companies and government employers are slashing the payrolls, anyone wanting to hang on to his or her job needs to know how to eat the right foods to stay alert during the day, how to effectively unwind at night, how to exercise safely, and how to keep from getting sick.

On a grander scale, the benefits of individual empowerment translate into a major economic force. Considering that it is no longer our defence budgets that are bankrupting our economies in the post-Cold War era, but rather our health-care costs, any program that reduces the incidence of heart attacks, cancers, automobile accidents, and work accidents is going to save us all a lot of money. A quick look at the budget deficits of the countries of the Western world reveals that not only have we been blowing all our money on medical cures for unnecessary and usually self-induced diseases, but we have also blown all our children's money, robbing them of the chance ever to attain our standard of living. The answer is not to try to trim a couple of percentage points from the health-care budget, but to shake up the whole way we have been looking at the problem. If we ask ourselves the wrong question ("How can we reduce the costs of modern health care?"), we will get the wrong answer ("Keep doing things the same way as we have, only increase taxes or insurance premiums to pay for it"). This is a modern exercise in futility, equivalent to shuffling the deck chairs on the *Titanic* as it sinks beneath the sea.

If, on the other hand, we can ask the right question — "How can we empower the individual to make informed choices to *prevent* disease?" — then the answer becomes at once possible and affordable: we simply need to give our heads a shake and change the way we have been viewing the challenges in our lifestyle. To continue to fund billions of dollars' worth of operations and treatments that never need to happen is folly. Not only does it bankrupt our health-care budgets, but it spills over into the rest of our economy as well. Companies are shying away from hiring extra employees and would rather pay overtime to current employees, just to avoid the burden of extra health-care expenses. As a result, unemployment is higher than it need be, lessening the base of taxpayers. Industries are looking to relocate their operations in third-world countries not only because labor is cheaper, but because our health care is unaffordable. This sends a chain reaction into our social structure, leaving many youth without hope for a job, and with crime as their only career. As the crisis in "health care" (read "incompetence") escalates, whole countries become uncompetitive, and whole populations feel the effects in their after-tax paychecks, even before it is their turn to get sick from their own self-induced diseases.

The *Counterattack!* plan will also address the issue of ecology, proving that the diverse goals of improved personal health, national prosperity, and global ecology can be addressed by the same simple approach. It's a complete win-win-win deal all around. Where's the catch? There isn't one. All it takes is for the informed reader to start with the right choices for his or her own body. By shaking off some of our old ways of viewing our lives, and finding the joy in new lifestyle habits, we can all be partners in a change that transcends the hollow promises of self-serving politicians and lobbyists, and unites us for the common good.

## Turning Back the Lemmings

North Americans are experiencing a health-care crisis. We are spending the majority of our health-care dollars during the final two months of life. We need urgently to reverse this trend and do more to keep people from getting avoidable illnesses. Delivering top-dollar health care at the bottom of the lemming cliff is bankrupting us, and still more waves of lemmings are hurling themselves needlessly — and expensively — over the edge. Prevention is the only thing that will stop them.

Demands for more prevention abound. There are TV specials, radio talk shows, print articles, and political speeches on the subject. There are multifarious government commissions to study the problem, trying to find out why we are so short on prevention, and so long on organ transplants. Insurance companies are scrambling to protect their turf as they sense government intervention in their fiefdom. Taxpayers anxiously look ahead, hoping for a quick fix, knowing full well who will have to foot the escalating bills.

The public turns for solutions to doctors and the medical infrastructure, insurance companies, governments, food companies — anyone who they hope will protect their families and their futures. Yet the sad truth is that the above institutions are not only unlikely to help, they are paid to continue the status quo and are roundly penalized for practising prevention. It is only by understanding this paradox that we can grasp the importance of empowering the individual to save his or her own life, and the lives of loved ones.

Let's take a look at the four entrusted groups that could be offering prevention, and see why they do not:

## Doctors

Right from the beginning there is a reason that doctors are not specialists in prevention. The admission requirements for medical school are usually driven by marks. If an applicant has perfect marks in biology, physics, and chemistry, he or she can be assured of a place in almost any medical school. While these marks may measure intelligence, surely one important criterion of being a doctor, they do not assess personality. There is little credit given in the screening process for communication skills, for being an athlete, for participating in school plays, for doing volunteer work, or for getting the joke. Yet the medical student is about to enter the one job that requires the most "people" skills of all.

---

### BREAKING THE PILL HABIT

A sixty-two-year-old gentleman presented himself in my office, having just moved to town. He was on a bagful of medications, costing him and his insurance company over $300 per month. He had pills for his blood pressure, then, because these pills caused potassium loss, was given potassium supplements. Because he couldn't sleep well, he also took pills for insomnia. Because these left him feeling groggy all the next day, he took iron pills, to build up his energy. Because these iron pills caused constipation, he took a stool softener. Because the stool softener caused cramps, he took an anti-spasmodic medication. Instead of feeling better for all these medications, he was feeling worse, although his blood pressure was fine. As part of my basic examination, I asked him about his diet, which turned out to be high fat and low fiber, with lots of meat. I suggested that he switch to my Ten-Step Counterattack! Diet Plan (see pages 87-88), which is 10–15% fat, vegetarian, with no dairy products, and start weaning himself off all his medications. At the end of the second week he came in to review his home blood-pressure readings, and to tell me he was now drug-free. His blood pressure had stayed down beautifully and he had more energy at home and at work. Another benefit: his monthly grocery bill was 25% less.

---

Once into medical school, the student learns little about prevention. Little time is spent observing doctors in the front lines of primary care, namely the busy family practitioners. Instead, emphasis is given to the highly technical world of the specialists. The University of Toronto (where insulin was discovered by Drs. Banting and Best) is representative of the best medical schools in the world and is on a par with Harvard. During my years there (I graduated in 1971), we had the finest professors, the most brilliant clinicians, and patients with rare disorders who had flown in from six continents. Indeed, many of the standard medical textbooks used around the world were written by our experts in anatomy, disease, and treatment.

We were trained (by the co-inventor of the cobalt bomb) to calculate the dose of radiation to cone into a lung cancer. Our surgeons taught us how to do a biopsy through a bronchoscope and how to remove a tumor and its lobe of the lung. Our hematologists showed us how to watch the blood counts for side effects during chemotherapy. All of the above was (and still is) world-class advice for the treatment of lung cancer — after the disease has already started.

Not once were we ever taught the words to say to a fourteen-year-old girl who smokes two packs of cigarettes a day. Not once were we taught how to motivate abstention in a middle-aged smoker who has just had a heart attack. Not once were we taught how to help stubborn patients abandon destructive lifestyle habits through behavioral and attitudinal changes. These are the best chances that we have to save lives in medicine, and we are ignoring them.

That's not to say that some medical-school deans are not introducing some elements of disease prevention into the modern curriculum, but overall medical education remains focused on learning about an ever-widening spectrum of diseases, and little time is left to ask what causes those diseases in the first place.

Once in practice, doctors quickly find that the system penalizes them for practising preventive medicine. Doctors are paid for givimg treatment *after* the disease starts, not for prevention *before* the disease begins. If a doctor sees six or seven cases of bronchitis an hour and simply writes out Amoxil prescriptions for each, he or she is more likely to be able to pay the office overhead and make a personal profit than if he or she spends that same hour trying to convince a patient to quit smoking. In socialized medical systems like Canada's the payment for such preventive counseling is less than the cost of the doctor's hourly overhead; in the United States private insurance companies often pay nothing for such counseling. So it doesn't take a rocket scientist — or a government commission — to figure out why doctors don't do more prevention. We are paying them not to!

When doctors do practise preventive medicine and are insufficiently paid for it, their efforts become "volunteer work" rather than prime sources of revenue. As physician incomes are being cut by new forms of managed health-care insurance in the United States, and by the failure of their earnings to keep pace with inflation in both Canada and the U.S., such doctors are less able to donate as much of their time to prevention as they would like; they still have to pay their bills, too. But experience shows that when doctors *do* counsel patients to change bad lifestyle habits, they are remarkably effective, in part because they already have a relationship with the patient, and also because they can paint a vivid picture of the consequences from their knowledge of other patients. If the system encouraged doctors to do more lifestyle counseling, through better training and financial incentives, we would see health-care costs plummet and public health soar.

## WHY DO CANADIANS LIVE LONGER THAN AMERICANS?

One of the most compelling arguments Americans have for adopting the Canadian system of state-run health care is that Canadians have a longer life expectancy than Americans. What these observers forget is that there are three other reasons for Canadian longevity that have nothing to do with the style of health-care insurance:

1. Canadians pay about twice as much for cigarettes as Americans currently pay, and as a direct result of these high prices (as well as a ban on cigarette advertising in Canadian media) smoke far less than their peers south of the border. Anyone who doubts the effect of cheap cigarette prices in encouraging young people to smoke should talk to Second World War veterans, who could buy cartons of cigarettes from their PX at a fraction of the normal price. Most became hooked and remained so even after the prices rose in civilian life.

2. Canadians have long enforced laws mandating automobile seat belts and motorcycle helmets, which have dramatically reduced deaths by accident, to the extent that organ transplant teams are experiencing a dearth of fresh donor organs.

3. Canadians are not permitted to carry handguns, which in the U.S. can turn any barroom fight or domestic quarrel into a bloodbath.

## Insurance Companies

If as CEO of a mega-holding company you bought a hypothetical airline with all brand-new planes, you could make yourself very popular among your shareholders. All you would need to do is stop all expenses for maintenance. Sure, the planes will eventually deteriorate and crash, costing your company millions, but by then you will be long gone into a comfortable retirement.

That is, unfortunately, the shortsighted reality that faces insurance companies. Why pay for smokers to attend smoking-cessation classes when their expensive lung transplants won't take place for a couple of more decades? Why pay for people with obesity or heart disease to learn how to cook, and how to shop for healthy foods, when their strokes or heart attacks won't happen for years? What really matters is the profit picture you carry into each quarterly meeting: investors are not impressed with programs that cost money now, but offer unquantifiable benefits in the distant future.

## Government

Governments have been so effectively lobbied by the pharmaceutical, insurance, hospital, and food and tobacco industries that their ability to take legislative and policy actions that favor prevention is acutely hampered. We reward our politicians by voting them in; they see no benefit in spending money now when the dividends will be accrued by future politicians. They would rather keep offering fatty foods to the poor through food stamps and school lunches (while accepting campaign contributions from meat and dairy lobbyists) than try to support the modest costs of public-education programs and tax breaks for people who sustain healthy lifestyle habits.

## The Food-Manufacturing Industry

The food industry isn't entirely malicious, but it is not in business to do good, just to do well. If company executives perceive that their customers want killer foods, it is their business only to see that the customer buys their particular brand. If they see their customers demanding healthy foods, they will be quick to respond in that direction. Similarly, Colombian drug lords say that if the American consumer craved turnips instead of cocaine, they would be smuggling turnips. Expecting the food companies to supply us with simple, healthy foods, while we continue to gobble up cheeseburgers and fries, is as unrealistic as a jungle rafter expecting to ward off piranhas by wearing a good-luck charm.

Prevention starts with you, dear reader. There are no institutions or government agencies that will ever have as much interest in *your* future as you do, and none that will protect you from the consequences of your own bad choices. It's up to *you* to take control, and to seek the information you need to safeguard your health. It's up to you to change the destructive and misleading mindset images manipulated by the special-interest groups and their advertising campaigns. It's up to you to protect your parents and your children, and yourself.

## The Ten-Step Counterattack! Action Plan for Fighting Back

### 1. Send a message to your insurance company.

Tell them you are fed up with having to pay the same rates as the truly high-risk people, the tub-chair potatoes who pig out on pork rinds, the two-martini lunchers, the substance abusers. Also tell your insurance company you want your doctor to be properly reimbursed for time spent on prevention of disease and follow-up visits for checkups. Remind them that it's a lot cheaper to do a mammogram than a mastectomy, and less costly to teach relaxation techniques than to treat a heart attack.

### 2. Speak to your politicians.

Why can't we deduct costs of prevention (health-club memberships, heart-healthy cooking classes, educational materials) from this year's income taxes? Why do governments insist on offering unhealthy foods to the poor? Why do they subsidize dairy, meat, and poultry industries, even to the extent of letting them chop down forests so they can plant vegetables we don't need to feed to animals we don't want?

### 3. Write your local grocery store.

Ask them for more organically grown produce and other healthy choices, if you find them in short supply. If you do find them in stock, make sure you buy them.

## 4. Write the food companies.

If enough of their customers request low-fat, high-fiber products, they will start to provide them.

## 5. Stand up for your rights at restaurants.

If you can't find any low-fat vegetarian choices, ask for them to be specially made. How can they tell you they are all out of "no meat"? If they do, tell them you would like "no chicken" instead. Can any pizza joint be out of "no cheese"? For fancier restaurants, phone ahead. If they can't do grilled vegetables, pasta, or other non-fat meals, go elsewhere. Most, in fact, will welcome the business and appreciate the advance warning.

## 6. Once you do get your healthy food, suggest that the restaurant offer it on their regular menu.

As their costs for ingredients are less, they stand to make even more money. It's already working at fast-food places like Burger King (baked potatoes), Taco Bell (plain bean burritos), and even McDonald's (veggie burgers, if you ask for a quarter pounder with extra lettuce and tomato, hold the mayo, hold the cheese, and hold the meat).

## 7. Speak to your local schools about the foods they serve our children.

Why is it that they serve so many meat and dairy products and deep-fried foods, yet make it difficult to find whole-wheat breads, vegetables, and other low-fat options?

## 8. Write to your school, college, and university about their curriculum.

Why isn't sound nutrition being taught to our children? Why are kids graduating into the work force without knowing which foods will sabotage their alertness on the job? Why are kids still being taught to eat a diet containing 30% fat when we know this level is dangerous? Why don't our kids learn which breakfast foods to eat before a stressful exam, or during a physically vigorous summer job? Why is home economics being cut from school curriculums?

### 9. Write to your local hospital.

Why do most serve greasy sausages to post-operative heart-attack patients? Why do they serve so much fat, lard, and grease in their cafeteria? Have they ever heard of whole-wheat bread? Why can't they at least make an effort to offer and identify good food choices for each course? Tell them you thought you were supposed to go to a hospital to get better, not to get sick.

### 10. Contact your travel agent and demand low-fat vegetarian foods on all your airplane trips.

Not only will you get an attractive meal or fruit plate (one that costs the airlines double the alleged "food" that they would have served instead), but you will be the envy of your seatmates. Refuse high-calorie snacks like peanuts, and instead, demand the pretzels (dust off the salt). Bring a large and ostentatious brown-bag meal if your airline refuses to accommodate you. They'll get the idea.

---

## ONE-STOP CHECKOUT

One of the most compelling advances in retail marketing is the "theme" shopping concept. I first noticed this when a new strip mall opened near our home, featuring a fried-chicken franchise right next door to an ice-cream parlor. Nice and handy: you can feed yourself a main course, then move just a few feet to find dessert, and *you don't even have to move your car.* A couple of years ago in Florida, I drove by another version of the theme mall, a grouping of three huge stores: one selling guns, the next selling live ammunition, and the third selling bandages. All this, and *you don't even have to move your car.* With today's trends in hospital budgets, many administrators are now turning over the cafeterias to commercial fast-food chains. Now you can eat in the hospital basement, filling your face with the fattiest of foods, then you can go up two floors to the cardiac operating room and have surgeons ream the Velveeta cheese out of your coronary arteries. All this and *you don't even have to move your car!*

---

*2*

# Imagining Your Way
# to Health

T ODAY WE SUFFER from a "time famine," while we are
simultaneously buffeted by the winds of change. In the
process, we are being ambushed by bad habits, made sick by
bad choices, and dying from the lack of information — ironical-
ly, in the midst of the Information Age. Our goal must be to
develop a strategy to protect ourselves from today's stresses
and to defend ourselves from preventable diseases, instead of
passively waiting for a breakdown in our health, then letting
the medical institutions decide our fate for us. As a first step
toward such a strategy it is illuminating to view our modern
lifestyle in its historical context.

## Hanson's Human History Minute

### PHASE 1: The Agricultural Era

For 100,000 generations human beings lived a primitive exis-
tence. Challenges were physical, and our salvation lay in the
"fight or flight" response to stress. These automatic reflexes,
carefully evolved over the millennia, are found in the lower

brain stem. None requires any awareness or active thought to function, and all could be activated in less time than it takes to blink an eyelid. Each of these reflexes was brilliant in response to the stresses of the day.

## PHASE 2: The Industrial Era

For ten short generations after the end of the Agricultural Era in the mid-eighteenth century, the Industrial Revolution changed our lives and forced us to rely on the left hemisphere of the brain. Now survival required the tools of instant recall and regimented behavior. Schools drilled facts into the left side of students' brains and demanded their recall at exam time. Bosses demanded that workers remember the rules to repair the assembly-line machinery and report for rigidly designated hours of work. With no reason to use primitive reflexes or creative thought, individuals were encouraged to follow the habits of their elders, to do things "the way things have always been done around here." These strategies were perfect for their (brief) time.

---

### THE BODY'S 12 NATURAL RESPONSES TO STRESS

1. Release of cortisone from the adrenal glands
2. Thyroid hormone increases in the bloodstream
3. Release of endorphin from the hypothalamus
4. Reduction in sex hormones
5. Shutdown of the digestive tract
6. Release of sugar into the blood and increased insulin levels
7. Increase in blood cholesterol
8. Racing heartbeat
9. Increased respiration
10. Thickening of the blood
11. Skin reactions: pallor, sweating
12. Heightened sensory responses

---

## PHASE 3: The Information Age

For the past *one* generation (since approximately 1971), we have lived in the Information Age, a new epoch that demands completely new strategies. If your neighborhood were threatened by an Information Age weapon, say, a computerized Scud missile, you would not want your defence left to the primitive spears and shields of the Stone Age, nor would you want to be armed with Industrial Age muskets. A sensible defence strategy would demand the latest Patriot missiles to offer a reasonable chance of survival.

In just the same way, the challenges of the Information Age demand that we come up with brand-new weapons, and for these we must turn to the right side of the brain. It is here that creativity and imagery are king. While Paul McCartney remembers the words to "Happy Birthday to You" in his left brain (as do we all), he makes his money creating new songs in his right brain. It is here that we find the paradigm, or mindset, that becomes the screen through which all left-brain facts must pass on their way to generating actions. If the images here are rigid, new facts won't get through, and new responses will be impossible.

Less than five hundred years ago, people still believed the sun revolved around the earth. When scientists like Copernicus and Galileo presented evidence to the contrary they were condemned by the church. Similarly, the flat-earth theory held for millennia, causing European rulers to order their ships to stay within the sight of land, for fear of falling off the edge. These now laughable theories were so entrenched in the right brains of the intellectual elite of the time that no new theories could be accepted.

It is precisely because we are in the era of rapidly changing information (entering our left brain) that we need to change our mindsets (in the right brain) to allow us to change our actions. Our grandparents were well served by the habits of their time, and our Neanderthal forefathers were well served by the reflexes of their bodies. We too could rely on these weapons if we faced their challenges. However, to face modern stresses like job insecurity, time famine, and information overload, we need to open all three avenues of change:

1. Process new facts ("knowledge") in the left brain
2. Replace outdated mindsets in the right brain
3. Develop new actions, skills, and habits.

## The Power of Imagery

The power of the right-brain image is clear when one compares the top-of-the-hill thoughts of two neophyte skiers, a three-year old and an adult. Such a scene occurred when our youngest daughter, Kelly, on the brink of her first run, stood beside a thirty-year-old man we'll call George, who was about to do the same. What George did not know was that Kelly had carefully prepared herself all summer by watching Warren Miller ski videos, and by wearing her miniature skis and boots around the house since her October birthday. Even though she was a mere three years old, she had a potently positive image of skiing implanted in the right side of her brain.

As both skiers paused to absorb the scene, into the left brain of each went the sounds of the chair lift, the touch of the wind hitting their faces from the west, the coolness of the snowflakes falling on their cheeks, the sights of skiers all around them, and the scent of pine. All this data had next to be screened through the mindset images on the right side of their brains. In Kelly's case, those images were of fun, of bending her knees and turning in the snow. In George's case, his right-brain image was of a hospital bed.

When they both pushed off and turned their images into actions, Kelly skied well, turning effortlessly, while George stiffened every limb and didn't turn at all (except when he careered off a hay bale and fell headfirst into a snowbank beside the parking lot). As he watched in amazement, Kelly skied through all the bits of his equipment that had been strewn down the hill, thinking she was skiing through a garage sale.

Afterwards, George joined us for a hot cider in the main chalet, and expressed his wish that he had started skiing when he was Kelly's age, because kids are so low to the ground they can't hurt themselves. I had to remind him of a simple medical fact: if an adult breaks a bone, it takes about six weeks for it to heal; if a child breaks a bone through a growth plate, it could take ten times as long to heal. So much for the myth of a child's invulnerability.

George missed the point by just two letters: the real difference in their performances was not their *ages*, it was their *images*. If Kelly had been imagining pain and suffering, she would have clung to her mother's ski jacket for dear life. If George had been imagining controlled turns, he would have been able to make his way down the hill quite safely.

Fixed mental images make people resistant to change. A mental image of being ridiculed in public prevents an adult from learning a new language. A mental image of being laughed at by secretaries keeps a boss from learning how to run a new computer. A negative image of healthy lifestyle choices keeps a smoker smoking, or a potential heart-attack victim spooning in triple hot-fudge sundaes.

The challenge today is not simply to feed more information into the left brain, but to remove the rigidly negative images in the right brain that block new habits. Let's begin our task by taking a look at the history of the image, and the power that it holds.

In the beginning, Primitive Man contrived to reproduce images of the animals he hunted on cave walls. These pictures served to establish a written culture and consoled hunters suffering through the slow seasons.

Gradually artistic images became more varied and more powerful in their ability to mold public opinion. The images on Michelangelo's Sistine Chapel ceiling inspired belief in the church's teachings; the gargoyles on the Cathedral of Notre Dame struck fear into the heart of the disbeliever. The images brought back from the New World by artists like Cornelius Krieghoff and Frederic Remington inspired generations of adventurous young people to risk Atlantic crossings to find new lives for themselves in North America. The imagery used to glorify war has long lured young men into going off to die or be maimed in old men's battles. In the First World War, recruiting offices on both sides of the conflict papered their respective countrysides with posters depicting the villainous enemy soldiers, juxtaposed with sappy scenes of mothers, children, and puppy dogs nervously anticipating invasion.

Be the cause noble or heinous, whole populations have been moved by the persuasive powers of imagery. In pre-war Germany, Hitler's propaganda minister Joseph Goebbels made brilliant use of images to incite hatred of the Jews, and to sweep Hitler into power. It was even the power of the image that gave Germany its excuse to start the Second World War, in September 1939. Goebbels arranged for civilian prisoners to be dressed in uniforms of the regular Polish army, then had them shot, both with bullets and with cameras, just inside the German border. Using these contrived images to show the world that they had been "invaded," Germany immediately launched a war that would claim over 50 million dead in the next six years. Once the war began, Goebbels continued to use images to manipulate millions of intelligent people beyond the bounds of reason. After all, what foot soldier would believe that a winter's march to Moscow was a good military move? On the other side of the battle, U.S. propagandists used images of the noble John Wayne defending Americans from humorless Japanese villains, while Nelson Riddle played patriotic music in the background. In Britain, it was Kenneth More and Jack Hawkins standing tall against the Hun, to the adulation of the most beautiful starlets in the film industry.

Every day, images broadcast by popular media like TV and movies inspire less dramatic human actions. Young boys act out their *Terminator* or *Star Trek* fantasies; young girls dress their Barbie Dolls and fantasize about being fashion models. I remember that when Davy Crockett rode the screen we all wore coonskin caps, no matter how hot the weather. The Beatles' manager, Brian Epstein, was a master of image manipulation. He arranged for thousands of pre-printed signs to be passed out to waiting crowds as the Fab Four stormed America in the early sixties. Succumbing to the choreographed hype, perfectly sensible girls and ladies degenerated into hysterical screaming and crying as soon as the music started.

While the Beatles did have phenomenal talent, even they were surprised by how quickly imagery brought them to the top. In an interesting experiment to isolate the role of imagery (without the talent) in creating mass hysteria, marketers reproduced the phenomenon with groups that did not write their own songs, could scarcely sing a note, and largely faked playing their own instruments. These *poseurs* would never have been successful if they had just released their music without the accompaniment of televised images. Witness the fiasco of the Milli Vanilli group: a multimillion-dollar campaign that made rock-video stars of two male models who lipsynced while real artists sang the vocals.

Simply put, in spite of being the most intelligent animal on earth, we are all real suckers for a seductive image. Television action heros and stunt drivers are never seen wearing seat belts, so a generation of macho drivers is manipulated into following suit, each leaving it up to his face to act as an air bag. When James Dean, Marlon Brando, and Arnold Schwarzenegger don't wear motorcycle helmets, their motorcycling fans mindlessly follow, ignoring the potential to become road pizza.

Even blatantly phony images exercise a potent attraction. Consider the difference between the mass appeal of World Wrestling Federation matches compared with the popularity of the true Olympic variation of the sport. People know the WWF wrestling is fake, and they know the Olympic wrestlers are finer athletes, yet millions turn out for the steroid-fed *poseurs*, while the real wrestlers grapple in empty stadia.

Today corporations around the world send their top employees on conventions, where they enthusiastically sport hats with company logos, participate in team-building challenges, and make group zoo noises. Political image-makers go to battle during elections, using images as their weapons. Even though the public may dislike many things about a particular candidate, they can be molded to vote for him or her anyway, after the spin-doctors implant a suitably positive image of their candidate in the voter's right brain. Few people today vote on just the issues. The power of the ten-second television image is so persuasive that many would not vote for a candidate with good ideas if she or he had some visible facial deformity, or was just plain ugly. (Abraham Lincoln would have ended his career as a political wannabe.) By the same token, if a candidate looks great (for example, John Kennedy), then the adoring public casts their vote in spite of misgivings.

## Advertising: Where Image Is King

Modern advertising is the master of the image, and nowhere more so than within the world of consumables. By this term I mean those products designed to enter the human body by being eaten, drunk, inhaled, applied on the skin, or absorbed through other orifices. Because these products enter the human body, any hidden agenda by the advertisers and producers has a great impact on the consumer. Among the most sophisticated and fiendish of image manipulators are the marketing gurus of the tobacco industry. These are the sleaze meisters who covered up evidence of thousands of smoke-induced deaths from lung cancer and emphysema for years, and who continue to spend millions for legal defences against any bereaved families who claim damages for the loss of their smoking loved one.

But the job of the cigarette marketer is no easy sell. Right from his or her first furtive puff of a cigarette, every teenager who has hidden in a locked bathroom with the window open knows the plain truth: smoking is asinine. It makes your eyes water, stomach heave, throat burn, tongue taste like Agent Orange, and clothes stink like moose fur. Not the sort of thing many would enjoy, were it not for advertising's powerful (right) brainwash and nicotine's addictive properties. More importantly, smoking causes lung and bronchial cancers, and kills hundreds of people each day with heart attacks. The victims are not only the smokers, but anyone who lives or works in the same building, or, in the case of pregnant mothers, the babies inside their wombs.

Young smokers know all this, and they feel all the signs of rejection from both their left brain and their organs, and yet they persist in this deadly habit. Why? Because of the power of the right-brain image to encourage wrong-headed choices. Not one cigarette ad has ever been directed at the left side of the consumer's brain ("No, our cigarettes don't really cause all *that* much cancer"). All tobacco ads are targeted to create unrealistic mindsets or paradigms in the right brain, strong enough to with-stand the counter-arguments of reason.

Let's examine some of these cunning ads. Now we know these smokers all have bad breath and reek of fumes so strong that their sports jackets could set off the overhead sprinkler sys-tem. But just look at them. Nary a loser to be found. All faces are wrinkle-free in spite of smoking's tendency to cause pucker lines and to age the skin. All bodies are handsome, and every-one is accompanied by a sexy companion; nobody is ever short of breath, and everyone else looks as if they are enjoying the second-hand smoke wafting up their noses.

It is of interest to note that tobacco industry lobbyists con-stantly maintain that their ads are not intended to entice new smokers; they're only "to get existing smokers to change their brands." But in countries like Singapore, where cigarette ad images are forbidden on the air, in print, or even on signs and posters, smoking has fallen dramatically, to less than 16%. In countries like neighboring Thailand, China, and Japan, where cigarette images abound, smoking booms.

While there are at least some restrictions on tobacco advertis-ers, the food industry, whose products are in some cases as lethal as tobacco, practises its deceptions largely unfettered. The Great American Food Machine has been working on us since birth and has been so successful in stenciling images into our right brains that we actively resist changing any of our food habits, no matter what new evidence is revealed. Using the most sophisticated of propaganda techniques, the Food Machine hires high-rent huck-sters and overpaid celebrities to sell their products, no matter what the consequences to their customers' bodies. While some of their food products are healthful, the sad reality is that the most profit is in the unhealthy food choices. That's why there is more money to be made having a sports star push candy bars than boiled potatoes. With so many billions of dollars at stake, the special food interests hire the best image-makers and role models to mold our right-brained paradigms, starting at the earliest possible age and keeping at us until we (often) kill ourselves with a knife and fork. Remember, these companies may have nice people working for them, but they are not paid to be interested in your long-term health; they are paid to look after their short-term profits.

## THE FOOD WHEEL OF FORTUNE

In school, we were all taught about the four basic food groups: meats, dairy, grains, and fruits/vegetables, each representing a quarter of the wheel. No meal could be complete without having half your plate covered with steaks, ham, chicken, or fish, along with cheese, a glass of whole milk, butter on your potato, then ice cream for dessert. In fact, in the United States, it is currently a government policy to give farmers artificial incentives to produce fatty foods that the market doesn't need, then fob them off on our children and our poor in the name of food stamps or cafeteria lunches at schools. In times of famine in parts of the world, we ship off some of this surplus milk and various meat proteins to be fed to starving children who often cannot digest it, and who frequently end up sick with diarrhea.

Parents who graduated with this food wheel imprinted on their right brains are programmed for life and will feel guilty if their children do not receive "enough protein" in the form of meats, milk, cheese, or eggs on their plates.

What we are not told is that the food wheel was the product of a plot by special-interest groups, especially meat and dairy producers, to have their foods given disproportionate representation. Against the interests of all these special interests, scientific fact is beginning to overcome marketing fiction. The result is that we now have a more truthful dietary model, the food "pyramid." In this model, healthy proportions are finally in balance. Fats and rich desserts are at the top, in the smallest amounts, while whole grains, fruits and vegetables make up the much wider base. The only thing missing is water, of which eight to ten glasses a day should be consumed.

In Canada, there is the new food "rainbow," which is a different graphic representation of the same message the pyramid gives.

---

Consumers are finally resisting the passive feeding reflex, where shopping choices become a passive extension of advertising images. People know they are being duped, and they know they need more information to make the right choices.

As a simple economic premise, the farther a food product is from its natural state (and the higher up the food chain), the more money the industry makes as profit. That's why a tube of squeezable Day-Glo cheese will be more widely advertised than plain brick cheese, and why we see so many ads for french fries and so few for the plain potato. When breakfast meals are advertised on Saturday morning cartoon shows, they are more likely to show candied, frosted, and puffed lumps of food additives than plain oatmeal porridge. Snack ads sell fruit-flavored roll-ups, but rarely real fruit.

Once kids get hooked on the high sugar and fat loads, the greasy cheeseburgers, and tasteless white breads that are so bad they need the adornment of fats like butter or margarine, they grow up to be adults with mindsets that resist new habits. Even if adults discover that candy bars are fatty, they might still seek one out every time they are depressed, because candy was used as a positive reward when they were children.

The Great American Food Machine does not let up on us once we reach adulthood. Now we are the targets of beer ads that show bare midriffs, but never a beer belly; cola ads that never show facial pimples or tooth decay; and fast-food ads that never have obese diners. We are not told to buy these products because they satisfy basic needs like hunger or nutrition (the left-brain approach), but because we will feel like losers if we don't step in and "join the party" (the right-brain approach). The price of admission is that you must use these products. In other words, drink our beer so you will be more attractive to the opposite sex; drink our cola so you will be "cool"; buy our candies because you love your children; and eat our burgers because you have a hectic schedule and "deserve a break today." By implication, these images tell us that those who don't swallow the bait will be impotent, lonely, crotchety, and depressed.

## Rebrainwashing Made Easy: The Kid-with-the-Crayon Principle

Given that the advertised image is so powerful and well financed it would seem hopeless for a single individual to resist it, the human spirit should not be underestimated. American prisoners of war in North Vietnam, tortured and locked in cramped dark cells for years, kept their sanity by using mental imagery to build a house, board by board, or to replay all of Mozart's piano music, note by note. Even though their senses were daily bombarded with the smells, tastes, touches, sights, and sounds of endless suffering, their own humble counter-images gave them hope.

It is to overcome the tremendous advantages of size and scale enjoyed by advertisers that the individual needs to be empowered to come up with counter-images to regain control of his or her own body. An incident from my childhood illustrates how easily a counter-image can reverse earlier perceptions. While I was still in elementary school in Vancouver, the young Queen Elizabeth came to town for a post-coronation visit, and a poster at the back of the classroom of Her Majesty in full regalia proclaimed the event. One day, when our teacher had ducked out of the room, one of my friends could resist this target no longer. A furtive glance to make sure the coast was clear, a few deft strokes, and presto: Her Majesty now sported a goatee, mustache, glasses, and big ears. In a few moments, the carefully crafted image of pomp and splendor was converted into one of silliness.

When the Queen did parade through Vancouver a few weeks later, I stood at the curbside, not five paces from Her Royal Highness. She might have wondered why one six-year-old in the crowd had such a daft grin; all I could think was that she looked a lot better without the goatee.

That's all it takes to fight back against the vast American Food Machine: a few deft strokes of the editorial pen can change the most appetizing images to revulsion and turn the product from a "must have" to a "who needs it" item. At my Peak Performance Clinic at Porter Hospital in Denver, I have found this relabeling exercise to be most amazing part of any diet process. One patient complained that he could do without his ice cream, but he really missed the taste of his cigarettes. I suggested he might lick an old ashtray, at which he positively blanched. His dream of the perfect smoke was effectively shattered by an ugly image.

Let's take a look at some popular images that have been drilled into our subconscious minds and see how we might change their impact with a few words.

| | Old Caption | New Caption |
|---|---|---|
| Breakfast muffin | Great start to the day | Lard puck |
| Hot dog | Take Me Out to the Ball Game | Processed Animal Lips |
| Southern fried chicken | Just like Mom used to make | Greasy Bird Lumps |

Got the idea? Then when you're about to eat the following items, try out some new names:

| | New Caption |
|---|---|
| Donut | Blubber-bagel |
| Cheeseburger | Orange-colored cow cookie |
| Ice-cream float | Cellulite barge |
| French fries | Grease-Dipped sponge sticks |
| Oysters/shrimp/clams | Sewage-filters for Boston Harbor |
| Thousand Island salad dressing | Pastel-colored oil slick |
| Chocolate bars | Jodhpur-filling thigh fat |
| Butter | Butt-builder |
| Chocolate mousse | Brown jowl wobbler |
| Bacon | Porky Pig's love-handles |
| Veal | Bovine child abuse |
| Cheesecake | Bustle-stuffing rump-raiser |
| Steak and kidney pie | Diced autopsy specimens |
| Steak tartar | Salmonella City |

Now let's start to override the nonsense of advertising with a little inside information that will help you more effectively resist bad habits. For example, let's consider the thoracic duct, a two-foot-long tube with the diameter of a drinking straw that drains all the lymph from around the intestines, leading it up toward the chest. Half an hour after a fatty meal, such as a cheeseburger, fries, or a milk shake, it quietly fills with creamy white fat globules and quietly carries them north, through the diaphragm, past the lower lungs, and in front of the esophagus. There the thoracic duct enters the subclavian vein, a couple of inches from the heart. Once in the ventricles, this greasy oil slick of cholesterol is then pumped into the fast-moving bloodstream, to end up lining every vessel in the body, coating every blood cell with a sticky shell, and sludging the flow of blood in every capillary.

The blood itself is a mixture of both solids and liquids. An hour after a blood sample is drawn, it will settle into its two fractions: the packed red blood cells will sink to the bottom, and the clear straw-colored serum will float on top — that is, unless you have eaten that cheeseburger and fries within the past thirty minutes; now, courtesy of the thoracic duct, the clear serum is completely clouded, the consistency of a vanilla milk shake. With every meal and every snack, the fat we eat courses up through our thoracic duct to pour its deadly pollution into our arteries. Is it any wonder that hardening of the arteries and heart disease are unknown in societies that eat low fats, and are endemic in North America? This clogging process can be observed in North American children as young as six years old!

Now, when we see the image of gooey chocolate layer cake à la mode, we can visualize the thoracic duct and its polluting oil spill and think to ourselves: *white death*. It sort of gives new meaning to desserts that are said to be "to die for."

The point of this re-imaging is not just to turn us off the bad foods, but to reverse the bad images we have ascribed to good ones. For example, let's take a look at the following images, and the connotations they most likely evoke:

| | Traditional Image | New Image |
|---|---|---|
| **Vegetarian** | pale, skinny body, eats only rabbit food, no fun, poor | Carl Lewis, Monica Seles. Lots of fun, great body, rich |
| **Exercise** | workout: sweat, showers smelly sneakers, wrecked hairdo, dirty laundry | play: running for a pass, swinging a bat, biking through a lush countryside |
| **Low-fat diet** | a plate with a sprig of parsley, a carrot, some lettuce | plates piled high with colorful, tasty helpings of food |

# 3

# Everything You Should Have Learned in Kindergarten

**W**HOOMPH!!! The explosion ripped through the tunnel like a tidal wave. A wall of flames rocketed along the shaft, consuming everything in its path. Indiana ran as fast as his straining legs could carry him. His arms pumped furiously, his feet pounded the uneven stone floor. He could see a small circle of daylight dead ahead, growing larger. A hundred yards to go. Faster. The heat of the advancing flames seared the back of his neck, and he could feel the air being sucked out of his lungs. Just another forty yards. He stumbled, and careered off the left wall, but somehow kept moving. Ten more paces. Five. Now! He dove headfirst for the soft ground outside, like a baseball player stealing home. He never heard the sound of his landing, because the tunnel entrance collapsed behind him with a roar, covering him in an avalanche of stones, soot, and smoke.

The hot African sun beat down as he dragged himself to his feet and assessed his body for damage. He wiped at his right eye with the back of his wrist, and coughed as he tried to catch his breath. His mouth tasted like zoo dust, and his tongue was as dry as a pinecone. His heart was pounding like a hammer inside his heaving rib cage, and his hat was soaked with sweat. His clothes were in filthy shreds, and his left sleeve was caked in blood, but he could still move his arm. Every muscle ached, and his skin felt numb from all the scrapes and cuts, but his luck had held. Miraculously, nothing was broken, and he was still alive. So far.

There was no time to waste. They would chase him to the ends of the earth to retrieve the sacred emerald in his breast pocket. There were thousands of lives at stake, people depending on him to return it to the King. Besides, he had to get back to rescue the beautiful Miss Veronica from those poachers. He was not going to let them all down.

His steel gray eyes scanned the horizon. The sky was cloudless, and the dry heat made the purple mountains shimmer across the open desert to the east. Down the valley, a buzzard cruised ominously, looking for a stray carcass. Indiana hoped it wouldn't be his.

Off to the right, no more than a mile away, he saw a dust cloud getting nearer. At first he thought it was caused by swirling winds, the beginnings of a small sandstorm. Then he heard it. A low thrumming sound, quickly getting louder. He squinted for a better view, and could pick out a dozen armored trucks leading the storm, each bristling with crack SS troops. Someone had betrayed his location to the Nazis, and they were coming straight for him. His pupils dilated like saucers and his nostrils flared, as he looked for a way to escape. There, an old motorcycle with sidecar, hidden behind a shed! He straddled it in a single jump, twisted the throttle, and kicked the starter lever with all his weight. *Vroom....* The engine almost caught.

The trucks were closing in on him. He could hear the rattle of machine guns, and his left foot could feel the vibrations in the ground. Another violent kickstart, and the engine burst into life. Bullets sprayed around him as he wheeled in a tight semicircle, and accelerated across the dry riverbed and onto the road on the other side. Two more miles of twisting valley curves, and then he could cross the open desert and escape to safety. He might just make it, as long as he didn't run out of gas.

Steering the motorcycle with his left hand, he unscrewed the gas cap with his right, and stole a quick look inside the tank. Damn! Almost empty. In the distance ahead he could see a solitary gas station. It was his only chance. With a glance over his shoulder, he skidded to a stop, almost knocking over the faded yellow sign that read Shell. The place was deserted. This would have to be self-service.

Without a moment's pause, he grabbed the hose from one of the two pumps and quickly filled his tank with diesel oil. *Spang!!!* A bullet hit his handlebar. This was no time to panic. Knowing he had only seconds to spare, he took one slow deep breath and gritted his teeth, his lips forming a tight smile. With the soft sands of the open desert ahead, those heavy trucks would bog down. In his gut, he knew he could pull this off. *Zing!!!* Bullets everywhere. Letting out an atavistic war whoop, he twisted the throttle and kicked the start pedal as hard as he could. *Splut ... splut ... splog ... kaff ... phut.*

"CUT!" The director stomped onto the set, hurling his beret to the ground in disgust. "Nice fuel choice, blockhead. You've just given your engine asthma. Motorcycles don't take diesel, they take gasoline. What did you think you were driving? A bread truck?"

The daily challenges we face may be a little less dramatic than those faced by Indiana Jones, but our poor choices can be just as disastrous. Like Indiana, we face one stress after another, with little apparent sense of control. However, at every meal and with every snack, we make important fueling decisions that we *can* control, decisions that will determine our fate. Simply put, we can choose either foods that are good for us or foods that are bad for us.

Once you have seen through the fog of misinformation and bad habits related to lifestyle and diet, it is important to continue to keep your eyes on the road ahead and choose the right fuel to keep your body running at top performance. To be sure, this is going to be extremely simple, but never easy. Eyebrows will be raised when you order at a restaurant, and questions will be raised by your friends and family members, especially those who remain slaves to their bad habits and need the "old" you as an accomplice to ease their consciences.

To stay on the road you will need up-to-date information, a willingness to re-image your diet, and practical tips for daily food choices. To that end, we need to look at specific food choices available on any menu, supermarket shelf, or on your own kitchen counter.

## Fat

If we were to put bad food components on the hit parade, fat would be number one. Weighing in at nine calories per gram, more than double the calorie content of protein or carbohydrate, fat is the "heavy" in our dietary battles. While some fat is needed to help us manufacture antibodies to disease, as well as cell-wall components, it is most unlikely that we will ever eat too little. The average person in the United States and Canada eats half their calories from fat, and most end up wearing the stuff, on the outside as obesity, or on the inside in their fat-clogged arteries.

There are common levels of dietary fat, which measure the percentages of calories in the diet that are made up of fat. We will look at each of the three — 50%, 30%, and 10 to 15% — in turn.

1. 50%: The amount consumed by the vast (and I do mean vast) majority in the United States and Canada. This is the diet that has brought the Western world an unprecedented level of obesity, heart disease, strokes, adult-onset diabetes and, because the high fats are usually accompanied by high animal-protein consumption, osteoporosis. In addition, this diet is implicated in many forms of cancer, such as breast cancer and cancer of the colon, that are far less common in societies that eat low-fat diets. In terms of its immediate effects, the 50%-fat diet causes a measurable "sludging" effect on the bloodstream, turning a liquid circulation into a molasses-like flow through the small blood vessels. Delivered into the aorta by the thoracic duct within 30 minutes of a fatty meal or snack, this fat coats each red blood cell, making it too stiff to bend through tiny blood vessels. This has an effect in every part of the body,

and explains in part why heart attacks and strokes are more common during the early-morning hours, because the biggest and fattiest meal of the day is usually in the evening. When one eats high fats chronically, the stuff deposits itself along the lining of the artery walls, and most importantly, in the coronary artery walls inside the heart muscle.

The reason fat is implicated in diabetes is simple: fat paralyzes insulin. When the body's insulin molecules are blocked in the bloodstream, blood sugar cannot be moved into the cells, and the blood-sugar levels rise. This shows up in blood tests and has led to the popular belief that diabetics need only watch their sugar intake to stay healthy. The reality is that diabetics very much need to watch their fat intake, as well. Indeed, while it is true that diabetics should not eat much apple pie, it is not only the apple-pie filling that harms the diabetic, but the lard-ridden apple-pie crust.

2. 30%: The amount recommended by the American and Canadian heart associations, the 30%-fat diet has been pushed for years by both doctors and nutritionists, and fobbed off on hospital patients as "low-fat." However, research done by Dr. Dean Ornish and others confirms that this is really still "high-fat" (the 50%-fat diet could be labeled "extremely high-fat"). His PET scans of coronary arteries showed that the 30%-fat diet can cause the arteries to continue their clogging, though at a slower rate than the 50%-fat diet. In fact, the doctors who settled on the 30% figure never believed it to be the best for us; but because they have no expertise in changing their patients' paradigms, they have wrongly assumed that the general public is too stubborn or too stupid to give up their cheeseburgers and spareribs and dairy products. These heart experts were frustrated by patients who gave up their very low-fat diets after a few short weeks or days, complaining that life was not worth living without their favorite fatty foods. The specialists may have had expertise in fixing the heart problems, but they obviously lacked expertise in selling new food habits to their patients. And so, the 30%-fat diet has become the norm for

"heart-healthy" and "lite" labels in restaurant menus and on labels. It is still being taught to nutritionists and, for the few minutes during their medical school years that are devoted to foods, to doctors. That's why hospital diets still include pork chops, cheese, ham, and chicken breast as part of the "low-fat" regimen. Needless to say, the special-interest food lobbies are keen to keep this fallacy alive and are happy to supply calendars, recipes, and sponsor-money to present their case to a gullible public. Indeed, they have allocated huge budgets for lobbying Washington and Ottawa to persist with the old-fashioned "food wheel," where dairy and meat/fish/poultry products form half of each meal, instead of allowing the more accurate food "pyramid" to represent our dietary needs.

3. 10-15%: The amount recommended by leading medical experts like Drs. Dean Ornish, John MacDougall, and Nathan Pritikin, who have shown the world how to reverse the progression of heart and artery disease. They've demonstrated that, not only do their patients show improved exercise tolerance, as well as increased blood supply to their heart muscle, they show a remarkable improvement in lowering high blood pressure usually without medications; their diabetic patients can lower or stop their insulin doses, and the obese can lose weight in spite of eating second helpings. In addition to reducing the need for open-heart surgery, these doctors have shown their patients to have reduced their risks of strokes, as well as many forms of cancer. The benefits of a true low-fat diet are greatest when started at an early age, but even middle-aged people with damaged arteries will see a dramatic improvement when they follow this guideline for fat intake.

## TYPES OF FAT

Fats are found in most foods, whether from animal or vegetable sources, and can come in different forms. Saturated fats are the ones most directly linked to cholesterol deposits in our arteries and are found in animal fats (cholesterol), as well as some vegetables (for example, palm and coconut oils, the so-called "tropical" oils). Unsaturated fats, (both mono- and poly-) are vegetable in origin. Once hydrogenated, these turn from liquid to solid form at room temperature. However, while the polyunsaturates have a theoretical edge over pure cholesterol, it should be emphasized that there is no such thing as a "healthful" fat in the context of our overweight society. Foods labeled "lite" or "cholesterol free" (such as muffins or granola bars) can still have tropical oils and be filled with fatty oils and margarines. As far as the human body is concerned, *all* fat should be kept in low proportion, namely no more than the 10-15% range of total calories.

---

The simplest way to look at fats is in terms of their percentage of the calorie content in various foods. Most people want a diet that does not require calipers and an adding machine to help them figure out what to eat, so a glance at this list makes it all quite easy. To adhere to a low-fat diet, choose endless quantities of foods from the low-fat section. Forays into the high-fat group should be done only with the greatest of caution, the smallest of portions, and the most selective of reasons. While it is true that most foods have something good in them apart from whatever fat content they contain (with the exception of pure fats like butter, margarine, and lard), one should be most wary of the siren call of "health" claims from high-fat groups. In most cases, their benefits can be obtained from other less fatty food sources.

For ease of reference, it is useful to think of foods in two arbitrary categories by fat content: high fat (over 15%), and low fat (less than 15%). Following each of these examples will be the number representing the percent of total calories found as fats. Note that this is a different number than total fats per volume; for example, whole milk is only 3.5% fat by volume, but once the water is removed, the biggest single component of milk is fat. Some margarines are labeled the same way, using water or inert filler to add volume and make it seem the spread is less than 100% fat.

## High Fat

Butter — 100%
Margarine — 100%
Almonds — 75%
Beef — 74% (some cuts are leaner, others, like hamburger, can be even higher)
Cheddar cheese — 73%
Whole eggs — 65%
Whole milk — 49%
Peanuts/peanut butter — 72%
Pork — 58%
Tofu — 54%
Chicken (without the skin) — 39%
Milk (2%) — 24%
Turkey (without the skin) — 32%

## Low Fat

Kidney beans — 2%
Whole-wheat bread — 8%
Brussels sprouts — 9%
Cabbage — 6%
Carrots — 4%
Corn — 8%
Grapefruit — 2%
Oatmeal — 15%
Oranges — 4%
Potatoes — 1%
Rice (brown) — 5%
Rice (white) — 3%
Spaghetti (whole-wheat) — 5%
Spaghetti, regular — 3%
Sweet potatoes — 2%
Tomatoes — 8%

In order to keep fat levels at or below 15%, one can eat without restriction from the low-fat list, and only dabble in foods from the higher lists. However, at the end of the day, it should all come out to an average of less than 15%. This means that if one is a lover of rich desserts, one can still have them, but should make up for it the rest of the day by sticking to the low-fat category. If one loves the taste of butter or margarine, by all means eat some, but know it will mean there is little room in your fat "budget" for any other treats. If you like butter and desserts, the only way to accommodate both is to exercise more. If you double the calories burned off in a day, then you can eat double the calories. That's why athletes who burn off 4,000 to 6,000 calories a day can eat some high-fat foods, as long as the rest of their diet keeps the average down to safe levels.

For the rest of us, the simplest thing to do is to tend toward the low-fat list most of the time. Because even breast of turkey (the leanest of the animal meats) is over 30% fat, the obvious conclusion is that most meals will need to be vegetarian. Tricks can help; for example, lovers of apple pie can still have the filling, heated with oatmeal crumbs on top, but they should avoid the pastry (mostly lard). Knowing that there will be occasions where such fat limitations will be impossible, try to keep the fats down on those meals where you do have control.

## NOTE TO PARENTS

The dietary advice given in this book applies to adults. Children under the age of two are built to be fed human breast milk, which happens to be very high in fat. I have seen examples of young babies placed on skim-milk diets who have become desperately ill. Please consult your pediatrician or family doctor about specific recommendations for your young children. However, once children in our society are beyond the age of two, they will likely suffer from too much fat in their diets. That means that growing children can join their parents in the low-fat foods recommended here and share the benefits to their health.

## Fiber

The father of medical awareness of fiber is unquestionably the famous British surgeon, Dr. Dennis Burkitt (affectionately known in the trade as "Dr. Stool"). Dr. Burkitt traveled the back roads of Africa and Asia performing surgery in small village clinics. In between villages, he would stop his party at any roadside deposits of human excrement while he got out his scale and scooper. He would then carefully record the weights into his logbook. (I have referred to this somewhat unusual endeavor as a "Turd World Study.")

His conclusions were dramatic. People who ate a vegetarian-based diet passed a pound of stool a day, while people on a Western diet passed only a quarter-pound a day. Dr. Burkitt then made a list of diseases he most frequently encountered in his clinics and correlated them with the two respective diets. The diseases were all familiar to us. The most common surgical emergency in the abdomen was acute appendicitis, and the most common elective surgery in the abdomen was gallstone removal. The list went on to include cancer of the colon, diverticulosis and diverticulitis, hemorrhoids, cancer of the breast, heart disease, and strokes. The part that was remarkable was that these diseases corresponded with the people who ate the least fiber and were extremely rare in those who ate high-fiber foods. Dr. Burkitt's conclusion was clear: The societies that have the smallest stools (namely ours) have the biggest hospitals. And we wonder why we are in the midst of an expensive health-care crisis.

Fiber comes in several forms, but it is essentially the undigestible residue from plant cell walls. It cannot come from, or through, an animal. In other words, there is no fiber in any meat, nor is there in cheese, milk, or eggs. Fiber accompanies all plant foods naturally (at least until Modern Man figured out how to separate the wheat from the chaff, throw out the chaff, bleach the living daylights out of the wheat, and market the pure white residual powder as "enriched" flour). That's why anyone eating a large variety of whole grains and vegetables need not worry about taking any fiber supplements.

## Protein

This is one food element, found abundantly in plant- and animal-based foods, that has been perennially awarded the MVP (most valuable player) status, mainly under false pretences. As we were growing up, our parents implored us to "eat your protein," usually meaning meats. They would look to examples such as Japanese immigrant children, raised on a high-protein (and high-fat) diet in America, who would tower above their Japanese-born parents by the age of adolescence. This supposedly demonstrated that protein builds tall bodies and strong bones. What really happened is the opposite. The elder Japanese, raised in Japan during the Depression and wartime, simply did not have enough food of any description. Particularly when bones are going through their growth spurt in adolescence, it is critical that enough fuel be provided to supply the body's needs. In other words, no matter what percentage of each meal is protein, if a teenager goes to bed hungry every night (having burned off more daily calories than have been eaten), then his or her bone growth will be stunted. There are many examples of vegetarian children rising to basketball-player heights, and, if they train correctly with weights, of developing incredibly muscular physiques. Indeed, most of the gold-medal-winning U.S. track team is vegetarian, following the lead of the legendary Carl Lewis.

Far from promoting healthy bone and body growth, the high level of animal protein in the Western diet has the opposite effect. While we do need some protein to sustain our normal growth of hair and nails, we can easily supply this amount from vegetable sources. When we eat high levels of animal protein, such as meats or organs (liver, kidney, brains), we cause our stored calcium to be washed out of our bones, and excreted through the kidneys. Effectively, this means that our skeletal systems are being washed out to sea. In other words, the quest for strong bones, both in growing adolescents, and in our elders who suffer from osteoporosis, is sabotaged by eating too much animal protein. Assuming one is not subsisting on famine rations, it is virtually impossible to have a protein-deficient diet, because protein is found in so many foods. Even broccoli has enough protein for us, as do all vegetables.

The livers and kidneys of those who consume a high-protein diet are also lumbered with the job of removing the nitrogen waste generated by the excess protein. Protein from plants is easier to digest than that from animals, partially as a result of the sulfur-containing amino acids that are more abundant in meats. That means that kidney beans are easier for the human to digest than beef, even though both have the same 26% protein content.

## Carbohydrates

The word "carbohydrate" is self-explanatory, at least to chemists. It derives from the words "carbon" and "water," the latter being hydrogen and oxygen. These three elements are brought together during photosynthesis, the process by which green plants make food. Some carbohydrates are stored in animal tissues (including our own) as glycogen, but the basic source of carbohydrates is vegetarian foods.

*Simple carbohydrates* are so called because of their simple molecular structure, and are more commonly known as sugars. Glucose is the most important of these molecules, or monosaccharides, and is the kind referred to in blood-sugar tests. Other simple carbohydrates are fructose and galactose, which often show up on labels of juices and milk products. When two such molecules are joined together, the result is called a disaccharide, and these sugars include sucrose, lactose (milk sugar), and maltose. Whenever these show up on a label, they mean simple sugars, or simple carbohydrates, and all quickly enter the bloodstream.

*Complex carbohydrates*, also called polysaccharides, are made up of many monosaccharides, or simple sugar molecules. These include starch, cellulose, and glycogen. Starch is the basic element of the healthy human diet, and is found in such foods as rice, wheat, potatoes, beans, and vegetables. Cellulose is the indigestible cell wall from plants, which give us our fiber. Glycogen, the animal form of stored carbohydrates, is how we supply our muscles with extra fuel for extensive athletic endeavor.

Complex carbohydrates cannot be handled directly by the bloodstream, but must first be broken down into their component molecules of simple sugars in the small intestine, then transported to the liver. There they are changed into glucose, or blood sugar, which fuels the engines of our cells. Unlike excess fat, which we end up wearing, excess carbohydrates in our diet are converted into glycogen to be stored in muscles.

## FAT SUBSTITUTES

Most families have a box full of old favorite recipes, and many people enjoy following new recipes from their favorite magazines. While these foods are often high in fat, there are some good tricks of substitution that will allow you to "fake it," and still enjoy a great-tasting recipe.

The following chart lists the regular ingredients first, then the corresponding low-fat substitute.

| When the Recipe Calls for | Use |
|---|---|
| *1 whole egg | 2 egg whites |
| * whole milk | soy milk (low fat) |
| * cake frosting | canned fruit-pie filling |
| * Baker's Chocolate | carob or cocoa powder |
| * oil, or butter, to sauté in frying pan | use oil in pan, heat, then wipe away with paper towel |
| * oil, to add to most recipes | water or fruit purée |
| * processed cheese (in an omelette) | light dusting of strongly flavored Parmesan or Romano |
| * cheese sprinkles | brewer's yeast or food-yeast flakes (use lightly) |
| * deep fry | bake at 400°F |
| * cream (in soups) | purée some of the vegetables or rice to thicken soup |

---

## Everyday Choices: The Good, the Bad, and the Ugly

### Fast Foods

#### Salad Bar

**Good:** fresh greens, chickpeas (garbanzos), kidney beans, carrots, topped with vinegar or "lite" dressing.
**Bad:** egg yolks, cheese, bacon bits, sliced meats such as ham and sausage, and standard dressings such as Thousand Islands, Roquefort, or Italian.
**Ugly:** Caesar salad (even uglier with anchovies).

#### Potatoes

**Good:** hash-browned (in a non-stick pan), baked or boiled, served plain, or topped with salsa, ketchup, barbecue sauce, marinara sauce, non-fat yogurt dressings.
**Bad:** baked potato served with butter or margarine, topped with sour cream, bacon bits, and cheese.
**Ugly:** french fries, or hash browns cooked in lard.

### Burgers

**Good:** all vegetarian, with pickles, tomatoes, relishes, ketchup, and mustard. A tofu or chickpea patty is optional.
**Bad:** burgers made with beef.
**Ugly:** cheeseburgers, garnished with mayonnaise and mushrooms sautéed in butter.

### Pizza

**Good:** loaded with vegetables, such as tomatoes, green peppers, onions, mushrooms. If available, also ask for broccoli, corn, peas. Ask for extra tomato sauce, no added oils, and *no cheese*. A crust made from whole-wheat is a bonus.
**Bad:** topped with any kind of cheese, or fatty vegetables like olives and avocado.
**Ugly:** topped with cheese and pepperoni, oil, anchovies, sausage, ham, or other meats.

### Sandwiches

**Good:** toasted or plain, whole-wheat or other multi-grain, high-fiber bread, filled with lean vegetables like lettuce, tomato, eggplant, sprouts, and pickles. Ask for mustard or relish on the bread to hold the ingredients together.
**Bad:** white bread, with butter or margarine, mayonnaise, cheese, ham or meat slices, or any prepared meat slices like bologna, sausages.
**Ugly:** grilled cheese, or "Dagwood" specials, which may even include fried egg.

### Pasta

**Good:** plain, especially when noodles are whole-wheat, and free of egg yolks. Top with tomato sauce (such as marinara), with vegetables of choice, such as mushrooms, peas, broccoli. A light dusting of strong cheese topping like Parmesan adds taste yet keeps the total fat content within bounds.
**Bad:** topped with meat sauces, or excessive butter and oil.
**Ugly:** cream- or cheese-based sauces, such as Alfredo. Watch out for lasagna, even the vegetarian variety, because it usually comes laden with fatty cheeses.

## Cold Drinks (non-alcoholic)

**Good:** water, especially bottled or filtered, fizzy or flat.
Alternatives are grapefruit juice, or sparkling waters flavored
with essences of fruits (for example, Clearly Canadian with
raspberry, Perrier with orange, and other low-calorie flavors).
**Bad:** sweet juice, such as apple, orange, and pineapple, or soda
pop.
**Ugly:** milkshakes, whole milk, chocolate drinks.

## Cold Drinks (alcoholic)

**Good:** abstinence, or a single standard serving of wine, beer, or
spirit.
**Bad:** anything with an umbrella, or served in a tropical fruit the
size of your head. Blender drinks usually disguise their alcohol
with froth, fats, and sugars.
**Ugly:** alcohol beyond legal sobriety.

## Hot Drinks

**Good:** herbal teas, or hot water and lemon juice. Hot tomato
juice is a good substitute for tomato soup and is low in calories.
Coffee and tea (black or with sugar, less than two cups a day)
are also fine.
**Bad:** coffee and tea served with cream, whole or 2% milk, or oil-
based cream substitute, or served in excess of four cups a day.
**Ugly:** eggnogg, hot chocolate (especially topped with whipping
cream).

## Frozen Desserts

**Good:** sherbets and fat-free yogurts; tofu-based varieties.
**Bad:** regular ice cream, and most toppings such as chocolate dip.
**Ugly:** any premium (high-fat) ice cream.

## Donuts

**Good:** bagels, especially whole-wheat. Serve dry, or with honey,
jam, or applesauce.
**Bad:** regular donuts. Same shape as the bagel, but soaked hot lard.
**Ugly:** coated donuts, dipped in fatty icings, or the ones with the

gooey fillings. Also beware most muffins, which often are filled with fats, egg yolks, and oils.

### Snacks

**Good:** popcorn, especially the plain kernel, popped in a microwave or air popper. Eat plain, or add fat-free flavorings such as salt or pepper. Pretzels (dust off salt), rice cakes, or *baked* tortilla chips with salsa (see Counterattack! Recipes, Chapter 10).
**Bad:** popcorn cooked in oil, topped with melted butter or palm oil; trail mixes laden with coconut flakes; potato chips.
**Ugly:** granola bars, roasted nuts, nachos with cheese sauce.

### Sweets

**Good:** dried apricots, raisins, hard candy (if you must) such as LifeSavers, candy canes.
**Bad:** chocolate bars.
**Ugly:** chocolates filled with fatty centers; licorice (can cause fluid retention).

## The Sit-Down Restaurant

### Breakfast

**Good:** egg-white omelette with vegetables, whole-wheat pancakes, hash-brown potatoes (cooked in a non-stick pan, no lard or butter), hot oatmeal cereal, dry whole-wheat toast with jam or applesauce.
**Bad:** regular hash browns, egg "muffin."
**Ugly:** regular omelette, with yolks, cheese, and sautéed in lots of butter or oil; scrambled eggs with bacon or sausages; eggs benedict; buttered white toast or pancakes.

### Lunch

**Good:** vegetarian burritos (hold the cheese), baked potato with salsa.
**Bad:** fish and chips, chicken fingers, hamburger.
**Ugly:** spareribs, cheeseburger, or bacon-cheeseburger.

## Dinner

### Appetizer:

**Good:** melon balls, grapefruit sections, salad (with vinegar or lemon juice topping), minestrone or gazpacho.
**Bad:** escargots, sautéed mushrooms, shrimp cocktail, creamed soups.
**Ugly:** deep-fried cheese.

### Main Course:

**Good:** vegetable plate with rice or baked potato; pasta; vegetarian chili.
**Bad:** fried chicken, steak, pork chop.
**Ugly:** lobster with butter dip, or served in a cream sauce; beef Wellington.

### Dessert:

**Good:** fresh fruit, sherbet, baked apple.
**Bad:** pastries, ice cream.
**Ugly:** chocolate mousse, pie à la mode, cheesecake.

## The Grocery Store: How to Save Over $300 an Hour

For most people, the struggle to eat the right foods will be won or lost in the grocery store. If the whole family wants to eat healthily, yet the person doing the shopping brings home bags of fat, then the family suffers. If the person doing the shopping is highly motivated to buy the right foods, but is not aware of the bad foods that wave a false flag such as "lite," or "cholesterol-free," then the results will still be poor. Good intentions cannot overcome bad grocery shopping.

The anatomy of the modern grocery is simple. The fresh produce lines the outside walls, while the packaged and frozen products fill the middle of the store. That's so the foods with the shortest shelf life can be restocked without causing major traffic jams in the narrow center aisles. The anatomy of the grocery shopper is also simple. The emptier the stomach, the bigger the eyes, and the greater the sense of urgency in filling up the basket. That's why the best thing to do when grocery shopping is to eat before you hit the store. Otherwise you can easily suffer "shopper's panic," and fill your basket with the worst possible foods. If you are shopping with young children in tow, make sure their stomachs have been topped up before entering the store or else they will be filling the lower rungs of your cart with products of the sponsors of all their favorite television shows.

Now, with a full stomach, and armed with information on the left side of the brain and open mindsets on the right, our smart shopper wheels his stainless-steel cart to the starting grid, taking his place among a gaggle of peers. A quick wave of the starter's green flag, *and they're off*, headed for the turn at aisle 1. The group comes to a clot as they round the dairy section, flinging butter, cheese, and milk into their carts. Our hero reaches around them to grab the grapefruit juice and the low-fat soy milk for his cereal. Now he slows down for the fresh-vegetable section, loading up on potatoes, rice, broccoli, carrots, and corn. The crowd passes on the outside.

He makes good time exiting the vegetable turn and sees the pack congealed around the meat counter. Dismembered animal pieces are dragged from the cooler, wrapped in cellophane, and labeled with extremely large numbers on the price sticker. Still the shoppers beg for more. The butchers, with faces as ruddy as their apron stains, smile helpfully.

Up ahead is the bakery aisle. Our hero selects the whole-grain bread, the loaves with the density coefficient of a bale of peatmoss. The crowd zooms in on the white wiffle-bread, after first giving it the approving squeeze test (also practised in the toilet-paper section). He picks up some oat-bran raisin bread; they reach for the cookies. He grabs the low-fat cinnamon cake, while they pick the lard-soaked pastries.

Now it's into the straightaway past the cereals. He loads up on All-Bran, shredded wheat, Cheerios, and hot-oatmeal mix. They slow down for Tony the Tiger, and the candy-coated fruit puffs.

(First rule of cereal shopping: never buy a box that features a cartoon character standing on the rim of the bowl.)

The pack closes in as they go past the mop handles to the drink stop. He picks out the bottled water, along with six-packs of flavored sparkling water. They load up on sweet soda pop and sticky fruit punch. The carts are riding heavier now, so it's a bit slower as the herd rounds the condiments corner. He grabs the mustard, salsa, relish, ketchup, and barbecue sauce, while they clutch the mayo and the tartar sauce.

He hurries up the next aisle, barely looking back as he selects the meatless spaghetti sauce and the egg-free noodles, then moves on for the canned beans and chickpeas, opening a significant lead. The pack is snarled in a traffic jam in aisle 7, over by the sample tray of canned ham.

One lap to go, and it's down to the wire. At the freezer section he scores some fruit popsicles, sherbet, and hash-brown potatoes, leaving the ice creams, onion rings, and french fries to the stragglers. Around the ripple-chip hairpin turn, correcting for a slight oversteering of the rear wheels and a wobble in the left front, it's down past the candy counter, maintaining speed through the aerosol-cheese display, and taking the checkered flag by the cashier at register 3. As the also-rans drift up to the finish line, the shock is apparent on their faces. One look at the bills tells the tale. Our hero, for all the filling, wholesome foods he has just stocked, comes in at under $130. The high-fat carnivores have to fork over $250 apiece. The first-prize money was $120, for just over twenty minutes' work.

## The Kitchen

Here is the final challenge. Now that we have screened out the bad foods from our shelves, the trick is to make the healthy raw materials into tasty meals. While not everyone is born with a chef's touch at the stove, and few have much time to devote to traditional food preparation, it is indeed possible for all to produce healthy foods, even when in a hurry. Recipes for our Counterattack! diet appear in Chapter 10, but first you should check out your equipment and supplies.

In addition to the normal array of knives, chopping boards, and wooden spoons, there are a few items that should be considered essentials for healthy cooking.

## Essentials for Low-Fat Cooking

* frying pan, small size, for egg-white omelettes.
* frying pan, huge, for doing big meals like vegetarian chili.
* saucepan, 2-qt (2-L) size, for soups and rice.
* saucepan, 2-gal. (8-L) size or bigger. The more water in the pot, the better will be the pasta. This pot also doubles as a great slow-cooker for party-sized quantities of vegetarian "stew."
* mandolin, for cutting quick julienne vegetables.
* wire whisk, for sauces.

All the above should be made of non-stick materials, such as coated aluminum (the coating prevents the aluminum from leaching into the foods) and come with thick bottoms and glass lids. It is useful if the saucepans have two small handles, which makes it easier to use them in the oven or to put them in the dishwasher.

* blender, free-standing or hand-held (ideal for creating fat-free salad dressings, soups, sauces, or whipping egg whites).
* food processor, for chopping vegetables, making whole-grain bread dough, and for puréeing beans for dips.
* Juice extractor, ideal for low-fat drinks (see page following).
* Kitchen scale, useful for those trying to monitor portion sizes to help them lose weight or to follow obscure recipes that use weight instead of volume measurements.
* Bread-making machine. For those who don't mind fiddling around for a few minutes in the kitchen, this is a most economical way of making bread while you sleep. Just toss in the measured ingredients, and the machine does the rest. This way you control the ingredients, insure the freshness, and get the best taste.

* Barbecue or indoor electric grill.
* Microwave oven.

---

## JUICE-EXTRACTOR CAVEATS

**P**opularized on television infomercials, juice extractors have become a national trend. The idea is to crunch the juice out of vegetables, such as carrots, celery, parsnips, as well as apples and other fruits. The resulting drink is low fat, and indeed contains lots of vitamins, minerals, and enzymes in a natural form. The caveats are simple. A vegetable is composed of two elements, juice and fiber, both of which are essential to our good health. When you extract the juice, then throw out the fiber, there is an easy tendency to have too little fiber overall. In addition, yellow vegetables like carrots and squash are high in carotene (which converts to vitamin A). When they are turned to juice, it is easy to ingest too much of them and turn skin yellow. This has often led mothers to think their kids have hepatitis or jaundice and even grown men to fear they've suddenly contracted yellow fever or AIDS. While the yellow staining of the skin is transient if the carotene overload is stopped, more permanent damage can be done if the staining is ignored, and if overdosing is continued. It should be remembered that even though vitamin A is an essential element in a good diet, it is highly toxic, even fatal, in large doses.

---

## Supplies

* Olive or safflower oil, which can be used to lubricate the frying pan. Wipe off excess with a paper towel after the pan gets hot, before food is added. The aerosol forms of oils are fine, except that they ricochet off the pan and may create quite a mess on the stove top, so one should spray the pans over the sink, or, better yet, outside the house.
* Garlic: who says healthy food has to taste bland? Garlic is great for our bodies and spices up a host of meals. As long as everyone eats it, no one will mind the odor.

* Dry grains
* Whole-grain flours
* Farina
* Corn tortillas (keep in the freezer)
* Whole-grain breads
* Pasta [2-3 lbs (2-2$\frac{1}{2}$ kg)]
* Arrowroot or cornstarch (thickeners for sauces)
* Frozen vegetables
* Frozen fruit and juices
* Canned tomatoes and beans
* Basalmic and rice-wine vinegars
* Mustards
* Fat-free barbecue sauce (check the label)
* Ketchup
* Salsa
* Low-sodium soy sauce
* Lemon and lime juice
* Fat-free condiments and dressings
* Dried onions and green peppers
* A range of spices and herbs

The challenge seems formidable, but you must recognize that the *Counterattack!* battle takes place every time you step up to the counter to prepare your food, and every time you approach the checkout counter to buy your ingredients. There are special-interest groups betting big money they can coerce you into eating foods that enrich corporate coffers, and encourage individual coffins.

We have been duped since childhood, starting with images of the Marlboro man and outrageous food wheels that hung on classroom walls, inculcating the idea that no meal is complete without animal pieces and dairy products taking up half the plate. But even in kindergarten, a part of us knew it was a sham. None of us smoked, and most of us would rather have had mashed potatoes than a tough old steak, and all of us ran around the playground like colts and fillies. But somehow that common sense was sapped out of us. Long hours of sitting in classrooms, followed by longer hours watching offensive TV ads punctuated by vacuous TV shows have turned us into slugs and lemmings. As adults we have been hypnotized by lifestyle ads that punctuate the ball game on TV, and by the medical-drug complex that tries to convince us that our self-induced diseases are really just an indication for more drugs or medical intervention.

It's time to take out our trusty crayons and change the intent of the ads that shape our lifestyle habits. Just like the schoolboy who drew a mustache on the Queen's portrait, we can write new punch lines to old ads, and relabel our images of good and bad food choices. It all comes down to selling, and it's time we started controlling our own sales pitches. Once you have been through the thin veil of deceit in the ads that surround us, victory is only a crayon stroke away.

CHAPTER

# 4

# Never Eat Anything
# with a Face

VEGETARIANISM HAS BEEN KNOWN for years to be a healthy lifestyle choice and indeed was the diet our primitive ancestors mainly followed. As gatherers they grew grains and picked berries. The hunters' weapons were too slow, and the prey was too fast, so by default, meals were largely vegetarian. Foods all contained natural roughage, and there were no fats to add in cooking. Heart disease and diabetes were rare, cancers were rarer, and obesity was most unlikely. In fact, the same continues to be true today in societies where people still eat the old-fashioned way. Select populations of vegetarians, like Seventh-day Adventists, although surrounded by carnivorous compatriots, maintain much lower rates of these "modern" diseases. We can no longer overlook the obvious: it seems these vegetarians are doing something right.

As the word implies, vegetarians eat vegetables, although there are various subdivisions within the category.

## THE FOUR TYPES OF VEGETARIANS

1. Vegan: eats only plant products, such as vegetables, fruits, grains.

2. Lacto-vegetarian: eats the above, along with milk and milk products such as cheese, butter, and ice cream.
3. Lacto-ovo-vegetarian: eats the above, along with eggs.
4. Lacto-ovo-oreo-nacho-vegetarian: eats the above in public, but when alone, pigs out on junk foods.

---

Around the world, vegetarians far outnumber meat eaters (and by "meat" I refer to chicken, fish, pork, beef, and anything else that once had a face). Recently, in the second half of this century, we began to raise meats in "factory" proportions. Advertisers cleverly linked meat products with the good life that the post-war public craved, while lobbyists inculcated the idea of meat being one of the four "basic" food groups, without which no mother was serving up a balanced meal. This brilliant combination of availability and propaganda contrived to increase Western meat consumption dramatically, to the point where it is now higher than at any time in history, and greater than anywhere else in the world.

This trend would be of merely anthropological interest, were it not for one simple fact: the human body cannot properly digest today's high levels of meat and fat consumption. True carnivores, like the dog and the cat, have intestines that are about the same length as their bodies. The cholesterol they eat very quickly passes through the gut, largely undigested. On the other hand, the human intestinal tract is over five times our body length, meaning that fatty foods like meats have more opportunity to be absorbed into the bloodstream. When we compound the problem by eating very little fiber (and letting our abdominal muscles turn to flab), then our stools become slow moving, tiny and carry out very little undigested food. Indeed, the transit time through the gut in many meat eaters is increased to the point of constipation. In other words, the human digestive tract is designed to process predominantly vegetarian low-fat foods, and absorbs far more fats out of meat than our bodies were meant to handle.

If the human digestive system could handle high meat intake, there would be no reason to question our diet, and our plentiful meat consumption would make us free of disease. The reality is quite the opposite. While we in the West do not suffer malnutrition and other diseases of dietary inadequacy, we have created a whole new category of diseases related to dietary excess. That's why we see so much obesity, heart disease, diabetes, strokes, and cancers filling up today's hospitals. We have become a society of the overfed and undernourished. It is not just that we eat too many calories for what we burn off, but that we eat too much fat, protein, and simple carbohydrates.

## DISEASE AND FOOD INTAKE

| Diseases caused by too little food | Diseases caused by too much food |
|---|---|
| starvation | obesity |
| poor immunity to infections | heart disease |
| rickets | strokes |
| beri-beri | gout |
| kwashiorkor | diabetes (adult onset) |
| liver failure | gallstones |
| kidney failure | constipation |
| anemia | many forms of cancer |
| poor brain development | back pain |
| poor bone growth | some forms of arthritis |
| insufficient hormones, including growth, sex, cortisone | |
| diarrhea | |

Even armed with the latest medical technology and drugs, doctors are powerless to fight starvation diseases, unless they can give their patients the right foods. By the same token, modern medicine is powerless to reverse the trends of overfeeding diseases unless they can empower the individual to make informed food choices.

While vegetarianism should be an easy sell — non-meat products are much cheaper and better tolerated by the body than meat products — its popularity has suffered from unappealing imagery and poor marketing. Many radical vegetarians have frankly put people off, taking the option far outside the mainstream of public opinion. Indeed, if one asks most people to describe the typical vegetarian, the collective description is usually quite depressing: "Someone who eats husks, disheveled, wears sandals and elbow patches, and drives an old Volvo."

In reality, vegetarians come in a variety of guises. Many people are vegetarian for religious reasons, such as Seventh-day Adventists and strict Hindus. Some are vegetarian simply because they cannot afford meats, or do not have access to any form of them. But when we use the term vegetarian in the modern health context, we are referring to those who consciously turn down animal flesh while they pursue a balanced diet. In Western society, this is very much a minority choice, although the ranks are expanding as people seek prevention, instead of treatment, of disease.

If you are not already a vegetarian, you should consider the benefits of becoming one. While I don't expect that most carnivores will change completely overnight, it is possible to start by eating vegetarian meals most of the time. If one eats twenty-one meals a week, then make at least a dozen of these meat-free. All too many people eat meat at all twenty-one of their meals, plus more at snack times, making their burden of fat intake overpowering for the bloodstream. Meat eating should be restricted to special occasions, like turkey dinners at Thanksgiving or Christmas, or dinner parties where it would be awkward to refuse what the host has prepared.

To present the reader with a better view of the subject and, perhaps, to find one reason out of many that will motivate change, let's look at several sound arguments for vegetarianism. While not all may appeal, there may indeed be one or two that will forever change your view of meat eating.

# COUNTERATTACK!

## Arguments for Vegetarianism

### 1. Killing animals is cruel.

As anyone who has ever loved a pet knows, animals have feelings. While the food industry pooh-poohs the idea that this applies to barnyard animals, there is no doubt that every animal can feel pain. I have witnessed the slaughter in a meat-packing plant and have seen the panic and fear in the animals as each awaits its turn. Whether the killing is done by slitting the throat or by firing a bullet into the brain, it is certainly not painless for the victim.

### 2. Raising animals to be eaten is inhumane.

Animals raised in factory or feedlot situations do not enjoy good living conditions. The case of the chicken illustrates how these animals are subjected to a "concentration camp" lifestyle before being killed. Normally a chicken walks around, getting considerable sunlight, fresh air, and exercise. Modern factory chickens are hatched and raised in cages, and force-fed until their bodies are the same size as their containers. At no time do their feet touch the ground (not unlike the average human couch potato), nor do they ever see the light of day. Some become injured or maimed as they try to beat their wings and move their legs against their cages.

At the time of dissection on the kitchen chopping block, the effects of the chicken's sedentary lifestyle are obvious and should at once alert the human to the consequences of sloth. As an experiment for those chicken fans who remain unconvinced, try purchasing two birds, one "free range," and the other the standard supermarket variety. As the chef's dissection of the carcasses progresses, it is dramatic to note the flabby, gray, greasy muscles of the unexercised bird, compared with the lean, toned muscles of the free-range variety. Closer inspection of the factory bird will reveal blobs of fat within the muscles, around the joints, and inside the arteries. The same findings are found when unexercised, obese humans come in for surgery or an autopsy.

The same conditions apply to any animal raised in factory conditions. Cattle that cannot roam, veal calves that are taken from their mothers and caged, or farmed fish that cannot swim freely are building up the same stresses and lifestyle disorders that Western society has developed in humans.

### 3. Vegetarianism eases world hunger.

Our food supply is plentiful. The problem is that we feed our vegetables to our animals, then we eat the animals. When one considers that a cow eats fifteen pounds of grain or corn in order to produce a mere one pound of meat, the world's alleged food "shortage" becomes more explainable. Even if we all ate a mere 10% less meat, it would go a long way to feeding the world's hungry.

### 4. Vegetarianism reduces water pollution.

While wild animals were once kept in check by natural and human predators, the modern process of factory farming has distorted the whole picture. Land that could naturally drain the urine and feces from a couple of cattle per acre is now seeing feedlots packed with hundreds of animals, standing shoulder to shoulder (and bladder to bladder). While extra food can be trucked in to feed them, the results of this food, once passed through the kidneys and bowels, is harder to deal with. The land can't drain it off fast enough, and the sewage pollutes the water table, running off into wells, streams, and lakes.

### 5. Vegetarianism conserves drinking water.

At a time when countries are already willing to go to war to seize potable water sources, it is odd that we should watch our barnyard animals guzzle our drinking water, wash it through their kidneys, pollute our wells and streams, and force us to chemically "purify" what's left for human consumption. The best way to preserve drinking water is not to turn off the lawn sprinkler, nor is it to leave one's car unwashed. The single most important way to save drinking water is to stop eating so much meat. To grow one pound of vegetables, the farmer must use about 20 gallons of water; to make a pound of meat, a cow must drink an astonishing 5,200 gallons of water. In other words, by *not* eating just one serving of meat a month, one can conserve enough fresh water to shower every day of the year.

### 6. Vegetarianism reduces air and soil pollution.

When we crowd our ex-forests with feedlots and import Arab oil to turn into fertilizer and pesticides to grow the crops to feed these animals, we use up a lot of fossil fuels. At the same time, we generate an unmanageable amount of animal waste. By going directly to the source, namely eating vegetables before they have been fed to animals, vegetarians bypass a wasteful process and contribute less to pollution and the abuse of our environment.

---

## THE VIEW FROM ABOVE

Our ancestors in the pre-industrial era were easy on their environments, but once we entered the days of the smokestack it became easy to dump toxic chemicals into the water and soil, and to pollute our skies. This habit of mindless soiling of our nests has taken its toll. Originally, only a few radicals protested, acting like canaries in the mineshaft. Today a lot more credible people are speaking out about the fragility of the planet.

I recently had the great privilege of spending time with the original Mercury 7 astronauts, as well as Virgil Grissom's widow, Betty, for a couple of hours in Florida. As the first Americans to view Earth objectively from outer space, they had all returned humbled by what they had seen. John Glenn said that one of his first thoughts once he was in orbit was, "What happened to the air?" As a boy he had stared up into the endless sky, as an astronaut he stared down at the blue planet covered by an extremely thin layer of atmosphere. Alan Shepard pointed out that at 35,000 feet, the altitude of a passenger plane, more than 80% of our atmosphere is below us. That's why all were appalled at the cavalier attitude we have toward our atmosphere. When smokestacks pollute an industrial town, the solution is not simply to build a taller smokestack to send the pollution elsewhere.

Wally Schirra also remarked that our space missions have given us new insights into our water, which covers three-quarters of the planet. Viewed from special cameras above, we can see currents under the oceans that travel at about twenty-five miles an hour, constantly mixing the waters in all seven seas. That means when one country suffers offshore pollution we all suffer it.

Only the most shortsighted or most foolhardy would ignore such realities in the global village. So when scientists point out that a reduction in our consumption of meat helps conserve the planet, more people are paying attention.

---

### 7. Vegetarianism conserves the world's forests.

Much scorn has been directed at Brazil, as it inexorably hacks down precious rain forests to make grazing lands for cattle to supply world demand for cheeseburgers. However, the pot should not be too smug in calling the kettle black: North American and European resources have also been ravaged, as forests are converted into feedlots.

### 8. Vegetarianism is safer.

Because blood is such a good culture medium (after all, we use it in hospital laboratories to grow bacterial samples), anything that bleeds becomes fertile ground for infection. That means that turkey that sits on the counter defrosting, fish that has been too long in transit from trawler to refrigerator, or meat that was touched by a food handler's dirty hands are all prone to breeding serious diseases. Shellfish can arrive with viral infections such as hepatitis, rump roast can have E. coli, and egg yolks (another good culture medium) can carry salmonella. By contrast, not much grows on a peeled carrot or inside an orange.

### 9. Vegetarianism enhances performance.

Vegetarian foods make exercise output more efficient and improve stamina. One of my earliest insights into the performance levels of athletes relative to their diet came early in my career, when I was the twenty-four-year-old assistant team doctor to the Toronto Argonauts football team, who were led by a young Joe Theismann to the 1971 Grey Cup game. Because I still had six months of internship left to finish before I assumed the title of team doctor, I had no input into the foods that were served during the week of hoopla leading up to the big game. The team, by far the richest in talent in the league, was fed bacon every morning, ham every lunch, and pork every dinner. This was repeated *every single day* for the entire week. On game day the entire team oinked its way onto the field. Instead of a runaway victory, they scored a narrow and disappointing defeat. (In retrospect, I wondered if the winner, the Calgary Stampeders, hadn't donated the food to the Argonauts.)

In the two intervening decades, enlightened athletes have started to clue in to the energy-sapping properties of a big meat dish. In just the same way that a three-martini lunch leads to massive afternoon snoring instead of performance in the office, so too does the giant plate of dead flesh lead to sluggishness. The key to athletic performance is to have carbohydrates (mainly complex ones such as vegetables, rice, pasta, breads, potatoes, and other starch-based foods) as fuel. Fat is too hard to turn into energy and ends up being worn, either visibly as cellulite, or invisibly, as lining of the arteries. Protein builds up excess nitrogen levels in the blood and urine. Carbohydrates, on the other hand, are the cleanest-burning fuels we have. That is why American Olympic superstar Carl Lewis, along with most of his Olympic track teammates, is a total vegetarian, adhering to the same low-fat levels we prescribe for victims of hypertension, heart disease, or obesity.

### 10. Vegetarianism makes you live longer.

Societies where people eat the low-fat vegetarian diet recommended in this book have remarkably low incidences of our most common Western ailments. As has been proven by Dr. Dean Ornish, heart disease can be reversed, and many forms of cancer can be avoided or diminished, by eating high-fiber/low-fat foods. Because even the white meat of chicken, about the most fat-free of all animal offerings, is still over 30% fat, it is clear that eating low-fat vegetarian foods is the best way to keep fat intake down.

## 11. Vegetarianism is cheaper.

Today the spendthrift 1980s have given way to the thrifty 1990s, and most people are having to count their pennies. That's why vegetarianism is beginning to make more sense (and cents) for daily food needs. Producers of beef are not necessarily making huge profits; the reason their meats cost so much more than vegetable foods is that ranchers first have to buy fifteen pounds of vegetables to feed their animals in order to produce a pound of meat. Even the most expensive, out-of-season fruits and vegetables are usually less expensive than meat, and in restaurants vegetarian dishes are often the cheapest items on the menu.

When all is said and done, there are many compelling reasons we should all become vegetarians or, at the very least, drastically reduce our consumption of living creatures. For me, it was a little of each, with a lot of reason number 9, that caused the final decision to be maintained: I simply have more energy and feel better when I don't eat meat, and I have the get-up-and-go of a slug when I transgress.

# Common Questions about Vegetarianism

### 1. Should I continue to drink milk?

Cow's milk has been long lauded (by dairy lobbyists and proponents) as "Nature's Perfect Food." This is absolutely true — if you happen to be a 375-pound heifer trying to gain another 400 pounds by spring. Even then, calves are smart enough to stop drinking the stuff and to convert to vegetarianism once they are fully grown. It is only human beings, alone among the whole animal kingdom, who have been conned into thinking they *need* to ingest the milk from another species well past infancy.

While it is true that cow's milk does indeed have many good features, such as calcium and protein, these benefits can be found elsewhere with less accompanying risk. Let's take a look at some of these hazards, which never show up on the label, and certainly not in the dairy industry's ads.

The first of these hazards is *fat*. While the dairy labels insist that whole milk is only 3.5% fat, and therefore over 96% fat-free, this ignores the role of water. If you put two pats of butter in an eight-ounce glass, you have 100% fat, which is obviously not a health food. If you now fill this glass with water, you have only 3.5% fat by volume. In terms of total calories (the rest of which come from milk's protein and carbohydrate components), whole milk is 50% fat, and 2% milk is 32% fat. If you must drink the stuff at all, the safest form of milk is skim. The same warning applies to such milk byproducts as cheese and yogurt.

Cow's milk *protein* can be a strong allergen. The percentage of people who experience allergic reactions to milk varies according to race and family history. Many cases go undiagnosed, or are written off as common colds, asthma, or chronic stomachaches. In individuals sensitive or frankly allergic to this protein, reactions to cow's milk ingestion can aggravate and, in some cases, even cause immune system disorders like asthma, some forms of arthritis, colitis, sinusitis, and skin rashes. The most common cause of a baby's colic among my 4,000 patients (and the 1,000 I delivered) was sensitivity to cow's milk. Indeed, my first step in relieving symptoms of asthma or chronic runny noses in kids or adults was to try a dairy-free diet for a couple of months to see if it made a difference (usually it did). As further proof that cow's milk protein affects human defences, no singer is ever offered a pitcher of warm milk between songs on stage; milk makes the mucous at the back of the throat thicken, producing cold-like symptoms.

While dairy producers like to pretend that all milk is pristine and pure, we know that government inspections are, at best, spotty. It is also known that the health and diet of the cow can (as in lactating humans) determine the quality of the milk. I recently talked to a dairy farmer whose local water supply was contaminated with a strong pungent smell of sulfur during one summer. The milk produced by his cows also was scented with the sulfur, but none was rejected as it went into the central mix, to end up in thousands of household fridges. There is also little control over the pesticides and other chemicals sprayed over grazing lands, and these can easily show up in the milk.

When one considers that there are now new strains of diseases infecting dairy herds such as tuberculosis, septicemia (from untreated scratches against barbed-wire fences), and even the bovine HIV virus, for which little is ever screened on routine testing prior to human consumption, one feels somewhat reluctant to recommend the unbridled consumption of milk.

The most significant mineral in milk is calcium, and many people drink it for that alone, knowing that calcium is essential to bone strength. But a healthy vegetarian diet can contain enough calcium for our needs, and a far more effective way of maintaining bone strength is exercise. When I had to treat a healthy athlete with a non-weight-bearing cast for a fractured leg, we could see the changes in bone density after just a few weeks; the leg that did the weight bearing retained its pure white shadows on X-rays, while the unused leg showed porous shadows, like that of an osteoporotic grandmother. When one considers that the average person in this country gets no exercise (and fights no gravity) during the work day, and none during the statutory five hours of "channel surfing" in front of the TV, it is no wonder that our elderly suffer bone deterioration. The calcium supplements that many people take would work a lot more effectively if their users walked instead of drove to the corner store to buy them.

---

## KIDS AND MILK

Even adults who have stopped drinking milk themselves feed it to their kids. When breast-feeding mothers wean their children onto cow's milk, the first thing they note is that the stools suddenly smell foul — simple testimony to the fact that humans were designed to drink only human milk. As kids grow up, milk gets in the way (or should I say "whey") again. Runny noses, thick coughs, asthma, and often diarrhea are often made better by stopping the milk intake.

In fact, Dr. Benjamin Spock, the best-selling pediatrician whose books urged my generation's parents to feed us cow's milk, has recently joined the battle to stop giving cow's milk to our children under the guise of "health" food. He has had the courage to keep his mind open to new evidence and has concluded that his old advice is making some people sick. His major concerns are that milk causes obesity and heart disease. However, an even more alarming risk of cow's milk is seen in its connection with juvenile diabetes. Studies done on the island of Samoa show a great discrepency in the rates of diabetes between kids raised on the island and those who emigrated to Australia, New Zealand, or North America. Samoans do not use cow's milk as a staple for their kids and have an extremely low incidence of diabetes. However, once these kids were exposed to dairy products, their incidence of diabetes rose to match that of the local population.

---

### 2. How can I get enough protein?

The amount of protein the human adult needs is extremely small, only 11% of our total calories. We can find all the protein we need in plant sources. Excellent ones include beans, lentils, garbanzos, and rice. Indeed, even broccoli has enough protein for our needs. All the various amino acids that make up our proteins can be found by eating a variety of vegetables and fruits.

### 3. How do I get enough iron without eating meat?

This question has been cleverly posed by the meat industry, anxious to undermine vegetarianism. Meat does have more readily absorbable iron than other foods; however, the human body doesn't need much of the stuff, and what it does need can be easily taken out of vegetable sources such as beans and green leafy vegetables. When one considers that experts are now touting "anti-oxidants" to reverse the oxidizing effects of excess iron in our bloodstream, it seems clear that there is no value in overdoing our iron intake. Excess iron is stored in our tissues and, especially in post-menopausal women, has been implicated in heart disease. The Red Cross is pleased with the new evidence, because it underscores that there are no risks, and now some benefits, to a healthy adult donating blood. Only those who are anemic are likely to need extra iron, and it is important for this condition to be investigated by your doctor during regular checkups.

### 4. What about all the pesticides sprayed on fruits and vegetables?

Here is one area that causes many consumers to throw their hands up in despair. Just when one is convinced to make the commitment to eating healthier foods and turn to vegetarianism, along come the latest reports on the dangers of pesticides and chemical fertilizers dusted onto the surfaces or incorporated into the substance of all our fresh produce. This is a classic example of the heavy-handed excesses and short-term thinking of our food industry.

The reason we dust, spray, and till so many chemicals into our growing crops is simple. We have been conned into thinking that all vegetables and fruits must have the most perfect shape and color (in just the same way that models for candy ads must have unblemished skin and beautiful lithe bodies). A quick look at the produce shelves confirms the uniform beauty that we have been lured into demanding. All oranges are orange, apples are shiny red or green, bananas are unblemished by bruises, and the vegetables glisten the way they do in the food ads.

What we have been conned out of realizing is that these foods are grown out of dead soil, with nary a worm, beetle, or microbe to be found. The soil is little richer than a bag of brown styrofoam chips and would probably not grow anything were it not for the tons of chemicals added to it, much to the delight of the oil-producing cartels, whose exports supply our need for these chemicals. The purpose is to produce "perfect" foods, but the reality is the opposite.

The whole idea of insecticides is to reduce the amount of crops lost to bugs. A generation ago, about 7% of all crops were lost to these pests. Today, after dumping billions of dollars of chemicals onto our food supply, we now lose about 13%. Those bugs must be having a good laugh at our expense.

Another advance fobbed off on us is seedless watermelons, grapes, and other fruits. All this has done is breed strains of these that are very fragile, requiring constant spraying to keep them from getting infested. The original fruits, with seeds intact, are much hardier, and can thrive without such additives, but the lazy consumer won't buy them.

Organic farmers are rising to the challenge. After about two years of work, they can develop "live" soil, with rich-smelling, fertile nutrients, that doesn't need the support of additives. Using fire to fight fire, or in this case, using pests to fight pests, they introduce harmless insects to prey on the bad ones, removing the need for expensive crop dusting. With proper crop rotation and harvest management, they can maintain the fertility of the soil without nitrogen supplements. By allowing natural microbes, worms, and insects to repopulate the ground, root systems are given ready access to oxygen. After a couple of seasons, organic farmers are seeing higher overall crop yields, with lower costs for labor, tools, and chemicals. By forming associations of like-minded growers in farming communities across the land, they pool the latest developments in organic farming, technology, and crop breeding.

The most important weapon of the organic farmer is public education. Consumers are realizing the hazards of picture-perfect "spray-painted" produce and are beginning to accept more natural foods. Many supermarkets are joining specialty stores in offering organically grown foods, and, as economies of scale improve distribution and costs, these may soon take over a much larger share of the stores. As families discover the hidden bonus of taste and texture that make up for an imperfect outer appearance, we may soon see the public leading the parade toward more healthy foods, leaving the shortsighted food industry scrambling. Remember, it takes about fifteen pounds of chemically grown vegetables to yield one pound of beef. That means that all the fat-soluble toxins eaten by barnyard animals are concentrated in their flesh. In other words, the effects of toxins are magnified by eating high on the food chain; our vegetables are far safer if we eat them first, rather than waiting until the animals eat them, then eating the animals.

## 5. Isn't vegetarian cooking time-consuming, complicated, and in the end, tasteless?

The answer here is a flat no. In fact, although we have been conned into thinking the fats add to the taste of a meal, they are largely neutral. The items that really give taste are spices, herbs, and condiments like ketchup, barbecue sauce, and salsa; all of these are fine on the vegetarian diet, and in fact are often the missing ingredients that make the meat diets tasty in the first place. Secondly, the vegetarian diet need not be complicated at all. A pasta dish is as easy to prepare without meat in its sauce as it is with. A baked potato with marinara sauce is as quick to make in the microwave as a tray of bacon. A platter full of lightly oiled bell peppers, zucchini, and onion chunks can make a fine barbecued shish kebab and is no more difficult to prepare than the meat variety. The *Counterattack!* recipes contained in Chapter 10 are all designed to require minimum effort while providing maximum taste.

In general, then, the best diet is clearly one high in fiber and low in fat. The simplest way to reach these goals is to eat the way our ancestors ate, which is mainly vegetarian. If you do wish to indulge an unrepentant taste for meats, make it modest, and remember to compensate by skipping fatty desserts or butter at the same meal. If all else fails, do as I do; periodically I declare salmon an honorary vegetable.

5

# Tubby or Not Tubby?
# That Is the Question

MOST OF THE WORLD is engaged in a food fight, although not the kind that conjures up images of fraternity parties and Three Stooges films. Great numbers of the world's people involuntarily suffer from malnutrition and the effects of famine, and they exhibit terrible related diseases like kwashiorkor and marasmus, chronic diarrhea, rickets, and kidney failure, to name but a few. For them, the fight is to find enough food to stay alive. At the same time, in the Western world, especially in the United States, Canada, and Europe, millions of obese people fight to lose weight, and in the process have created an "epidemic" of self-inflicted diseases, such as constipation, heart disease, back pain, gallstones, and many forms of cancer. The solutions for involuntary undernourishment are outside the scope of this book and lie largely in the political, military, and international public-health arenas. The solutions for voluntary overnourishment are more easily within the grasp of the individual.

The reasons for obesity are as complex as the human psyche, but the resulting fat is a matter of simple arithmetic. When more calories are eaten than are burned off, the excess is stored as fat. Obesity on a mass scale is a disorder unique to twentieth-century humans and, tellingly, to the household pets that we also overfeed. All other members of the animal kingdom have the sense to stop eating when they have filled their needs. Clearly the problem is not with intelligence, where humans outrank "mere" animals, but with our computer-age lifestyle, with its absence of exercise, new forms of stress, and foods that have been processed to remove the fiber and increase the fat content. In the face of these new realities, all our old habits, including the "food rules" that we were taught in school, are completely inadequate in overcoming our fatal attraction to fat. That's why the plethora of diet books pumping more information into the left brain may add to the store of intelligence, but do nothing to overcome the paradigms or mindsets in the right brain. In consequence, obese people, often highly intelligent, continue to inflate their bodies, clog their arteries, and give themselves deadly diseases. While many may pause in their lemming-like march for a temporary diet or two, most rejoin the herd, headed for sure disaster.

Another reality of our time is the short attention span, fostered by images that change every two seconds in televised music videos, ads, and even newscasts. Most obese people have a sense of urgency about losing weight. This is one of the attractions of the word "fast," because it implies an element of speed along with weight loss. Diet books have leapt into this breach with misleading titles that titillate the dieter's desire for an instant cure: *Thin Thighs for the '90s* (of course, all the weight shifts to your stomach); *Willpower — Who Needs It?* (the inside story of liposuction); or *Lose 50 Pounds in 50 Days* (and wind up in the hospital).

In fact, new evidence shows that these fad diet books are not only useless, but may indeed do more harm than good. Recent studies confirm that "yo-yo" dieters may be giving themselves a far greater risk of heart disease than their peers who maintain modest levels of obesity.

## YO-YO DIETERS

**D**ieters often lose weight in cycles, for example, in January after a New Year's resolution, or prior to the summer bathing-suit season, and most put the weight back on just as quickly thereafter. Some chronic dieters have literally lost a half a ton, then gained it back. Not only do these yo-yo dieters experience intense frustration as they alternate between denial of the foods they crave and guilt for the pounds they regain, they also increase the risk of heart disease. Dr. Kelly Brownell, a psychologist at Yale University, published a study in the *New England Journal of Medicine* showing that yo-yo dieters have a 70% greater risk of dying from heart disease than those who maintain moderate obesity (up to an excess 25 pounds or 10% of their ideal body weight).

Unfortunately, while this research reveals a very real problem that must be addressed, it also offers false consolation to the obese. The fact that frequent temporary weight loss is more dangerous than moderate obesity does not mean that a single *permanent* weight reduction is dangerous. In fact, Dr. Brownell's finding only underscores the importance of going on just one diet, no matter how many you have been on in the past, and sticking to it for life. Fortunately, you will find my Ten-Step Counterattack! Diet Plan for Guaranteed Safe Weight Loss (see pages 87-88) to be the easiest regimen you have ever tried, and once you have gone past the first few days of it, you will never think of yourself as being on any kind of a diet at all.

To rid our bodies of excess fat once and for all, we should look at the big picture. Obesity comes in many sizes, from medium to XXXL. Many people of normal weight consider themselves obese because of a problem area such as big hips, or a flabby stomach, or simply because they have a distorted self-image or deeper psychiatric problems. When these people follow a diet designed to fight true obesity, they become malnourished and weak, or succumb to eating disorders like anorexia and bulimia.

When I refer here to obesity, I mean the true medical variety. In textbooks this is defined by actuarial tables of weight ranges for particular heights and ages.

## FAT BY NUMBERS

To calculate your (very) approximate "ideal" weight, start with 100 pounds if you are female, and 115 pounds if you are male. Then simply add five pounds per inch of height over five feet. Thus, a five-foot-one-inch woman should weigh about 105 pounds, and a six-foot man should weigh about 175 pounds. In recent years insurance companies have increased these numbers somewhat, mainly because the "average" weights are higher in our culture.

---

Of course, any weight chart can be wildly inaccurate unless consideration for muscle mass is given. In other words, Arnold Schwarzenegger in his body-building prime would have found himself listed as "obese" on some charts, because he weighed 75 pounds over his suggested maximum. However, the old "swim-suit" test shows that his excess weight was anything but fat, and indeed his health might have suffered if he'd arbitrarily starved himself down to 170 pounds. By the same token, many who are their "ideal" weight have let their muscles disintegrate through disuse and, much like factory-raised chickens, have replaced peripheral muscle with central fat. Typically, this body shape looks like four toothpicks stuck in an avocado, with skinny legs and arms, maybe a skinny face, but lots of fat around the waist or bottom. Even if the total package comes in at the "normal" weight, this is clearly an unhealthy state.

When a doctor wishes to detect those patients most likely to have a sudden heart attack, the best equipment is not the EKG, the stethoscope, or the blood pressure cuff. Nor is the best measure found by expensive tests like stress EKGs, angiograms, or PET scans. The most revealing test of all requires the humble tape measure. This test can be done right now, by you, dear reader, in the comfort of your own home. All you need is two measurements: the circumferences of your waist and your hips. If the hips are larger than the waist, as they are intended to be in both men and women, then the cardiac risks are low. For women, the waist should be no greater than 80% of their hip measurement; for men, no greater than 95%. If the waist is larger than the hips, then the risks are high. This ratio is also denoted by the shape of the torso. The safer configuration when you inspect your reflection in the mirror is to see the "pear" shape of your waist and hips. The dangerous shape is the "apple" configuration. This, in part, explains why your large-bottomed Aunt Tillie was able to survive her extra blubber much longer than did your late Uncle Fred, whose beer-barrel belly forewarned of his heart attack.

In men, this dangerous fat accumulation around the waist can often be buried deep inside the abdomen (in the omentum, or "fat apron," that lines the peritoneal cavity). That's why tub-shaped men are often deluded into thinking they are not obese, because their total weight might still be the same as in their earlier athletic careers (when their arms and legs rippled with muscles). Now that their mass has retreated centrally, much like a turtle retracting into its shell, their abdominal skin and underlying muscles may be just as firm as ever, even if their belt size is five notches bigger than it used to be. These pre-cardiac ex-jocks can be tricked into complacency by their "underground" fat, often with tragic consequences.

## The Results of Obesity

While organizations of fat people complain that they are discriminated against, the real consequences of obesity are its health risks. Obesity places a tremendous burden on the body, and on all our pocketbooks in health-care costs. At a time when governments are scrambling to reduce the health-care bills, and insurance companies are trying to contain premiums, obesity is a classic situation where individual empowerment can be a lot more cost-effective than liposuction clinics and heart-transplant wards.

Obesity gets riskier by degrees. Modest obesity of an extra ten or twenty pounds is not nearly as harmful as the morbid obesity of those who sport an extra hundred pounds. Young adults who weigh double or even triple their ideal weights are not likely to live to see their fiftieth birthdays. While the cause of such deaths is usually a massive heart attack, the severely obese usually suffer from other conditions that contribute to a lifetime of ill health, long before the final whistle blows.

## Conditions Made Worse by Obesity

### Head and neck

Headaches
Thyroid disorders
Strokes

### Abdomen

Diabetes (almost guaranteed by severe obesity)
Liver failure
Gallstones
Kidney failure
Diverticulosis/diverticulitis
Hiatus hernia
Stomach and duodenal ulcers
Bladder infections
Prolapsed uterus and bladder in women
Hemorrhoids
Constipation

### Chest

Heart attacks
Pneumonia
Asphyxiation/choking (it's much harder to do effective CPR or Heimlich maneuvers on obese bodies; in addition, overeaters have, by virtue of the frequency of their intake, far more opportunities to choke on food)

### Limbs

Varicose veins
Gout
Arthritis, made worse in the back and legs by carrying the burden of extra weight around

"Fallen" arches, bunions, and otherwise painful feet, ankle, and knee joints

## Skin

Acne

Fungal infections in the nether regions. These usually show up as a foul-smelling red rash deep in redundant skin folds, such as in the groin or under the breasts. Because these valleys of skin never see daylight or air, infections here are hard to treat with medication.

## Cancers

Many cancers are believed to be caused by our high-fat diet. While some controversy exists as doctors try to prove the links with specific cancers, one fact is clear. It is easy to detect a small stone in your bed if it is just under the top sheet, but very difficult if the stone is beneath eight inches of mattress padding. For this reason, a small abdominal tumor hidden under a thick slab of blubber is likely to go undetected until it becomes massive or starts to cause obvious symptoms. With virtually all cancers, early detection enhances the cure rates, meaning that the obese are often diagnosed too late.

## Energy and Fatigue

Hikers carrying heavy backpacks feel elated when they can finally unload their burden. Their energy levels improve, they have more spring in their step, and they feel optimistic. When the load is back in place, they tire much more readily. The obese are carrying even heavier loads, but are unable to set them aside for even a minute. Every time an obese person rises from a chair, climbs a stair, or even bends over to tie a shoe, he or she is lifting the equivalent of a backpack full of rocks, in addition to the normal body frame. It comes as no surprise, then, that many obese are chronically tired and not at all inclined to exercise their already exhausted muscles.

## Fertility

Many couples are infertile today, for a variety of reasons, and clinical obesity can be one of them. For reasons not yet fully known, grossly obese people seem to have a reduction of their sex hormones. If both partners are severely obese, there is also a practical anatomical problem with contriving to have intercourse at all. One of the first steps advised by infertility specialists is that obese patients lose weight. (It should also be noted that infertile patients who are underweight are given the opposite advice. It seems that fertility is optimum when one falls within the recommended range of body weight.)

## Psychological Effects

There is no question that the obese are a visible majority. Apart from wearing a tarpaulin and a fencing mask, there is no real way to disguise true obesity. Being overweight has a definite negative effect on self-image, causing many to feel ostracized, anxious, depressed, and lonely. These negative feelings fuel the rush to a food fix, and reinforce the cycle of obesity.

While many obese people appear to be among the "happy fat," who have so many other positive qualities that their obesity doesn't bother them, most will privately admit to wishing they were thinner. The stigma of extra pounds can be especially hard on teenagers, and for social reasons girls feel more pressure to be thin than boys. Sadly, "thinning" options such as anorexia, bulimia, and smoking have been on the rise among young women.

## Job Discrimination

Some obese find themselves victims of discrimination when they apply for a job or when they apply for a promotion. Their employers may assume that the fat employee is not only out of control of his or her food intake, but lacks discipline, ambition, and character as well. Sometimes this discrimination is sexist, such as that shown by male airline executives who formerly insisted that all flight attendants be model-trim. Often the prejudice crosses gender borders (when was the last time you saw a

300-pound TV news anchor of either sex?). Usually such cases are unjust forms of prejudice and can be appealed legally, but the psychological and economic damage they cause to the overweight person is hard to undo.

## The Causes of Obesity

I have long observed, in the thousands of cases of obesity that I have treated, that obesity itself is never the problem. Obesity is always the *result* of a problem, and unless the underlying reasons are treated, the extra poundage will never disappear for longer than a few weeks or months. Obese people have nothing wrong with their intelligence, and virtually all know that ice-cream sundaes are fattening, while celery is not. The real causes of obesity are often invisible to the individual, but once he or she is presented with the possible culprits, he or she can easily identify the ones that apply. This is usually the first step toward a lasting cure.

## The Twelve Underlying Causes

### 1. Too Little Stress, a.k.a. Boredom

This is common, especially among the recently retired, or among career parents who choose to quit work to stay home and rear their babies. With too little stimulation from other adults, many turn to food for solace. They will camp out in front of the fridge, nibbling their way to the big time. These patients usually have at least three bookshelves full of disused diet books, drawers full of used coupons from diet centers, and files of sophisticated nutrition articles clipped from magazines. But if they don't lessen the boredom in their daily routines, no diet will ever work. Food, like nature, abhors a vacuum.

### 2. Too Much Stress, a.k.a. Burnout

Here we see the exact opposite cause of obesity — too much stimulation. In these cases, the individual is overwhelmed by so many challenges at work, or at home, that he or she discards personal care from the priority list. Food is usually an absent-minded afterthought, such as gobbling peanuts over the sink, nibbling chips and cheeseburgers at the desk, or secretly scarfing a row of Oreos and a brick of ice cream after the kids go to bed. These patients will never cure their obesity permanently unless they learn some basic skills of stress, time, and priority management.

### 3. Too Little Food on the Plate

Here is a paradox: obesity caused by little or no food at mealtimes, especially at breakfast. Many obese patients are so full from their midnight snacks that they wake up feeling like a python that swallowed a hog. Because they can cruise through the first few hours of the morning without adding more food to their stomachs, breakfast seems an easy sacrifice to make. However, by mid-morning the stomach starts voicing its emptiness, compelling its owner to ingest ill-advised "panic" snacks. Because these snacks are usually high in fats and low in fiber, they don't fill up the stomach for long. Cunning manufacturers add sugars and salt to snack foods to enhance the stomach's rebound cravings (as the advertisers say, nobody eats just one potato chip or one cookie). The mid-morning donut by the coffee urn usually starts a daily avalanche of food that will not stop until bedtime.

### 4. Too Much Food on the Plate

This is an obvious sin, one that only occurs after the obese have come out of the (kitchen) closet. The overloaded plate is easily observed at the smorgasbord meal, where the overeater can tank up on second and third helpings for all to see. But full plates alone are not a cause of obesity. It is possible to eat huge quantities of the right foods, if they are low in fats and high in fiber, but most overeaters are fueling their bodies with high-fat, low-fiber foods. Because the stomach is an expandable bag (just like the bagpipe), it becomes larger with habitual overfeeding, creating increased appetite. In general, it is advisable to keep the size of a meal down to a single plateful, to avoid the temptations of overeating.

## 5. Insufficient Information

While most people know the obvious sources of fat in their diet, it is remarkable how many are deceived by false advertising. When one needs to aim for low fat, in the 10 to 15% range, it is important to be able to recognize the hidden fats lying in ambush.

Many patients tell me all about their miniscule meals: "I only eat two slices of radish for dinner. Do you think that's what's making me fat?" they ask. However, they may be blissfully unaware of the 500 calories and 40 grams of fat that lurk in every handful of peanuts, nor are they aware of the two grams of fat in almost every cookie. Still others carefully watch their foods, but ignore calories in drinks. Piña coladas, even without the alcohol, are terribly fattening. Indeed, most juices (with the exception of grapefruit, cranberry, and tomato) are full of calories, yet, because they contain no fiber, are no more filling than water.

Oat-bran muffins may have more fat than birthday cake, and an avocado is a veritable lard grenade. More than one alleged dieter has passed on the restaurant main course, choosing instead to suffer through the Caesar salad like a martyr — a fat martyr, that is. It turns out that the Caesar salad, with its oil, egg yolks, anchovies, and bacon pieces, has more fat than cheesecake. Meanwhile, most dieters avoid the humble potato, without realizing it has no more calories than, and just as much fiber as, an apple.

## 6. Poor Self-Image

This is a very important element in obesity, one that can range from a mild affliction to deep-seated psychological trauma dating back to childhood. When a person has a poor self-image, he or she doesn't see the point of treating the body as a temple. Instead, there is often a perverse sense of pleasure in treating the body as a garbage dump, eating damaging foods, and lots of them, with a sense of self-punishment. Celebrities like Oprah Winfrey, who courageously exposed the traumas of early child abuse that undermined her battle to lose weight, have increased public awareness about the connection between mental wellness and physical health. Many obese people need the support of professional counseling to overcome the root causes of their eating problems.

## 7. Peer Pressure

Many obese people are surrounded by family, friends, and even whole communities of the similarly afflicted. For them, obesity is a cultural problem, not simply a problem of lack of information about food and health risks. The situation usually starts in childhood with the infamous admonition to "finish everything on your plate," even when the child is past the point of satiety. Among adults, this peer pressure manifests itself in feeling compelled to finish all courses when out for dinner, or to partake of a friend's home-baked goodies when you have just popped by for a brief conversation.

Members of the obese person's "non-support" group may feel threatened when he or she starts to lose weight, fearing that it reflects poorly on their own lack of self-discipline. In much the same way that it is hard to quit smoking if all your friends are heavy smokers, and hard to quit boozing if all your friends are barflies, it is difficult for an obese dieter to lose weight permanently if he or she is embarrassed to ask for off-the-menu meals at a restaurant, or afraid to seem rude by turning down fatty foods at dinner parties. The successful pound shedder needs to develop a strategy to replace group habits with individual choices.

## 8. Eating by Association

Here we see overeating blamed on outside events, such as going out for dinner, having company in, attending a banquet, or going to a wedding. For some, the Pavlovian association is between televised sporting events and potato chips and beer, while others get the midnight "munchies" watching late-night talk shows. Some overeat every time they walk past a favorite deli or donut shop during the week, but never feel the temptations for those foods when they are in a different environment during the weekend or holidays. These reactive responses must be first identified, then changed into proactive eating habits.

## 9. Sabotage

Mom sees her teenaged daughter start to turn a few male heads and may perceive this attention as a threat to her own image. This is particularly true when men (including Dad) who used to favor Mom with attention are now bypassing her to notice her younger edition. One common response is for the mother to try to fatten up the daughter: "Here, dear, you can eat all the rest of these chocolates, you don't have to worry at your age." Sometimes the successful weight loser's obese friends start to get pressure from their own spouses to shape up ("If she can lose weight why can't you?"). The response is to attack the now-thin peer with calories: "Oh, do try a piece of this cheesecake, I baked it especially because you were coming over. Besides, you are so thin now you don't have to worry about your diet any-more." When dieters find themselves to be a slender reed, alone in a forest of stout peers, they need added resourcefulness to bend in their own direction.

## 10. Paradigm Paralysis

Many obese have read every food fact known to humanity, have a vast knowledge of the foods good and bad, yet they still fall prey to the lure of the fudge bar, or the siren call of the soft cone. These are the people who have been duped into the food industry machine's association between bad foods and good images, all firmly ensconced in the right brain as paradigms. The phenomenon is easily recognized by the persistence of an old food habit in times of stress. For example, all might go well for the three meals during the day, but the dieter turns to fats when anxious, tense, lonely, or simply feeling the munchies at midnight. In other cases the bad habit is associated with a particular location, or group of friends. For example, the pre-shift coffee with co-workers at the donut shop. This urge for a bloated lard muffin would never crop up in a different setting.

## 11. Binge Eating

This is a condition where the obese person eats apparently modest meals, yet will periodically binge on high-fat foods.

These binges may be infrequent, but substantial (not unlike the alcoholic who stays sober for a few weeks between bouts of heavy drinking). When these obese bingers are on holiday with thin friends, it may be noted that they eat no more, publicly, than their companions for a whole week, but their excess weight has come from prior feedings. Often such incidents of feeding frenzy are absent-minded (munching a whole box of cookies in front of a late-night movie), or blocked from conscious recall, but the body remembers every last calorie.

### 12. Obesity

One of the least-known causes of obesity is obesity itself. Once fat, the obese person has more difficulty being active. Even the simplest of movements, such as walking across the room, burns off fewer calories. Indeed, there is little spring in the heavy person's step, and a greater temptation to stay down once settled in for the evening. There may also be a lowering of the overall metabolism, which, in combination with the fewer calories burned off through daily activities, means that it is harder for a severely fat person to lose weight than for a person who needs to lose only five or ten pounds.

## The Cures of Obesity

Obesity may look the same in every fat patient, but it has so many causes no one treatment will work for all. Similarly, tonsillitis might look the same in each patient, but it can be caused by many different bacteria, with each responding to a different antibiotic. If one uses the same penicillin on everyone, the results will not be as good as if one customizes the antibiotic choice to the culture report. By first examining the list of causes, the dieter can then select the appropriate cure(s) from the list following and avoid wasting time and energy on strategies that are useless or harmful, or don't apply to his or her situation.

## 1. Empty Stomach Diets

### a) Starvation/Fasting

This one is very popular among the obese. After one pigs out, whether chronically, or on a recent binge, it is easy to get mad at oneself, and the easiest punishment is starvation. In the process, no new information is gained, no new food images are formed, and no underlying causes are addressed. Fasting is absolutely useless as a practical and long-term strategy for obesity. To make matters worse, once the empty stomach lets its displeasure be known through cramps and loud growls, it is difficult indeed to withstand the temptations of the wrong foods after the fast is over.

### b) Liquid Diets

These have been around for a long time, and were originally invented as a food supplement to help underweight people gain. It was soon found that these liquid foods could be sold to dieters, with the proviso that they stop all solid foods. The liquid diets are hugely profitable, and come in powders or pre-mixed forms. While celebrities such as Oprah Winfrey have popularized them, they clearly do not work in the long term, unless the underlying causes are treated. Besides, our teeth need something to chew on, our stomachs need something to break down, and our bowels need solid fiber to keep them moving. Predigested foods like these are unsatisfying from one end of our digestive tract to the other.

### c) Reduced-portion Diets

This one is a real pain. Portion control basically requires weighing all foods on a set of scales prior to every meal. No matter what foods are on the plate (even if they are low-fat vegetables), these diets tell you to count everything and eat only meager quantities. If one is active (as one should be to lose weight), these arbitrary small meals contrive to cause fatigue, and the dieter never has a feeling of satisfaction after a meal. Besides, with today's time famine, who can afford the extra hours for doing food calculations?

### d) Teeth Wiring

This dieting method was born from the observation of patients who had fractured their jaws and had their teeth wired together for several weeks to allow the bones to mend. It is almost impossible for these patients to maintain their weight, especially if they are overweight, because all foods must be taken through a straw. By dint of the tiring effects of all this suction, overeating becomes exhausting. Some obese people have undergone teeth wiring in a desperate attempt to control their urges. I have seen several such patients, all of whom lost weight when the wires were on, none of whom addressed the paradigms that kept them eating the wrong foods, and all of whom gained back their weight (and more) after the wires were removed. There are additional risks, such as inhaling vomit.

### e) Stomach Stapling or Intestinal Bypass Surgery

Many who are chronically obese and fed up with being fed up find the idea of surgery attractive. Staple or cut the stomach so that it can hold only half as much, and there is no more need for willpower. But even the stapled stomach can stretch, and the determined overeater may focus on concentrated fatty foods, negating the effects of the surgery. The surgical bypass has also been tried: great lengths of intestine are bypassed so that no matter how much food enters the stomach, there is not enough bowel to absorb it all into the bloodstream. This "treatment" has been shown to be fraught with serious digestive complications. The only bypass that would work is the unviable option of hooking up the throat directly to the rectum.

## 2. Full Stomach Diets

### a) Bulimia

The obese bulimic decides that eating is not the problem, rather swallowing is. The dieter ignores all the underlying causes of the obesity, carries on eating willy-nilly, then quietly regurgitates between courses. "Biofoodback" is my name for this serious psychological disorder, which can result in serious physical complications.

### b) Liposuction

Here the trick is to eat all you want, deposit the excess calories in your hips, stomach, or chin wattles, then report to the plastic surgeon for $10,000 worth of fat suction. The surgeon makes a few small incisions in the skin, inserts one end of a metal nozzle, turns on the vacuum, and fills a glass bottle with greasy yellow fat blobs, tinged with blood. The dieter, having learned absolutely nothing at all about the laws of cause and effect, can then proceed to eat all the wrong foods until the next treatment. It would be safer to vacuum the dieter's plate, *before* the food enters the body.

## 3. Flossing

This seemingly odd dieting method can be useful, especially for those suffering from late night munchies. After a good session of gargling, flossing, and picking, brush your teeth (and roof of the mouth, gums, cheek linings, and tongue) with a minty toothpaste. Having gone to all that trouble, it seems easier to resist snacking on that piece of gooey cake sitting in the fridge. This works best for late-night snackers if one turns off the television and takes a book to bed; if one stays awake for a few more hours, the taste of toothpaste will wear off.

## 4. Hypnosis

This works well for those who are obese because of poor self-image, peer pressure, or sabotage, and is also useful in cases where eating is done by association. Post-hypnotic suggestion is a powerful way of introducing new habits, such as substituting what I call the "dieter's trilogy": a slow deep breath, a firm "no thank-you," and a quick U-turn or change of subject away from the proffered excess calories.

## 5. Acupuncture

One of the fastest-growing obesity treatments is acupuncture. Acupuncture releases the body's own molecules of morphine, called endorphins, and these act as a powerful appetite suppressant. In effect, acupuncture works because it converts an individual's food addiction into a morphine addiction, but because the morphine in question is *end*orphin (from the patient's own body), there are none of the dangers inherent with the bottled drug.

I have successfully used acupuncture in my office for years to treat obesity, but never as a stand-alone cure. If it were that simple, there would be drive-through acupuncture shops where the patient would simply stick an arm through the window for each treatment. Along with the other cures mentioned in this chapter (selected according to the causes of each patient's obesity), acupuncture can help keep the dieter on the right path. Typically, I use a needle in each ear, as well as one in each hand or elbow. I stimulate each pair with a low-intensity current, and afterwards supply the patient with adhesive stimulation points for each ear. In between weekly treatments at my office, the patient occasionally rubs the patch, which has a small steel pellet underneath. The patch seems to generate a moderate endorphin effect, which supplements the endorphin generated by electrical stimulations. My patients tell me their appetites are suppressed and their self-control is improved. In most cases, their excess weight is steadily lost.

## 6. Information: Left-Brain Food

There are many people who do regular exercise and never eat more than a plateful of food at a meal, and yet who are obese. As we have seen, for some the problem can simply be a lack of information, in particular about the high quantities of fats that may be hidden in so-called health foods. These people falsely assume that their problem must be bad genetics or slow metabolism, when in reality they are being sabotaged by the huge levels of fats in muffins, Caesar salads, or even vegetarian lasagna. For these patients, I conduct seminars (and have written this book) to help correct misconceptions. Input from a dietitian who is skilled in making low-fat foods tasteful is also critical to the educational process. The patient needs to learn new cooking techniques, recipes, and menu selections. At Porter Hospital in Denver, where I practise, we have the nutritionists take groups of obese patients to the supermarket for "front line" shopping lessons.

## CAVEAT EMPTOR

My wife recently brought home a can of vegetarian chili, picked out by one of our children on a busy shopping trip. Although she quickly spotted the ruse, she brought it home to add to my collection of examples to show patients. The label is festooned with health buzzwords, such as "cholesterol free," "vegetarian," "chili," and "...with beans." The fact that the contents are extremely high in fat is cleverly hidden in the fine print on the back. While new labeling laws make it easier for customers to find the right information, an inspection of the back of this label is instructive. First of all, most of the information on a label is "filler" and, by its very presence, tends to dilute the key facts. The only two numbers we need are the total calories per serving, 320, and the total fat per serving, 20 grams. Now we need to multiply the fat grams by nine (because there are nine calories in each gram of fat) to get 180 calories. This means that 56% ($^{180}/_{320}$) of the total calories come from fat! Considering that the portion size is only half the container, the daily recommended fat intake could be exceeded by this one can, meaning that any additional fats during the rest of the day would be worn, either on the body or inside the arteries. When the consumer realizes this, he or she can then inspect the regular can of beans (in tomato sauce) sitting next to this one on the shelf. Here the total calories are 18, and the total fats are one gram, netting a fat level of only about 5%. Both cans of beans are equally filling. By simply keeping the 15% fat level in mind, it is easy to switch to low-fat options when presented with such choices.

## 7. Paradigm Shifting: Right-Brain Exercise

One of the most important shifts of paradigms in the right brain is that of one's self-image. If the obese person visualizes himself or herself as thin, then the goal of an ideal weight becomes sustainable. If that goal is reached but the dieter finds his or her thin reflection in the mirror to be in conflict with a self-image of plumpness, then the weight returns. This urge to be at one with our self-image is so strong that no amount of compliments or rewards will keep a dieter suffering this dissonance in the thin state for long. In fact, the newfound attention often frightens the dieter back to the safety of a more "comfortable" plumpness.

Another paradigm shift needed to fight obesity is to recognize that it doesn't take superhuman effort to make the right choices. Often the obese view healthy foods as "boring" or picture them served in such ridiculously small portions that they wouldn't satisfy anyone's appetite for long.

But perhaps the most difficult paradigm shift is to acknowledge the fine tastes and feelings associated with the old favorite fattening foods while divorcing yourself from overindulgence in them.

## The Ten-Step Counterattack! Diet Plan for Guaranteed Safe Weight Loss

**1. Eat three meals a day, at normal mealtimes.**

**2. Fill your plate at each meal.**

**3. Drink at least ten glasses of bottled or filtered water a day.**

**4. Choose only foods high in fiber, low in fat.**

**5. Eliminate meat, poultry, and fish, or restrict them to infrequent occasions.**

**6. Avoid drinks with calories.**

This gives you more room to fill up on healthy low-fat, high-fiber solid foods.

### 7. Skip dairy products, order pizza without cheese, and avoid butter.

Also skip non-dairy substitutes. They're usually no better for you. Margarine is just as fatty as butter or lard, and non-dairy coffee whiteners have a surprising amount of aluminum. It's also wise to get in the habit of using non-stick cookware, and using the most miserly dose of light oil, wiped away with a paper towel.

### 8. Skip food substitutes, like artificial eggs or artificial fats.

While I heartily approve of the principle of recycling, I am loath to eat any chemically derived "food," for fear that, in its former life, said polymer might have been a tread on somebody's old snow tire. It's better to keep buying eggs, but throwing out the yolks, or to keep buying tinned peach slices rather than "lite" peach ice cream.

### 9. Keep healthy snack foods handy.

One of my favorite nibbles is a bowl of Cheerios, or other fat-free cereal. Low in fat, with no milk necessary, these become a great substitute for peanuts or potato chips during a ball game.

### 10. Cut out all fatuous excuses for fat.

Don't tell yourself you can't lose weight; say you haven't yet lost weight. While the former takes away all hope of success, the latter implies you are ready to learn new habits. Don't kid yourself that your problem is a slow metabolism, or that it must be glandular (a few simple tests at your doctor's office can rule this out). It has been shown that most obese people greatly underestimate how much they eat and wildly overestimate how much physical activity they do. If you are fat, you are eating too much and/or burning off too little. Remember that weight loss is a slow process. If you lose a pound a week, that's a respectable fifty-two pounds a year. Beware of diets that promise a fifty-pound weight loss after six weeks; they usually deliver a one-hundred-pound weight gain by the end of a year.

# 6

# Hazards Lying
# in Ambush

HEALTH HAZARDS ARE ALL AROUND US, and they come in three forms: the obvious, the known, and those lying in ambush. Obvious hazards are easy to identify, usually marked with a skull and crossbones. When we see such products in our household cleaning cabinets, we know not to ingest them, and to keep them locked up and out of the reach of children. In the case of accidents, the ingredients are clearly marked, so your emergency doctor can tell you whether to induce vomiting, and whether there is an antidote. Other hazards bear no such warnings but, due to widespread publicity, they are still recognized by the public. Examples of these unlabeled (but known) threats are second-hand cigarette smoke, air and water pollution, poisonous toadstools, and radiation from the sun. Even though many choose to ignore such overt health hazards, their actions do not stem from the lack of available information.

Ambush hazards are the unmentioned and unnoticed dangerous products that have somehow slipped through the net of product warning labels and government regulation. We can protect ourselves from these hazards only through information, and it is to *counterattack* these hazards that we shall expose them in this chapter.

## Chance vs Choice: Avoiding Known Hazards

**D**eath and illness evoke much sympathy, and are most often attributed to chance by friends, relatives, and victims. "It's too bad Mrs. Brown got Alzheimer's disease," or "What bad luck that Grandpa has lung cancer." Once the tragic *effects* of these diseases have been attended to by modern medicine, it is useful for the rest of us to consider the real *causes* of these disasters to see how few of them were inevitable (attributable to chance) and how many were avoidable (attributable to choice).

Most of our medical resources are spent either researching obscure diseases or, more commonly, treating long-standing lifestyle diseases during the last thirty days of a patient's life. In order to maximize the lives saved with our medical dollars, we must question our quixotic tilting at esoteric windmills and face this fact: illness and premature death are usually determined by choice, not by chance.

---

### HOW DO YOU MAKE CHOICES?

**A**n old system of sales training uses four categories to describe the ways people make choices. These are just as relevant to health choices as they are to business decisions. In ascending order of desirability they are:

1. Unconscious Incompetent: Makes poor choice because the left brain lacks enough information; is then surprised when things turn out badly. Humphrey Bogart inspired a generation to smoke, but had no idea he would pay for his habit with his life.

2. Conscious Incompetent: Has plenty of knowledge in the left brain, but consciously makes wrong choices anyway, and ends up with things turning out badly. The late Richard Burton knew full well the dangers of his addiction to alcohol and cigarettes, but because he held (right-brain) paradigms of how insufferable

life would be without these crutches, he proceeded to self-destruct nonetheless.

3. Unconscious Competent: Has insufficient information (in the left brain) but, because of luck or instinct, makes the right choices anyway. As a result, things usually turn out well. Coco Chanel, the legendary couturière, knew nothing of the medical risks of suntanning (skin cancers, moles, wrinkles, and premature aging), yet actively avoided all exposure to the sun. She kept her youthful complexion until her seventies.

4. Conscious Competent: Has sufficient information in the left brain, and accommodating paradigm images in the right brain. To no one's great surprise, good choices now produce good results. Bob Hope continues to work at the age of ninety. Among his many smart choices, he eats a healthful diet, doesn't smoke, has a stable marriage, and exercises daily, followed by a massage.

Clearly, there are a lot of people who are in categories 1 and 2 who are becoming ill simply because of the lack of participation of both sides of the brain. Incompetence, conscious or otherwise, is hardly a prescription for excellence in any endeavor. However, even the competent people in category 3 are not safe. In today's changing world, new challenges demand good decisions all the time. The chances of an unconsciously competent person being able to continue with lucky guesses are slim. The only option that offers a modicum of security is category 4; it is only by assimilating the latest knowledge, then passing it through flexible paradigms, that competent actions and habits can be initiated and sustained.

Bad choices originate in the human brain, but it is important to know *where* in the brain the problems lie. In just the same way that a forensic autopsy can reveal causes of physical trauma to the body, a closer look at the functions of the brain will reveal causes of disasters of choice. Understanding the post-mortem is the best way to avoid the same mistakes again.

## Left-Brain Disasters: The Information Deficit

Take for example the case of a fifteen-year-old girl our hospital recently saw. Her father had remarried, giving her a new stepmother and two stepsisters. What with the trouble she was having in school and the new dynamics in her home, she desperately needed to get her father's attention, but seemed unable to communicate this need to him. One Saturday morning, in the depths of despair, she walked to the local grocery store and purchased 500 aspirin tablets, on special for a few dollars off. Once home, she took a couple of handfuls of the pills, hardly making a dint in the total supply. A few hours later she was brought into the emergency department, and her stomach was pumped out. But it was too late. The aspirin had already done its damage, leading to metabolic acidosis, coma, and, in spite of everything doctors could do, death within forty-eight hours.

Now, this suicide might pass through a physical autopsy to become another tragic statistic and be ascribed to the hazards of teenage stress. But it should be given special mention because it was an *unintentional* suicide. This girl did not mean to kill herself; she thought that these pills were relatively harmless, especially considering that she only took about 10% of the bottle. Had she taken Drano or some other toxin that was clearly labeled with a skull and crossbones, she would have known the consequences of her gesture. However, the fact that she died from the left brain's *lack of information*, in the middle of the Information Age, makes her death an especially cruel irony.

The same judgment could be made of another tragedy that came into our pediatric emergency department. A pregnant mother was taking a standard vitamin pill with iron, as prescribed by her obstetrician. She left these in plain view on her kitchen counter, often with the lid off. While she was taking her morning bath, her two-year-old daughter managed to climb up onto the counter and swallow eight of the pills. In spite of urgent treatment in hospital, the child absorbed a fatal dose of iron and died on the second day. While the mother had taken great pains to lock away all the known poisons in the house, she had no idea that these seemingly harmless vitamins could be so deadly. Once again, an infuriating and senseless tragedy, caused simply by the left brain's lack of information.

## Right-Brain Disasters: The Immovable Paradigm

On ward rounds during my internship, we had a twenty-four-year-old law student who suffered from Berger's disease. This is a terrible (and fortunately rare) disease afflicting young men, where the peripheral circulation is extremely sensitive to inhaled tobacco. Smoking will cause such severe constriction in the arteries that gangrene can occur in the tip of a toe. If the patient does not immediately quit cigarettes, the toe must be amputated. If he then stops smoking, all will be well. However, if he smokes even a few cigarettes, the stump of the amputation develops more gangrene, and the surgeons must amputate higher up on the foot. If the smoker resumes his habit, the surgeons resume their amputations until, in the case of this patient, his leg was amputated six inches below the hip. I watched his wound dressings being changed and noticed two alarming facts: his stump wound was developing more gangrene, and his bedside ashtray was full of cigarette butts.

Although his left brain was endowed with tremendous intelligence, and he knew that he could save his leg by stopping cigarettes, he had powerful images in his right brain that prevented this sensible action. His paradigm images showed life with cigarettes as wonderful, and life without as intolerable. His actions were therefore predetermined, and I was not surprised a year later when I asked his surgeon how he was doing. Sadly, he had not quit smoking and, though blessed with a fine intellect, he did not live.

## An Ounce of Prevention

The training of a medical doctor is to treat diseases after they occur, but we can save a lot more lives if we also prevent diseases *before* they occur. To be sure, some of the work of prevention is being done by others. Bacteriologists test our water supply for impurities, and chemists then treat any contaminants. Pharmaceutical company scientists develop immunization shots for measles and flu viruses. Scout leaders prevent stomach infections when they teach their kids to dig latrines *downstream* from the camp water supply. Neonatal nurses teach new mothers how to bathe a newborn child to prevent diaper rashes and other skin infections. Environmental ozone specialists warn us all about the dangers of exposure to the sun, and an endless stream of celebrities warn us of the dangers of unprotected sex.

However, in spite of all this information bombarding us through the media, a lot of vital prevention facts are being missed or misread. Part of the reason for the confusion lies in the nature of published medical research. A lot of people have told me they are so confused by medical reports that they don't know which way to turn. First we say that fish is bad for the heart, then we say, no, fish have omega-3 fatty acids that are good for the heart. Then we say, oops, fish may have some good elements, but they still have too much of the bad. One researcher says that red wine is good for our health (look at the French), the next one says his research shows it to be totally unhealthy (look at the French). It seems we cannot open a newspaper or magazine without being deluged with dozens of conflicting medical alarms, replete with controversial headlines.

When the popular press gets hold of research articles, they often lack the appropriate criteria to judge whether the research is sound. Valid breakthroughs gain the same headline ink as do flaky, outrageous "studies." This is especially true on slow news days. However, the informed reader can tell the sensible from the silly by knowing what to look for between the lines. Over the past five years, I have researched and written hundreds of such items for my syndicated daily radio show and have developed some guidelines for sifting through the rubbish and focusing on the real.

## How to Spot "Junk" Research

When you are confused or alarmed by a press report of a new medical finding, ask yourself the following questions:

**WHERE** was it done? Look for the name of the institute performing the study to see if it is impartial and reputable. Conclusions reached by the East Elk Snout Laboratory and Aluminum Siding Company should not take precedence over those reached by the universities of Stanford, Harvard, or Toronto. Also beware of innocuous-sounding organizations such as the Tobacco Research Council or the Dairy Bureau, which are fully funded by their industries and whose results are inevitably biased.

**WHO** was studied? Good research uses a reasonable number of subjects to rule out anecdotal evidence. Junk research often uses only a handful. A study of 50,000 patients should mean a lot more than gossip assimilated from the other three players at your bridge table. Another tip-off is the species of animal. Rats never seem to die of natural causes; with even the slightest provocation they are prone to die of some nasty disease. This does not always mean the results will apply to humans. That's why we see some truly assinine headlines like "DIET COLA CAUSES CANCER," or "CLASSICAL MUSIC MAY CAUSE WHISKERS."

**WHEN** was this done? If something was proved in 1924, that doesn't make it wrong today. However, many fad-diet books have been written that conveniently ignore modern research and cling only to outdated references. These are especially common among non-medical doctor/authors, and can entice readers into some inappropriate decisions.

**HOW LONG** were the subjects studied? In general, a longer term yields more reliable conclusions. A retrospective review of many years gives better results than a test following blood-cholesterol levels for only one week after starting a new food supplement.

**WHY** was the study done? Sometimes the story will give away clues of a hidden agenda. For example, a story on the benefits of beef may contain a quote from a spokesperson or "nutritionist" for the beef industry. This is especially obvious in cases where the news release is accompanied by suggested recipes.

**WHAT SENSE** does it make? If the article reports so-called dangers of being tall, what is the point? Should all tall people go in for bilateral leg amputations? The original studies that prompted articles on the dangers of artificial sweeteners used ridiculous doses of the stuff; if a rat is forced to drink an Olympic swimming poolful of diet cola every two hours for a year, are we to be surprised that it dies of cancer of the bladder? Besides, the researchers did not consider the weight gain (and subsequent mortality) that would occur when millions of Americans switched back to real sugar in their food and drinks. If a story guarantees life past 120 if the reader sends in $3,000 for a six-month supply of Dead Sea kelp, does this seem reasonable?

Here are some examples of alarmist medical headlines and some impartial analysis.

### "Male Baldness Causes Heart Attacks"

This finding was released by the prestigious *Journal of the American Medical Association* in March of 1993. It studied 665 men between the ages of twenty-one and fifty-four who had been hospitalized for their first heart attack, and compared them with a control group who were in the hospital for non-cardiac reasons. The conclusion was that men who were balding at the top of the scalp, or vertex, were anywhere from 30 to 300% more likely to have a heart attack, compared with those who had a full head of hair. So far it sounds like a plausible account. But who commissioned the study? None other than Upjohn Co., in 1989, the manufacturers of Rogaine (minoxidil), the only prescription brand of hair restorer on the market. The fact that Rogaine happens to work best for vertex baldness is an even greater coincidence that taints the conclusions, even if they are valid. (If the study showed that hair loss reduced the risks of heart disease, do you think Upjohn would have still paid all that money to release and promote it?) As if bald men didn't have enough to worry about, this study serves only to add worry about something that is beyond human control, and may prompt some balding men to figure they will have a heart attack anyway, so why bother with a low-fat diet?

### "Birth-Control Pills Proven to Be Killers"

Back in my internship days, in the 1970s, this headline shocked the public. The study flew in the face of all prior works and talked of the women who had died from blood clots while on the pill. They did not mention that the chances of dying from these same clots during routine pregnancy (an obvious option when the pill was not used) were many times greater. Indeed, it is estimated that over 100,000 unplanned pregnancies followed this headline as women dropped the pill and, sure enough, far more of these women suffered fatal consequences than they would have if they had all stayed on the pill. Investigators found that the "researchers" were three pathologists who had heavily invested in a company that made intrauterine devices.

### "Secondhand Smoke Causes No Harm to Others"

This one comes from several studies funded by the tobacco lobby, using astonishing logic that totally contradicts all known medical knowledge. Japan has also produced several such studies, and it should be noted that the Japanese government sells cigarettes at the same time as it officially denies that there are any side effects. Consider the source, and consider a possible agenda before you ascribe any merit to the conclusions. Would you ask a new car salesman to "study" your old car to see if he thinks you should buy a new one?

### "Red Meat an Excellent Source of Iron"

Yes, and the nuclear warhead is an outstanding source of heat, but I wouldn't want one in my furnace room. This partial truth about one of meat's elements should not be taken to endorse the healthiness of all its other components, such as cholesterol. There is also no mention of the fact that most people in this country have plenty of iron stored in their bodies, and that excessive iron may pose risks of heart disease. Indeed, iron is an "oxidant" that we go after with "antioxidants," such as vitamin E, to protect us from heart disease.

### "Egg Yolks Good for You"

True, if you happen to be a yet-to-hatch chick, but not true if you are among the millions of North Americans who suffer from obesity, heart disease, and cancer related to high fat intake. Countless reports in medical journals quote credible heart specialists telling us the opposite — that we should restrict our fats, including yolks. This headline was extracted from propaganda hatched by the Egg Marketing Board of Canada, and their researchers were unnamed. Does this sound like an unbiased conclusion?

### "Magnets, Iron Therapy Help 75-Year-Old Woman Deliver Triplets: Only Problem Is Kids All Point North"

What did you expect?? This one is from the *National Enquirer*.

So, amidst this avalanche of medical drivel and facts, it would be helpful to focus on those health hazards that are not labeled or commonly known, the ones I have dubbed ambush hazards. Many of these will surprise you.

## ALUMINUM

Once thought to be an inert metal, aluminum's safety in the human body is now being questioned in conjunction with Alzheimer's disease, a degenerative neurological disease that causes premature aging of the brain, memory loss, early senility, and premature death. While genetics and other causes may play a role in Alzheimer's, high levels of aluminum ingestion are likely also implicated; autopsies of the brains of Alzheimer's patients show plaques containing aluminum lining the cell walls. While the link between dietary aluminum intake and eventual aluminum deposits is still being investigated, no research is claiming that aluminum is likely to become a health food. Until the impact of aluminum on the human body becomes clear, the prudent consumer should be aware of some of the foods and skin-care products (most elements are easily absorbed through the skin into the bloodstream) that are high in aluminum, especially when alternatives exist. Where no alternatives exist, I don't recommend being paranoid; the purpose of this section is simply to illustrate some easy choices that will minimize potential risks.

Dr. Donald McLachlan, professor of physiology and medicine at the University of Toronto, notes that we should eat about two micrograms of aluminum a day, but that most people average at least four times this amount, and some inadvertently consume forty times this amount. Those of us who remember our grandmothers boiling rhubarb or spaghetti sauce in a shiny aluminum pot were watching the pot dissolve into her food. Although today's non-stick and anodized coatings over aluminum cookware, and the coating over aluminum soft drink cans, make these items quite safe, the old shiny aluminum pots were not.

Aluminum is added to some food because, among other properties, it helps remove the lumps. When we recall the early days of non-dairy creamers for coffee, we remember the powder turning into floating islands, requiring deft strokes with the heel of a spoon to squish them against the side of the cup or, if that failed, some kind of an eggbeater to help make the clods dissolve. Today, one can pour non-dairy creamer from a great height, and the stuff dissolves like rain as soon as it hits the coffee. The reason is that we now add aluminum silicate, a dandy anti-caking agent. Aluminum phosphates are the most common food additive, but are not highly soluble, so may not be as serious a source for humans. Alum, another source of aluminum, turns up in some skin-care products, including deodorants.

The secret is to read the fine print, and avoid the products listing aluminum where alternatives exist. In general, aluminum is only added to processed foods, so the best choices are foods closest to their natural state. However, some spurious discrepancies exist. For example, Dr. McLachlan's research found Crest Sparkling Gel toothpaste to have over 10 times more aluminum than Crest Freshmint Gel or Aquafresh.

The conclusion here is that we should be lobbying our politicians to insist on full disclosure of all ingredients (including aluminum) in consumables, so that we can make informed choices.

## THE DIET-DRINK MYTH

An astute observer at the grocery store checkout line would note that most of the diet colas and other diet drinks are being purchased by people who look as if they should be on a diet. So if these drinks have only one calorie, how come the people that drink them are fat? The reason is simple. The artificial sweeteners, such as aspartame, trick the tongue into thinking sugar is entering the body. In a fit of enthusiasm, the body sends reflex messages from mouth to abdomen, excitedly warning the digestive organs to get ready for a treat. The liver pumps out more of its bile, which the gall bladder gets ready to squirt into the duodenum; the stomach starts churning and secreting its acidic digestive juices; the pancreas fires up its enzymes, which are poured into the duodenum, and its insulin, which is dumped directly into the bloodstream to move sugar molecules from the blood into the cells. Even the intestines start their peristaltic movements in anticipation. The diet drink then gets swallowed, heads down the esophagus and into the stomach, where — wait for it — *nothing happens!* After all that preparation, the abdomen is victimized by a false alarm. Disappointed, the abdominal organs demand satisfaction, which begets the most incredible urge for food. So, while the diet drink may only have one calorie, the dieter often finds its ingestion is followed by the megacalorie munchies. Other studies show that people who drink large quantities of diet drinks can be prone to osteoporosis. While an infrequent glass of the stuff is not going to cause grave danger, it is best to limit your intake beyond this point. If you are thirsty, there is still no better drink than water.

For those who find drinking only water reminiscent of a prison regime, fruit juices can offer a good alternative. Those that are high in calories, like orange, apple, and pineapple, should be consumed moderately, and it's wise to dilute them with carbonated water to reduce the calorie content. For a low-calorie taste, try tomato juice (cold or hot) or grapefruit. If you crave the sweetness and bubbles of soda pop, the regular ones, rather than diet drinks, are fine for an *occasional* treat.

## FIZZY OR FLAT: WHICH WATER IS BEST?

Essentially, water is tasteless, except for its mineral content. When I suggest drinking ten glasses a day, I mean you should find a brand of bottled water (or filtered tap water) that you like, whether it is fizzy or not. The carbonation process adds acid to the water, which some people prefer, but its bubbles can offend sensitive stomachs. The only medical criteria for choosing one or the other are the following:

When flying in an airplane, drink still water. The bubbles in carbonated waters expand in the gut, and may become entrapped and cause pain until the plane lands.

When traveling in the tropics, drink carbonated water. The acidic pH helps to prevent diarrhea by killing infectious microbes that often taint the food.

## LEAD

This highly toxic substance leads to medical complications such as headaches and neuritis. In some instances it can be fatal. The recommended safe daily dose is zero. Lead used to be used in paint, and children who eat flakes of it in old buildings have been documented to have lead poisoning, which can lead to mental impairment.

### Wine

Connoisseurs beware: Any wine that has a lead-foil wrapper over the cork should be treated with care. Enough lead remains on the lip of the bottle to contaminate your drink (especially if the wine is white, and for some reason French whites seem to be the worst offender here). The best precaution is simply to insist that the end of the bottle be rinsed and wiped before the cork is removed.

### Crystal Decanters

Fine crystal decanters, such as those listed in most bridal registries, are made with lead crystal. Any port, brandy, wine, whiskey, or other spirits stored in decanters will absorb the lead. It is safer to use cheap glass containers (like the original bottle) to store all alcohol. If you insist on flaunting the crystal left over from wedding gifts, make sure you drain the contents back into the bottles as soon as the company leaves (that's assuming the company has left sober and not drained the decanters themselves). If you insist on showing off your decanters year-round, keep tea or other colored liquids in them; it works just fine in the movies.

## China

Unknown to most consumers, even those who turn the hostess's plates upside down to look at the label, chinaware is a major source of lead that can leak into every meal served on it. Fine china or cafeteria plates, any quality of china can do the trick. Most raised decorative touches add to the problem. Recently the whistle was blown by the attorney general's office in California, and the Environmental Defense Fund, which sued the top ten fine china makers, including Wedgwood, Royal Doulton, and Lennox. In consequence, the china makers have agreed to reduce the lead content in their dishes so that no more than .5 micrograms can be released into each meal. In spite of this so-called "moderation" in lead leakage, it seems reasonable to exhibit restraint: one should still beware of using china routinely to store acidic foods like juice, tomato sauces, or coffee. It also makes sense to scrape leftovers into a glass or plastic container to refrigerate. If you have questions about your own china, write the Environmental Defense Fund, 1875 Connecticut Avenue, NW, Washington, D.C., 20009.

## Drinking Water

The standard lead levels for urban and rural (well water) supplies used to be 50 micrograms per liter, but currently public utilities in the U.S. are required to survey consumer homes, and test finished tap water at levels less than 15 micrograms per liter. Current tests cannot detect levels below 2 micrograms per liter. The home tests are on first morning samples, after the water has rested in the pipes for six hours. The worst offenders are old pipes, especially the galvanized ones that often have lead solder in the joints. Levels of lead here are often 20-30 micrograms per liter. To lessen your lead risk, let the cold water tap run and do not fill up your container until the water is very cold. In some large buildings this may take a few minutes. If you are in doubt, ask your public health department about local testing. For greater security, consider a reputable brand of bottled water, or filters that have been tested to confirm that metals are being screened out.

### Calcium Supplements

With our aging population, many people, especially women, are taking calcium supplements to stave off osteoporosis, often without any medical indications, and without having first addressed the most likely causes of osteoporosis: too much protein and too little exercise. Others are prescribed calcium for hormonal disorders.

New research by Dr. Alfred Quattrone, staff toxicologist at California's department of health services, shows that a large number of calcium supplements being sold over the counter have unacceptably high levels of lead in them. The worst offenders are some of the "organic" products made from shells and bones, which can have ten times the lead content of synthetic calcium supplements. If your doctor does prescribe calcium, make sure you take the purest synthetic variety, like calcium carbonate.

## MOUTHWASHES

Most mouthwashes are over 24% alcohol, which is why they "kill germs on contact," and one study now confirms that these alcohol levels in mouthwashes increase the risk of oral cancers by 60%. This certainly makes sense, from all our knowledge of cancer experiments with animals. If one has open sores inside the mouth (even from biting the inside of one's cheek by accident), the alcohol irritates the sores and, just like any irritant in chronic contact with an area of inflamation, can eventually cause a predisposition to cancer. A more serious threat from mouthwashes is that consumers are not aware of the high alcohol levels and glibly put them in bathroom cabinets. If a youngster gets the cap off (note that it is not a childproof cap), it is easy for toxic amounts of alcohol to be ingested, sometimes with fatal results.

If you feel the need to gargle, use plain or salty water, or try one of the new alcohol-free brands of mouthwashes. If you prefer the taste of your current brand, keep buying it, but get in the habit of diluting it half-and-half with water, even weaker if you have open sores in your mouth. If you have young children, do not leave mouthwashes in the bathroom cabinet.

## COFFEE

Wildly popular, coffee is often consumed with something of a guilty conscience. It turns out that while excessive quantities of caffeine can indeed be unhealthy, modest doses for most people are quite harmless and, in some cases of asthma and jet lag (or shift work), can even be helpful. While some individuals are highly sensitive to even a cup of coffee a day and may develop insomnia, tremors, facial tics and, rarely, excessive cystic breast lumps related to high caffeine intake, most people tolerate up to three or four cups a day of regular coffee, although I generally advise patients to consume no more than two cups daily.

The highest caffeine content is found in the cheapest beans. The ordinary *robusta* variety comes with about twice the caffeine of the more expensive *arabica* bean. The coffee that sits all day in the office percolator has virtually no caffeine left in the grounds; all of it is in the drink. Arabica beans, ground finely and exposed to water for only a brief single passage (such as a few minutes in a coffee filter, or fifteen seconds in an espresso machine), are the lowest in caffeine. Make up for the extra expense by having less of it. Die-hard fans of cappuccino should ask for skim milk, because it builds a tremendous head of foam, compared with 2% or whole milk. For those sensitive to caffeine, try a bean that has been decaffeinated using the Swiss water process, to minimize chemical ingestion.

## JAVA JAG

**A** woman came to see me for a problem of recurring breast lumps. She was thirty-five years old, and had already had six breast biopsies, all benign. Her surgeon had told her that because she had such a "gravel-like" consistency to her breast tissue he could not be sure of any new lumps just by palpating them. His only recommendation was that she have bilateral mastectomies, with implants. As part of my new-patient routine, I asked her to fill out our questionnaire. In the section on coffee intake, she entered thirty-two cups *per day*. When I had her quit, her breasts became less painful at the time of her periods, and the cystic texture improved dramatically, making it much easier to examine her for new lumps. She did not need any surgery. While not everyone is this sensitive to caffeine, it is wise to consider any such dietary excesses in the quest for prevention.

---

While it seems that there are a hopeless number of hazards lying in ambush on every store shelf and food counter, the best defence is very simple: start reading labels. To review, here are some simple steps:

• In foods, the percentage of calories from fat is now to be listed on most foods, which obviates the need for mental arithmetic to convert total grams of fat into calories. Make sure the fats are below 15%, or, if higher, make sure you take them in moderation, and make up the rest of the meal with low-fat foods.

• Look for the order of the ingredients listed, because they are lined up according to quantity. In other words, water often shows up first, followed by the rest of the ingredients in descending order of amounts used. If oils or fats are among the first listed, chances are the item is high in fat; if the oils are listed last, the food is likely fine.

• Contact your local public health department, consumer advocate, or grocery store, and demand full disclosure of the elements not listed on labels, such as aluminum in non-dairy coffee creamers, and lead contaminants in "organic" supplements. Patronize those stores and restaurants that offer organically grown foods.

- When in doubt, ask your doctor or nutritionist for specific information about a particular product.

In the end, the safest path is to eat low on the food chain, both in terms of vegetation instead of animal meats, and in terms of organically grown rather than chemically processed products. A few indiscretions are not going to kill anyone, but we should be aware when we shop, so that we are not thumbing our noses at the gods.

*7*

# Living Well Is
# the Best Revenge

L IFESTYLE HAS ASSUMED AN IMPORTANCE today that was unknown in earlier times, because we now have so many choices. In the earliest stages of human history, the basic survival duties of hunting and gathering took every waking hour. In the industrial era, nobody thought much about lifestyle because nobody had one; they just got up, went to the factory (or looked after the kids at home), and set about the tasks of staying warm, clothed, and fed. While a few of the rich may have had options, the vast majority were more worried about having a life than picking out a lifestyle. However, now that we are in the computer age, there are lifestyle options aplenty for everyone, and no shortage of enticements for us all to make poor choices.

We've already discussed the unhealthy options of a poor diet and obesity and, in the next chapter, we will examine the healthy options of exercise. In addition to these critical aspects of our lives, there are a lot of other choices that can make a big difference to our quality of life. To gain some insight into these, let's take a look at two neighbors who share similar salaries, ages, and family responsibilities. They are both under pressure in their respective jobs, but have made different lifestyle choices and, as a result, have developed quite different stress levels.

Jill is cool. She is disciplined enough to go to bed early every night, so that she can rise two hours before she is due at the office. Before turning out the lights, she makes sure she has laid out the clothes she will wear in the morning and reviews her schedule for the coming day. She starts off the morning with a slow stretch under the covers, then another one standing beside her bed. After a twenty-minute yoga routine with emphasis on breathing, stretching, and meditation, she showers and gets ready for work. Then it's time for a nutritious breakfast. Once she is ready for action, and only then, she sets the timer for ten minutes, as she reads the morning paper. Then she attacks the rest of her mail and dictates replies on her portable machine. On the way in to the office, she goes through a list of calls that she makes from her car phone. Once that is done, she catches the morning news on the radio, then plays a tape of a recent lecture by one of her favorite authors. She arrives at work fifteen minutes early, prepared to cope with whatever stresses the day deals her.

Meanwhile, Jack, next door, was out till 2 a.m., drinking with the boys, then had to take three sleeping pills to nod off. He sleeps through the alarm twice, then slowly lifts his aching head off the pillow. He shuffles into the bathroom and startles himself by looking at his reflection in the mirror: eyes like a road map, and hair like a chicken hawk. Because his mouth is so dry from his hangover, he has trouble swallowing the two prescription painkillers his doctor gave him for his chronic back pain. He gropes for the newspaper at the front door, then gets so engrossed reading the sports pages he suddenly realizes he is going to be late for work. Time for a quick shower, then it's into the clothes closet. Let's see, one blue sock and a pair of brown. That means the brown shoes, and the camel pants, but where is the white shirt? His tweed jacket won't do, one of the buttons is off, and he has beer stains on the left pocket. So it's the blue blazer. That means the brown shoes won't do. So where is an extra blue sock? Nuts, it's back out to the laundry bin, to try to find a matching pair of dirty socks to go with his black shoes.

Ten minutes later and he still looks like hell, squinting his aching eyes to discern which of five ties looks better in the mirror. He puts his mail, unopened, on the avalanche already on the kitchen table, and grabs his briefcase and a donut for a sprint to the car. Now that he has left it so late, he has to screech around every moron he finds driving the speed limit, honking furiously.

Luckily he has left his electric razor on the passenger seat, so he can shave while he drives. The radio plays the same news several times over, so he punches one station after another, as he curses the road construction up ahead. The parking lot at work is full, so he has to park down the street and run to the front steps, wrenching his back muscles as he goes. He elbows his way through the crowd and charges through the revolving door, but has to stop when the latches to his briefcase pop open, dumping a trail of unfinished business on the floor. Late again, his headache not letting up, he holds all calls until he takes another pain pill and two tranquilizers to settle his nerves. He can only hope his boss didn't see him arrive, because this is the month when five people are being let go, and he sure doesn't want to be one of them.

The stresses we face at work are often beyond our control, but, as we can see from this example, the lifestyle choices we make are usually voluntary and will largely determine the outcome when we battle our stresses. In Jill's case, her organizational abilities and planning have removed a lot of the anxiety from her day. In Jack's case, his poor time management and substance abuse guarantees that his stresses will seem insurmountable. If his boss is paying attention, Jack will be one of the first to be laid off.

I recently did a survey for a large New York brokerage firm, prior to speaking at their convention in Bermuda. Each of the 300 participants was extremely successful by any financial measure; most exercised and ate well. However, they were surprised to find that their performance at work could have been even better had they paid closer attention to the laws of cause and effect in making their lifestyle choices.

About 35% of the audience reported difficulties with their spouse/significant other that prevented them from focusing on the job. The same people had taken no meaningful holidays in the past two years. So much for the myth of the workaholic who outperforms his peers. Some 45% admitted to serious fatigue from eleven to twelve o'clock every morning, and not one of this group had eaten anything for breakfast. Over 50% became deeply fatigued every afternoon between three and four o'clock, when insulin levels are at their peak, and blood sugars are lowest. Of this group of dozers, none had eaten lunch or, if they had, they were sabotaged by the fatty desserts they ate, or the sweet buns the company put out by the coffee urn at two-thirty; following these their blood sugars rose quickly. Then, an hour later, they fell like stones, taking performance and energy levels down with them. The whole group had consumed full dinners of meat and fatty desserts, in fact a little too full and a little too late in the day. Most slept fitfully as a result, and many woke up feeling like a python that had swallowed a hog. Needless to say, these respondents could not face breakfast, so they skipped it and found themselves dozing off at eleven in the morning ... and the cycle began again.

A large percentage (58%) of the group admitted to insomnia, and of these none knew how to shut down their consciousness with power-nap techniques or self-hypnosis. Of the 47% who said their family lives were a source of stress that kept them from concentrating at work, almost all spent less than twelve minutes a day in heart-to-heart conversation with their spouses, and less than three minutes a day talking to one of their children at a time. Significantly, the top 10% of the money earners in this group all reported being happily married, took regular vacations where they didn't talk shop or bring along their briefcases, and those who had young children were actively involved in their activities. The peak performers without children found time for hobbies or volunteer work. As one might imagine, few of these peak performers wasted much time channel-surfing; only 10% watched more than one hour of television a day.

The lesson for the young bucks aspiring to big earnings was clear. Those who do the best over both the short and the long term are the ones who do not go it alone. Each of us needs to make smart lifestyle choices and to enlist the support of family, friends, and neighbors in our downtime. This strategy forms the basis of the counterattack against the potential hazards of stress.

The problem is that most of us have too much stress happening at the same time to focus on stress-management techniques. At the end of a busy day, most people are too pooped to ponder how they could improve their choices; they are just glad to be through another sunset. But very few poor lifestyle choices have to be permanent; there is always the potential for change, no matter how entrenched our bad habits may seem. I have been impressed by the fact that most of my patients who have been making smart choices learned the hard way, by first suffering the consequences of the wrong choices.

It's time to recognize that the habits of our Industrial Age mentors and role models are obsolete, and that the fight-or-flight reflexes of our primitive ancestors are largely useless except in the simplest situations of physical danger. Today's stresses demand that we contrive new strategies to cope and to triumph.

In fact, while people equate stress with such events as corporate mergers, loss of a job, divorce, and other messy issues, and thus conclude that stress is at an all-time high, the reality is the opposite: daily stress has never been so trivial as it is today. Consider the plight of our forebears. They were under constant threat of attack by wild animals, weather, and famine. Today, we sit on hold on a telephone, cool our tempers in a traffic jam, or fumble with the instructions of a new software package. Without doubt, our new stresses are aggravating, but they are not in the same league as the emergencies faced by our ancestors.

Today's stresses can be made harmless, and can indeed be used to produce greater productivity, health, and happiness, but they require creative and innovative responses. With heart disease becoming more prevalent in younger people, and with the costs of looking after stress-related diseases bankrupting our health-care system, it is painfully obvious that modern stresses are not responding to old habits, obsolete reflexes, and inflexible mindsets.

Let's take a look at some of the new stresses we face, and see how the strategies have changed since the dawning of the Information Age.

## 1. Maintaining Job Skills

**Industrial Age Reality:** Once established in a career, work never changed. One career would last a lifetime.

**Industrial Age Strategy:** Study during your learning years, then work during your earning years.

**Information Age Reality:** Today, young workers can expect at least ten job changes in their lifetimes, each requiring them to start the learning process all over again.

**Information Age Strategy:** We never graduate from the learning years, and indeed we frequently need to *un*learn, then *re*learn in order to stay competitive.

## 2. Eating a Good Diet

**Industrial Age Reality:** Most available foods were natural, full of fiber and nutrients. Because there were no refrigerators, foods were picked fresh daily. Because meats were so expensive, most meals were vegetarian-based and low in fat. What meats were consumed were raised from "free range" animals, which had more muscle and less fat than modern feedlot "factory" animals.

**Industrial Age Strategy:** With few exceptions, the foods that were handy were healthy.

**Information Age Reality:** Fried and fatty foods abound at every street corner. The media saturate our subconscious with images of fattening foods consumed by admirably fit models. With today's time famine, most people have little time to cook, or even to read labels in the store, so end up with processed, pre-packaged microwave meals, or drive-through fast foods on the way home. Fiber and color are gone, fats and chemicals are added, and the body pays the price with obesity, heart disease, and many forms of cancer.

**Information Age Strategy:** Now the consumer needs to exercise personal control, to make informed choices, to know where hidden fats are found, how to get enough fiber, which foods promote alertness after a working lunch, and which foods assist sleep just before bedtime.

## 3. Getting to Sleep at Night

**Industrial Age Reality:** Most people worked hard, getting muscular exercise during the day. Before cars, they walked daily to shop or visit. To stay warm, they had to chop wood or carry coal.

**Industrial Age Solution:** Before electricity, sundown brought its own treatment for insomnia. Because of muscular activity during the day, sleep came a lot easier.

**Information Age Reality:** Work gives no exercise to the muscles, commuting even short distances is done by car, bus, elevator, or moving sidewalk. On the other hand, mental activity is frenetic, with new software to learn, new jobs to train for, and phones and faxes ringing off the hook. Bombarded by the omnipresent TV screen beaming hours of crises and bloodshed into our homes, and by the sensory overload from computer games and music videos, our brains are working overtime by bedtime.

**Information Age Strategy:** To avoid the trap of getting prescriptions for sleeping pills or relaxants, one now needs to learn the skills of relaxation, such as taking power naps, practising deep breathing, or yoga.

## 4. Staying Awake During the Day

**Industrial Age Reality:** This never used to be a problem, because with work so intense and physical, wakefulness was a given. Few harvesters fell asleep while pulling out stumps, and few hunters nodded off while being chased by a wounded moose. Indeed, even during the first half of this century, drivers seldom fell asleep at the wheel of a car, because the roads were mainly unpaved, the car's suspension was stiff, the seats were uncomfortable, and gears had to be constantly changed.

**Industrial Age Strategy:** Just get out of bed; the rest of the day was contrived to keep you awake.

**Information Age Reality:** Today we do our work from a squat position, usually on a swivel chair, staring numbly at a cathode-ray tube, with a phone in our ear. Elevators remove the stimulation of stair climbing, and our modern freeways have straightened the bends and paved all the bumps that used to keep us awake. Cars have cruise control, the seats have gone from hard bench to upholstered tub chair, and the shock absorbers remove all feel of the road. As a consequence, people are falling asleep in droves (or drives.)

**Information Age Strategy:** To avoid falling asleep at work, we need to make sure we have breakfast and lunch. To avoid falling asleep at the wheel, try pinching your earlobe. I learned this trick from midwives in England during my days as a medical student. If one touches a sleeping patient on the arm or leg, the patient is apt to respond with a reflex jolt (in the case of the arm reflex, we call this the "Gordie Howe Elbow" response). So as a matter of self-defence, midwives quickly learned to wake their patients by pinching an earlobe, gently at first, which has the effect of interrupting sleep without any jerking or flailing of limbs. Sleepy drivers can activate their "awake" switch by reaching across and pinching their opposite earlobe as hard as it takes to keep them alert.

Another trick is to use the power of music. This is best accomplished by singing (boisterously is good) along to songs on a favorite tape or radio station.

A third way to stay awake at the wheel is with audio sound effects. In my *Driver Alertness* tape I have reproduced all the disturbing noises that were reported to me by my insomniac patients over fifteen years. This means we have the sounds of the snoring spouse, the crying baby, the dripping tap, the flushing toilet, the neighbor's demented German shepherd, and the garbage pickup at 5 a.m.

## 5. Getting to Work

**Industrial Age Reality:** In the early stages of urbanization, homes and factories were built in close proximity. Those who worked the land were even closer to work. Commuting, when necessary, was done on foot or by horse over short distances. Even after the automobile's arrival, traffic jams were rare in the first half of this century.

**Industrial Age Strategy:** Just go to work and come home.

**Information Age Reality:** Gridlock. Urban sprawl has driven most new home building far into suburbia, and most families now need two incomes to pay for those houses, multiplying the number of cars on the road. Our commuting distance lengthens and, all the while, the car radio bombards us every fifteen minutes with news of fresh disasters, getting us steamed up about events beyond our control.

**Information Age Strategy:** We need to plan for traffic. Drivers can purchase tapes for learning a new language, listening to a favorite author, or laughing with a favorite comedian. Train or bus commuters can read novels, do paperwork, or meditate with soothing music on their Walkmans.

## 6. Social supports

**Industrial Age Reality:** When families all worked the land, and when there was no birth-control pill, adults could look out every window and see parents, aunts, uncles, and children living nearby. In the cities, with only one parent leaving the home to work, the woman of the house was able to establish vital networks of friends and neighbors, a sort of surrogate family unit, who would be there to help in times of need.

**Industrial Age Strategy:** When a crisis came, whether a minor matter of a need for someone to watch the kids for a couple of hours, or a major one, like looking after a bereaved widow, it only took a word for the support groups to close ranks. Even in the event of the tragic death of both parents, most children were taken in by family or friends.

**Information Age Reality:** At the dawn of the Information Age, we added two complications to the normal social-support patterns. One was the birth-control pill, which saw the size of the family dwindle from ten to two children, and the other was the transience of the worker, which caused some families to disrupt their lives to move from city to city, even around the globe, every year or two. Today it is not unusual for parents to be in different cities from grandparents, and for their own children to be scattered all over Christendom. There is a constant stream of new faces in the neighborhood and in the classroom.

**Information Age Strategy:** To replace the closeness of the former neighborhood scene, where everyone knew everyone else from birth, we need to reach out to welcome newcomers, or if we are the newcomers, to summon the nerve to introduce ourselves to new friends. My family has lived in both kinds of scenarios, one with reclusive neighbors who pulled a face if a child's ball rolled onto their lawn, and today in suburban Denver, where I recently encountered twenty-three bikes and trikes in our driveway, and five adults chatting in our kitchen.

The folks who hold annual street parties, or the old gang that hangs out at the community tennis courts, fitness club, or golf course, are showing the rest of us that it is in our own best interests to take an interest in each other. This may be particularly difficult for working couples to accomplish due to time constraints but, especially when there are no family or long-term friends at hand, it can be a worthwhile investment of time and effort. We need to join activities that will keep us in abundant company, whether the activities are related to school, local politics, sports, or hobbies. It is the support of others that helps keep us healthy.

It may be impossible to turn back the clock, but it is not that hard to turn ahead our strategies. Today's stresses can indeed be conquered, just as we conquered those of yesterday. The one response that is sure to be fatal is apathy, so plan your own counterattack on the problems that confront you today, rather than waiting to pay the price in poor physical and mental health tomorrow.

# 8

---

# Ladies and Gentlemen, Start Your Engines

THE ENGINE OF A RACING CAR consumes its fuel supply and defines the functions of the car. While some of the fuel's energy is sent to run the generator and the electric gauges, most of it is spent in forward motion, assuming it is in the hands of a competent driver. The engine of the human body is our muscle mass (40% of a man's weight, 32% of a woman's), which consumes our fuel of choice, namely the available fat stores. But neither the car nor the body will burn off anything unless we heed the admonition of the official starter of the Indy 500 trace track: "Gentlemen, start your engines." Not only do gentlemen and ladies need to start them, we need to run them at the appropriate pace. The racing car engine is built for speed, and the car suffers if it is held at idle, or only at parade-pace. Indeed, such a car would quickly develop deposits of carbon in its pipes and pistons, which could only be burned off with some regular driving at the speeds for which it was designed. Our body's muscles are also built for motion, and by idling in swivel chairs at work and tub chairs at home, we are clogging up our pipes (arteries) with cholesterol. It is not enough to address the epidemic of arterial cholesterol deposits by simple focusing of our food intake; we also need to take ourselves out for some regular exercise.

## THE VALUE OF EXERCISE

Exercise benefits every part of the body. It improves the way we look to others, the way we see ourselves, the way we feel, and the way we function. Let's take a look at the impact of exercise on various aspects of our physical and mental health.

### Muscles

Exercise works our muscles, and muscles are the engines of our metabolism. Some muscles work while we sleep or rest, namely those that control our vital functions of breathing and circulation. The amount of energy these muscles burn off is minimal, and is included in our "basal metabolism rate." Unless you have a thyroid or other endocrine disorder, there is nothing you can do about your inherited rate of basal metabolism, a fact that causes great frustration and envy among obese people who watch slim people pig out and not gain weight. When we choose to get up and move our bodies, more metabolism is required of our muscle mass, and we effectively start our engines. Depending on the type of exercise we choose, we can build muscle mass or endurance.

*Aerobic* exercise is the kind of exercise that one can do while breathing more or less regularly. This means the lungs are able to deliver enough oxygen through the bloodstream to fuel the combustion of fat in the muscle cells. It's as if the lungs were a wood-burning stove and when you open the doors to let the oxygen in the fuel burns at a high rate. When we do regular aerobic exercise, we burn fat, which, with oxygen, converts to water and carbon dioxide, both of which are readily transported back to the lungs for exhalation.

When exercise is *anaerobic*, which means "without oxygen," the rate of metabolism in the muscles exceeds the supply of available oxygen in the bloodstream. With all the oxygen being spoken for by the muscles, breathing becomes difficult. This is the stage at which we grunt or gasp rather than breathe comfortably. It's as if we had shut the wood stove's doors and vents, thereby slowing down the process of burning fuel. That's why anaerobic exercise is useless as a way to burn off excess fat.

But the human body has another way of delivering energy to the muscles, other than burning fat as a fuel: it can also burn sugar, stored as glycogen in the muscles. This fuel doesn't need oxygen, but it doesn't burn as cleanly as fat. Instead of producing harmless carbon dioxide and water, anaerobic exercise produces lactic acid, which can remain in our muscles to cause stiffness over the next couple of days. This is why any anaerobic exercise, such as weightlifting, should be followed by aerobic exercise, such as easy jogging or bike riding, to wash the muscles free of their lactic acid. It is also helpful to start any exercise session with aerobic exercise to gradually heat up the muscles and tendons before exposing them to anaerobic strains.

---

## FIT OR FAT

One of the simplest and most eloquent descriptions of the fuels we burn during exercise was given by Dr. Covert Bailey, author of *Fit or Fat*. Bailey alludes to fat molecules as being the logs on the fire, while sugar molecules are the kindling. He notes that during typical aerobic exercise we burn about 80% of our calories from stored fat and about 20% from sugar. This also explains why many athletes and coaches find that plain water is not as effective for fluid replacement as sugar-water solutions.

On the subject of metabolism, Bailey agrees that there is nothing we can do about our metabolism, but he notes that after five months of regular aerobic exercise, we can almost double our supply of fat-burning enzymes in our muscles. Of course, the reverse is also true: a chronic sedentary lifestyle also decreases the number of fat-burning enzymes in our muscles, making it easier to gain weight. This explains why sedentary obese people may note that their exercising peers are able to eat a lot more food and still not gain weight.

---

The most important muscle to benefit from *aerobic* exercise is the heart. Endurance is improved in time, meaning that you can gradually tolerate more exercise with less racing of the heart, and less rising of blood pressure. In addition, the frequent repetitions of aerobics benefit the tendons and joints.

It is important to seek good instruction, as many of the celebrity aerobic exercise videos show poor technique. Some novices trying Jane Fonda's original videotape ended up with terrible backaches. (To Miss Fonda's credit, she did correct this by seeking expert consultations in her subsequent tapes.) It is best to ask your doctor, physiotherapist, or fitness professional about the best video program for your body type.

One look at Olympic athletes will reveal that there are two different kinds of muscle effects gained from exercise. Marathon runners have legs and arms as slender as bamboo poles, while 100-meter sprinters have limbs like tree trunks. This is because the muscles have two ways to burn fuel, with or without oxygen, and each way determines whether the muscles build strength (bulk) or endurance (lean).

## WAIST DISPOSAL

Why sit-ups don't work: People suffering the dreaded middle-age spread often resort to sit-ups to lose fat around their midsections. However, sit-ups are anaerobic, and do not burn off fat. While they do tone and strengthen the abdominal muscles, they will not lose inches. If you are trying to reduce weight around the waist, try any aerobic exercise, preferably using the bigger muscles such as the quadriceps (thigh) or gluteus maximus (buttocks). That's why jogging, biking, or step aerobics are far better to burn off "love handles" around the stomach.

Anaerobic exercise enhances performance, prevents injury, and builds a better physique. One of the reasons that today's records in track are much improved over those of a century ago (apart from the illegal use of steroids) is that athletes now train with heavy weights, incorporating anaerobic exercises into their routines. World-class sprinters bench press over 400 pounds, and do power leg lifts to improve their explosive starts. Downhill ski racers squat with hundreds of pounds on their shoulders to prepare themselves for the tremendous gravity forces they will endure as they enter a turn at eighty-five miles an hour. Olympic swimmers start regular weightlifting even before their bones have stopped growing, in order to shave seconds off their entry dive and to add power to each stroke.

## USE A REAR-VIEW MIRROR

One of the most common flaws among novice weight lifters is that they look at themselves only in a frontal mirror. This means they work on all the muscles they can see, and end up with huge biceps but skinny triceps, and the same inbalance applies to the rest of the body — strong front, weak back. Professional trainers can spot such misguided training at a glance and warn that it can lead to tremendous injury risks.

Muscles are designed to move joints and generally all work against the opposing muscles that return the joints to their original position. When the hamstrings are weak but the thigh muscles (quads) are overdeveloped, the knee changes its natural dynamics with every step. This can result in increased strain on ligaments, grinding on cartilages, and more chance of needing corrective surgery in the case of an impact injury.

That's why it is important to use weights properly, preferably with a skilled instructor to take you through each set of movements. In sum, the best technique is to remember that for every muscle that is exercised, always work the opposing muscle(s). Once you have determined the number of repetitions and sets (low repetitions for building bulk, high reps for building lean muscles), you should lift enough weight to cause noticeable muscle fatigue by the end of each set. This need not be a "burn," but should not be effortless. When turning to the opposite muscles, your weight tolerance may be considerably different, but use the same number of repetitions and sets. In other words, you may be able to lift thirty pounds in a biceps curl, but only fifteen pounds for the triceps. You should not try to get both muscles lifting equal weights, but rather should aim for both muscles being equally tired at the end of each set.

## Joints

Joints are meant to move, and this has never been better demonstrated than after a long ride in the back seat of a small car. I recall one such ride as a young medical student, during which my legs were so cramped I couldn't move them. After the car pulled to a stop, I unfolded my limbs and discovered what old age must feel like. My hips, knees, and ankles were so stiff they almost squeaked as I tried to straighten them.

The same thing happens when our joints are imprisoned by a cast, or by pain. One of my favorite professors at the University of Toronto medical school was the world-famous orthopedic surgeon Dr. Robert Salter, of the renowned Hospital for Sick Children. He told me of his early research into the healing of joints. Up until this point, we had always been taught that joint cartilages lack blood supply; therefore they are "dead" and, once damaged, cannot heal. Indeed, torn knee cartilages that were treated in casts and then re-examined weeks later showed no sign of improvement. This formed the basis for the removal of thousands of cartilages, until Dr. Salter and his colleagues discovered the real story.

His researchers inserted small instruments into the knees of rabbits and scraped out tiny pieces of cartilage. Half of these injured knees were treated conservatively in casts, the other half were connected to a continuously moving contraption (not unlike a bicycle pedal) that gently straightened and bent the leg in what is now known as continuous passive motion, or CPM. Six weeks later, the casts were off, and the knees were examined through an arthroscope. As predicted, the casted knees showed no improvement; the original damage remained intact, like footprints on the moon. However, the CPM knees showed complete healing, and the cartilages were restored to their normal baby-smooth texture.

Dr. Salter and his team showed that cartilage, like all living tissue, needs the nourishment of food and oxygen to survive and repair itself. They demonstrated that this nourishment is delivered not by the blood vessels, but rather by the synovial membrane that surrounds each joint and bathes it in fluid. This fluid tap is turned on by motion and shut off by immobility. CPM machines now grace every orthopedic hospital in the country, and surgeons are getting their patients up and walking sooner after operations. Mercifully, we no longer see young athletes walking around with post-operative knee scars the length of the River Nile.

Now let's consider a joint imprisoned by sloth. The same thing happens as in the back seat of the small car: the synovial fluid stops flowing, the joint dries up, and the cartilages rub together like sandpaper. This is particularly true if one has an old injury or a case of arthritis. That's why simple movement can make all the joints feel better, because it activates the lubrication and nutrients in the synovial fluid. While it may not be the gateway to eternal youth, exercise certainly oils our hinges.

## Tendons

Tendons are the stringy ends of the muscles that attach to the bone. Anyone who has eaten a chicken leg knows exactly how tendons look (and how rubbery they feel if you inadvertently bite into them). While they look like opaque plastic, they can easily lose their elasticity if not properly stretched with movements. Just consider what happens to most adults who sleep lying on their stomachs, with their toes pointed, thus shortening their Achilles' tendons. As soon as they are jolted up to answer the doorbell or the cry of a baby, the toes want to stay pointed, resulting in an "old man shuffle" for the first few steps. In women who wear high heels, this tendon shortening can become chronic and leave the leg prone to injury. One of the most devastating injuries to mature athletes is a ruptured Achilles' tendon, because it needs to be repaired surgically, and often keeps the individual from sports for over a year. I have seen several such injuries to football players, especially those who off the field habitually wore cowboy boots, with their two-inch heels.

The simplest protection for tendons is to stretch them daily. Just as athletes stretch prior to their sports activities, we should all get in the habit of starting each day with some gentle stretches.

## TAI CHI

Every morning millions of Chinese start each day with a ritual of stretching, toning, and balance. This is done alone at home or collectively in city parks or town squares. Because the movements are gentle and slow, they can be done by all ages, and do not involve impact or injury. Westerners attending expensive spas are learning the merits of tai chi and finding that it not only limbers up joints and improves the circulation through muscles, but it can even improve energy levels. It is this energy "flow," called *chi*, that Chinese practitioners seek to stimulate in all their medical treatments.

## Heart

The heart is the most important beneficiary of regular aerobic exercise. With increased demand for oxygen to feed the muscles, the heart opens up its vessels and pumps to its best capacity. Cholesterol is burned off from the inside of the arteries. There is one caution, however: when one tries too much exercise, the opposite can occur. The coronary arteries can go into spasm, causing minute scarring that will later provide the repository for cholesterol. That's why moderate exercise is best, with regular checks of the pulse rate. Aim for at least three hours out of 168 each week, either in half-hour sessions, or spread out through a few minutes of walking, stair climbing, and other routine aerobic activities.

## Arteries

Arteries that carry ingested cholesterol end up wearing the stuff. When each fatty meal turns our blood to sludge, it is important to realize that exercise can provide a partial antidote. By burning up some of our ingested cholesterol we can help open the arteries to every organ in the body. *However, if you have significant artery blockages and develop severe pains in the lower legs when walking (known as claudication), do not push yourself to exercise past the point of pain. This is a very serious condition which requires medical supervision and, if diet alone is not sufficient to reverse the process quickly, surgery is often needed to replace clogged segments of artery with artificial tubing.*

## Veins

Varicose veins, especially in the legs, are partially prevented and to a degree improved by regular exercise. The veins of the legs are fed their blood from the arteries, but they must return this blood against the flow of gravity. To help the process, each vein has a back-flow valve every few inches from the feet back up to the heart. However, these flimsy valves need the support of firm leg muscles to withstand the five or six feet of blood pressure above them. The regular exercise gained in activities like walking helps the pumping action of the veins.

## Lungs

Lungs need to be given their own workout. If lung capacity is not fully used, only a fraction of the alveoli open up; the rest are not needed. When the body metabolism is lowered by sloth, or lowered even more by a general anesthetic, the chances of these alveoli shutting down increases. In fact, one of the major causes of post-operative fever after general anesthetic is atelectasis, or infection in these collapsed alveoli. Exercise reopens the air sacs, improving the overall lung function and capacity. (It should be noted that in some asthma sufferers, exercise can have a reverse effect, causing bronchial spasm and wheezing; in these cases careful medical management is essential.)

## Digestion

If the stomach wall muscles are left to flab, constipation often results. Our intestines run through the compartment of our abdomen, and if the pressure inside this compartment is zero, then the bowels have to do all the work of moving along the food. If the intra-abdominal pressure is kept high, by intermittent exercises as well as by increased resting muscle tone, then the bowels can do a bit less of the work. This is one of the reasons even healthy athletes can become constipated if they are confined to bed.

Routine post-operative orders often call for codeine or other opiates for pain relief. These leave the patient feeling drugged and often constipated, and less inclined to leave the bed. The resulting lack of exercise means more costly days in hospital. When patients can restart exercises quickly after surgery, their chances of constipation are remarkably reduced. While the abdominal muscles benefit directly from stomach crunches, virtually all exercise will help tone the stomach muscles; even simple walking requires that the stomach muscles contract to tilt the pelvis, to prevent the lower spine from swaying forward.

## Weight

The best weight loss comes from aerobic exercise that involves the bigger muscles, namely the quadriceps (thigh) and the gluteus maximus (buttock). The secret for effective weight loss is to have lots of repetitions of these movements, such as walking, jogging, and aerobic step classes.

## Mind

One of the best examples of the mind-muscle connection is endorphin, the body's own molecule of morphine. Just as morphine from the poppy plant can treat pain and elevate mood, the same molecule can be generated with the release of endorphin following exercise. This is the basis of the so-called "runner's high" experienced by marathoners, and the reason habitual exercisers often feel depressed when denied a couple of days of their routine.

Transference occurs when we transfer anxieties from one source to another, such as coming home mad at the boss, but kicking the garbage can. Exercise provides an ideal outlet for this pent-up energy to be spent in non-violent ways. Whether we hit a punching bag, pound the pavement, or whack the cover off a baseball, athletic activity offers a great way to seek revenge for all the day's frustrations.

## Sleep

To sleep effectively, we must dive down to our deepest levels of sleep, during which we have rapid eye movements (rem) and frequent dreams accompanied by muscle twitches. It takes a couple of hours to reach this stage of sleep, and if you have trouble falling asleep, your rem time is also being cut short. On the other hand, take a look at the family dog after a day of brisk running; once he lies down, sleep comes almost instantly, followed a few minutes later by the grunting and muscle twitching of deep sleep. The reason dogs do this so well is that they exercise; dogs kept in tiny apartments and denied any exercise have just as much trouble sleeping efficiently as underexercised humans. Physical exhaustion from exercise benefits the whole body, including the mind. The only caveat is that exercise also releases adrenaline, which can keep you awake if you exercise vigorously too close to bedtime. Try to confine exercise to earlier parts of the day when you want to enhance your alertness.

## Sexual Function

One of the unspoken benefits of moderate exercise is that it helps improve both the adult libido and, in couples having trouble conceiving, may help fertility. However, the operative word here is *moderate*; excessive exercise, as done by marathoners or triathletes, often has the opposite effect, especially in women. Not only might the libido decrease, but many of these dedicated athletes stop having periods altogether. In the case of young girls, excessive exercise may delay their onset of periods by a couple of years. In both cases no permanent harm is done; once the vigorous daily exercise moderates, the reproductive functions return to normal.

## THE LONELINESS OF THE LONG-DISTANCE RUNNER

One apocryphal story that has made the rounds of medical conferences since the time of vaudeville illustrates both the importance of exercise in sexual function, and of communication between doctor and patient. A middle-aged man complains to his doctor that his sexual function is inadequate, and that his wife is getting very frustrated with him. The doctor suggests that he run ten miles a day, then call back after a week for a progress report. Seven days later the patient calls in, announcing that he has followed the prescription to the letter. "Great," says the doctor. "Now, how's your sex life?" "I don't know," replies the patient. "I'm seventy miles from home."

## The Dangers of Exercise

The good news is that while it has many benefits, exercise has only two dangers. The bad news is that these are pain and death. Fortunately both are preventable.

### Pain Caused by Equipment

The biggest cause of injury is the unrealistic demand that people make of their bodies. Forgetting the limitations of age, size, bone structure, or conditioning, weekend athletes routinely push themselves to achieve goals better suited to younger, fitter bodies. Too often they seek to achieve these unrealistic goals with inappropriate equipment. This is most easily illustrated with the simple running shoe. Properly designed, it should have ample room in the forefoot and a well-padded, rounded heel. Depending on your foot shape, you might also need metatarsal arch supports, and wedges to ensure a stable contact with the ground. Unfortunately, many runners run in ill-designed shoes, sometimes in street shoes with squared heels that make each step seem as if each foot is still wearing the shoe box. Skiers who wear ill-fitting boots and poorly set release bindings have only their equipment (and their judgment) to blame if they get injured.

Injuries can also result if you buy good equipment but of a quality that is beyond your ability to match. Tennis superstars like

Pete Sampras, Boris Becker, and Jim Courier hit serves over 125 miles an hour and use racquets and string tensions suited for the purpose. Weekend amateurs who try to copy their heroes find that these racquets are ill-suited to a thirty-mile-an-hour "cheese-ball" serve, and indeed they may send bone-jarring vibrations all the way from the arms through to the teeth. The same applies to golf clubs, downhill skis, and squash racquets; overbuying can often lead to underachieving, with preventable injuries as a result.

## Pain Caused by Technique

The second source of injury is using the right equipment, but in the wrong way. Former Canadian Davis Cup star Peter Burwash now heads a company of tennis pros in forty countries called PBI. As a teacher and regular contributor to *Tennis* magazine, he has developed a great eye for injuries in the making. When Boris Becker stormed Wimbledon at age seventeen, Peter told me to watch the extreme arch in Becker's back during his serve. He correctly predicted that Becker would eventually suffer back pain if he did not change that habit. Burwash also has a couple of facetious and highly effective tips on how to *give* yourself tennis elbow. This is most efficiently caused by holding one's thumb up the shaft of the racket on the backhand, or by having lazy feet and hitting backhand shots off the hind foot (which requires a flick of the wrist).

A common cause of knee pain among cyclists, including devotees of the home stationary bike, is the seat shaft that has partially slid back into its housing, making the seat too low. The result is a rider who is forced into a semi-squat, making him or her look rather like a circus bear riding a unicycle. A regular check will reveal whether the leg has enough room to reach nearly complete extension; if it does not, then adjust the seat to a higher position.

Other injuries occur when athletes use good equipment but omit key protective parts. For example, the best cross-country bike won't prevent a head injury if the rider refuses to wear a helmet, and the best goalie pads won't protect the face if the goalie forgets his mask.

When I see a painful foot, I am trained to treat the pain, but if the patient has a stone in his shoe, his pain will soon return, no matter what treatments I give. That's why part of the job of a skilled doctor is to look beyond the symptoms, to look for the simple clues that might cause complex troubles. In the case of athletic injury, sometimes this requires a non-medical referral to a coach in a particular sport. Even the best pros will take a lesson from one of their peers if they are developing bad habits that lead to physical pain. I often remind my golfing patients who suffer from, say, a sore elbow, that they should imagine what would happen if they were on television and Jack Nicklaus was doing the color commentary on their swing. Even if Nicklaus did not know of their injury, he could predict it from the most subtle flaw in their technique.

One of the classic examples of technique analysis is for the simplest sports of all, walking and running. The first clues to trouble are obtained by asking the patient to wear old shoes into the office. The doctor can examine the patterns of wear, to see if one foot is dragging its toes, or if the heel is being worn down off-center. After this preliminary search for clues, a foot specialist can perform a "dynamic gait assessment" using a video camera and treadmill. By using the freeze-frame and slow motion replays, podiatrists, orthopedists, and kinesiologists can assess the nature of the heel-strike, the angle of the push-off, the angles of the leg bones during each step, and the forces along the sides of the foot. Any amateur athlete with leg pains or back aches made worse by standing, walking, or running should consider a thorough examination of the mechanics of his or her movements.

Often we see examples of part-time athletes who have suffered years of back, hip, knee, or ankle pains, perhaps resulting in tens of thousands of dollars' worth of operations, still with no improvement in symptoms. Imagine their chagrin when the solution turns out to be as simple as $2 worth of felt wedges underneath the insole to correct pronation, or a $30 heel lift to correct a leg-length discrepancy. Even if the problem turns out to need $300 worth of molded insoles or modifications to the footwear, it is always cheaper to do surgery on the shoe than surgery on the foot.

---

## TEST YOUR OWN RUNNING STYLE

**A** simple experiment to test your own mechanics of running can be done on soft ground, or on a sandy beach, where you can leave footprints. To prove the importance of arm movements, simply run at top speed for ten paces with your hands in your pockets. Then, after circling back to the starting line, run another ten paces beside these footprints, this time pumping your arms like a sprinter. Now go back, and measure the distance between the footprints in each set. In my own case, my stride length was four feet between heel strikes with my hands in my pockets, and fully seven feet when I used my arms. Try the same thing running up a set of stairs two at a time; the legs seem heavy if the arms are immobile, whereas they can fairly fly up the stairs when assisted by the arm action. Amateur runners can get leg injuries even with perfect leg mechanics if they are not enlisting the support of coordinated arm movements.

---

## Death

The human body was built to handle moderate exercise levels, occasionally interspersed with maximal output, but repeated severe exercise bursts, especially if they are sudden and without sufficient warm-up, can lead to spasms in the arteries of the heart. These coronary spasms eventually become scar tissue that initiates a cholesterol build-up along the artery walls. Death can follow with little warning, and may not come during exercise, but during periods of stress or after a fatty meal.

A far more dramatic form of death is the sudden heart attack during exercise. Typically, this is incompetence in its simplest form. If a race-car driver ignores his tachometer and constantly changes gears beyond the red line, the engine will soon blow. If this pattern is repeated, the driver is held up for ridicule and will likely have a short career. The human tachometer is our pulse (or heart rate), and if it is ignored during exercise, the engine that blows is the heart.

Most people check their pulses at their neck, placing a couple of fingers over their carotid artery. This is usually because they have been taught to do so by some steroid-fed television personality, a grown man dressed in rubber shorts, jumping up and down on a mat, telling his adoring audience to check their pulses at the neck. But there are only four arteries that supply the brain, each the diameter of the little finger: the two carotids in the front of the neck, and the two vertebrals at the back. If all four are open, there should be no problem closing one of them. However, if three of the four are plugged with cholesterol and you block off the fourth artery to check the pulse, the result can be disastrous.

A far safer place to check the pulse is at the wrist, but most people have never been shown how to do this properly. Here's how: Turn your left palm up, then, with the middle finger of your right hand, follow the crease between palm and wrist to the bony ridge on the thumb side of the left wrist. Press firmly against the bone for a few seconds, until the nail starts turning white. Then, with the index finger barely touching the skin, feel the bounding pulse beneath. The principle is same as kinking off a garden hose, which backs up the water pressure, causing the hose to bulge, and in the case of the radial artery at the wrist, making the pulse more easily felt.

To find out your own "red line" level of pulse, the simplest way is to have a doctor perform a stress ECG to find out your maximum safe heart rate, and your recommended "target zone" for typical exercise. In the absence of this definitive test, a conservative estimate can be made from the following formula:

**220 – your age  =  your maximum, or "red line" heart rate**

A conservative estimate of your ideal target zone is 75% of this number. In other words, if we take the age of 40, subtracted from 220, the red line is 180, and the target zone is 135. A six-second pulse check that shows fourteen or fifteen beats indicates that the target zone has been reached. At this point, it is a good idea to pause in the activity, or get out of the hot tub.

The above is definitely playing it safe with the pulse rates. Some experts suggest we should be using the number 220, and subtracting *half* our age to reach our red-line value. Indeed, fit athletes can routinely run with heart rates much higher, and many marathoners can run all day with pulses over 200. However, considering the poor state of fitness of the public at large, and the fact that it is better to strive for more minutes of endurance rather than the highest possible heart rate, it is best to underestimate your maximal pulse until you have checked with your doctor.

## The Seven-Step Counterattack! Exercise Plan

### 1. Assess Your Body

To plan a realistic exercise routine, you should start by categorizing your body. If your shape is mesomorphic, or muscular, then power exercises, such as sprinting, body building, and football, might be appropriate. If your body is endomorphic, or obese, then swimming or water polo would neutralize the weight problem. If you are ectomorphic, or reedy, then long-distance running might be the best choice. If you love speed, then pick a sport that offers it, such as downhill skiing; if you love heights, climb mountains; if you love quiet, try scuba diving. I had a patient whose young son had trouble with most sports because he had one leg two inches shorter than the other. After trying several activities, he turned out to love water-skiing on a slalom ski. His leg-length discrepancy was no impediment and he was able to improve his self-esteem, while getting plenty of good exercise. As a fourteen-year-old, he went on to win the regional championship title in his age group.

Another patient had trouble with a bad back, even when she was swimming. It turned out that she was always breast-stroking with her head out of the water, to keep her contact lenses dry. In consequence, her back was arched like a banana, and the strain was painful. A simple switch to the backstroke solved the problem.

## 2. Assess Your Goals

Ask yourself a simple question before deciding on a particular exercise program: "What am I trying to do?" Are you trying to build muscle mass in the arms or lose inches in the waist? Are you trying to build endurance for the Boston Marathon, or simply trying to keep up with your nine-year-old on a bike ride? Are you hoping to make the track team, or to maintain muscle tone in your back and legs? Are you trying to combat afternoon fatigue at work, or are you simply obliged to take the dog out for a walk?

## 3. Assess Your Weakness

Ask yourself another question: "What has caused me to fail with past exercise plans?" Perhaps it was the lack of discipline, or a short attention span. Perhaps it was inertia; the thought of having to change clothes, mess up your hair, and have another shower seemed too imposing. Perhaps you chose a sport that fit into a former lifestyle, but was no longer practical; this happens often to old football or hockey players who can no longer find a dozen people to play with the way they could as teenagers. Perhaps it was sheer laziness; the stationary cycle purchased in a fit of optimistic zeal now lives up to its name and gathers cobwebs in the furnace room.

In other cases, the weaknesses may be physical. An arthritic spine or knee joint may dictate a non-impact sport such as swimming or biking. Obesity may prevent all land sports, leaving only the gravity-reduced world of aquatics. Asthma that is induced by exercise may prevent severe sprints, but endurance events might still be possible. Asthma that is induced by cold air may preclude outdoor winter sports, but permit indoor tennis. Make sure you take a realistic look at your limitations before committing to a particular program, but don't use these limitations as an excuse to avoid all forms of exercise. Courageous role models like Canada's Terry Fox and Rick Hansen, and Wheelchair Olympic athletes, should inspire the rest of us to use our imaginations to find something active to enjoy.

## 4. Assess Your Budget

The most important part of an exercise strategy is the budget for time and money. If a shortage of time seems to be the reason that exercise gets put off day after day, then identify a couple of your top time-wasters. In some cases the problem is that the entire activity is wasteful, such as TV "channel surfing." In other cases the activity could be done in less time. For example, the morning news can be found on television, radio, and the newspaper. You don't gain anything from hearing the same news repeated on all three sources. Besides, by definition, it can only be called "news" the first time you hear it.

Even within the print media, the rule of 80/20 applies: 80% of the information will be gleaned in the first 20% of the time spent reading it. If you find yourself reading the paper or magazines so thoroughly that you are even reading the paid political ads, the soap-opera gossip, and the eggplant recipes, it's time to get a life. Set a timer for five or ten minutes maximum before reading the first word (or read/watch/listen while doing your exercises). All you need to find is a mere three hours out of a 168-hour week (only 40 seconds out of every waking hour) that could be diverted to exercise.

Exercise should also fit into your monetary budget. There is no point picking sports that require equipment or a lifestyle that you cannot afford. That's one reason that I have passed on polo and yacht racing, and instead focus on skiing and tennis. Even if the sport is affordable financially, it may take up too much of your time, thus causing other problems in your personal life. Weekend golf can be one of the most expensive hobbies if you have a young family; not for the costs of the clubs and green fees, but for the potential costs of the alimony. ("Bye, honey. Have fun with the kids while I slide off for eight hours of quality weekend time on the greens.")

The easiest exercises to budget for are those that are most handy. In other words, if you live on the beach, go for long walks/run/swims. If you live in the North, learn to snowshoe. If you live in the mountains, try to ski, or, in summer, try hiking or biking. If you are certain you will use it, and if it is not far out of your way, consider buying an annual membership in a fitness club.

## EXERCISE — OUT OF THIS WORLD

Astronaut Wally Schirra once explained to me the difficulty of manned space travel to Mars. Even at almost 18,000 miles an hour, such a trip would take three years. Until scientists figure out fully how to reproduce the effects of gravity in space, the astronauts would arrive on Mars, where gravity is greater than on Earth, with bones and muscles like noodles. The idea that the first Earthling arriving on Mars might be reduced to doing an impersonation of an amoeba does little to stir the imagination of the taxpayer. The importance of exercising our bodies against gravity should not be lost on sedentary Earthlings.

### 5. Pick a Time

Mornings are the best time for exercise, preferably before the first shower. Early exercise will improve the circulation, and cause the release of more endorphine and adrenaline, at a time when both are needed. If mornings are out of the question for your exercise time, then pick any other time of the day that is practical. However, do not exercise too vigorously within two hours of bedtime, or you may have trouble getting to sleep; walking the dog before bedtime is fine, but don't run a two-mile foot race.

### 6. Pick a Partner

With so few aging yuppies having time to maintain their social contacts as they did in school, exercise can offer an effective way of combining a workout with team building. Besides, there is less chance of sleeping in past your alarm if your buddies are pounding on your door every morning to haul you off to aerobics or to the tennis court.

## 7. Pick a Sport or Activity

Mercifully, the choices are legion: everything from jogging to bird watching, and from weight lifting to bicycling. After reviewing the above criteria, all you need to do is to "sell" yourself on one or two activities that fit the bill. Remember that the more side benefits you can contrive, the more likely you will be to stick with the activity. So unless you have the self-discipline of a martyr, try to find an activity that gives you the right kind of exercise, while satisfying your other needs as well.

9

# Beyond the Fringe:
# Good and Bad
# Alternative Medicine

THE SUBJECT OF HEALTH CARE has never been so prominent in our daily headlines. Once defence spending started to decline, health care surged to the number-one expense in Western economies. In the United States, for example, there are now 25,000 different prescription drugs, for which 1.7 billion prescriptions are written annually, at a cost of over $67 billion. The explosion of technology has led to astronomically expensive tests and investigative procedures, and the cost of a hospital stay has gone through the roof. It now costs three or four times more to sleep overnight on a rubber-lined mattress than it does to stay at the Waldorf. Health-care expenses are expanding far more rapidly than inflation, and they show no sign of peaking. We all end up paying the bills, whether we are self-insured, privately insured by an insurance company, or insured by the state.

There are many reasons for spiraling health-care costs, including the escalating costs of legal insurance that doctors and hospitals pass on to their patients, and the inefficiencies inherent in the medical bureaucracy. However, perhaps the biggest reason we are running out of room at the top of the health-costs graph is the technology of medicine itself. A chest pain in 1959 used to cost about $20 to investigate: $10 for the doctor's visit, and another $10 for the EKG. If the test was normal, the patient was told to take a day off and rest in bed.

Today, the same chest pain can cost hundreds of times more to investigate. The cost of the doctor's initial visit and EKG has now risen to $150, as one might expect with the effects of inflation. However, technology has added the rest of the costs: $1,000 for the thallium scan, $990 for the MRI, $350 for the stress EKG, $400 for the echocardiogram, $1,500 for the PET scan, $3,000 for angiograms, and, just to be on the safe side, $3,000 for a couple of days in the coronary-care unit, with follow-up by a twenty-four-hour home monitor. If these tests turn up something, the arteries can be ballooned open in an angioplasty ($9,000), a quadruple bypass might be needed ($35,000), or, if things are really bad, a cardiac transplant could be performed ($175,000). These costs apply in Canada, too, though they're buried in taxes and medicare payments.

Of course, if I were to experience a sudden chest pain I would want the latest treatment, just as millions of other North Americans would. In response, the health-care bureaucrats simply shrug and expand their budgets to fund the costs, even if no end to the escalation is in sight. As a practising physician who has worked in the state-run Canadian system, and who now works within the largely privately run American system, I have been frustrated by the sight of politicians and "experts" flailing away to answer the impossible question: "How do we keep paying for this?"

One truth is clear: if we change the question from funding health care to funding disease prevention, the solution is more attainable. We must empower individuals to prevent illness and reward them for doing so. Right now, virtually all countries subsidize disease (for example, through artificially cheap tobacco and booze prices, and special benefits granted to producers of fats such as the beef and dairy industries), and penalize health — just try to deduct the cost of your fitness-club membership or diet classes from your next tax return.

Governments pretend to be interested in protecting the public from hidden dangers, yet the shelves are filled with misleading or inadequate product labels (or, as in the case of meats, eggs, dairy products, and prescription drugs, virtually no warning labels at all). We have funded private and public health insurance plans that disallowed prevention, waited for the self-induced illnesses to follow, which they did, as inevitably as a lit fuse leads to an exploding firecracker, then stuck the bill to the next generation, which is now us. Then, true to the bureaucratic maxim of cutting red tape — but only lengthwise — the paper pushers set up new commissions to "study" health care.

Every time a smoker buys a pack of cigarettes in the U.S., non-smokers are subsidizing them to the tune of about ten dollars. In Canada the subsidy is about five dollars. The true cost of smoking should include the costs of looking after the heart and lung diseases caused by tobacco (including secondhand smoke), the costs of lost work days due to smoking-related illnesses amongst smokers (and those forced to breathe their fumes), the expenses of treating childhood allergies and asthma directly related to parents who smoke, the costs of maintaining the tragically charred patients on burn wards (smoking in bed is still the greatest cause of severe burns), and the costs of all the buildings that have been torched by careless butt-heads. Some of the true costs of cigarettes should also be earmarked for smoking cessation expenses, which, at the time of this writing, are still not allowed as a tax deduction. Indeed, many insurance companies are no longer paying for nicotine skin patches; rather than absorb these minor costs into their current year-end budget, they prefer to stick the lung-transplant bill to future administrations in their company. Still more of the real cost of cigarettes should include money to fund equal time for anti-smoking promotions and ad campaigns to counter the billions of dollars spent luring children around the world into nicotine addiction.

The same case could be made for the true costs of alcohol. Consider the carnage of the drunken driver (or ship's captain, or train engineer), and the terrible domestic violence perpetrated by abusers of alcohol. These costs are being borne by all of us, so that tobacco and liquor can be sold at unrealistically low prices. The consequence is predictable: health care is now sold at an unrealistically high price.

Exactly the same chain of events can be seen with regard to the "fat" industry, including producers of meats, cheese, milk, cookies, fried potatoes, and deep-fried chicken. The true costs of our traditional national diet should be borne by those who choose to follow it and not passed along to the rest of us, added to our escalating health-care bill. If Joe Beerbarrel decides to eat half his calories as fat, then why should the rest of us have to pay for cardiac surgeons to scrape the Velveeta out of his coronary arteries? Fats may be a cheap form of calories to feed into the body, but they cost thousands of dollars an ounce to ream out of an artery.

Clearly, our past strategies have been outrageous failures, and we are going to have to use the other side of our brains to find new solutions. I hope that this book can in some way empower each reader to make those changes needed to stay out of the clutches of the medical machine. One strategy is to make judicious use of the various non-traditional modes of treatment that not only work to prevent disease, but in many cases offer a powerful cure after the disease has happened. None of these is written on a doctor's prescription pad, and none requires cutting open the body for surgery. All are a reflection of the powerful connection between mind and body. The effectiveness of many of these "natural therapies" serves as a potent reminder that the link between the mind and the body is a key factor in health, and that the two can only be separated on the autopsy table.

Alternative medicine has now moved from the fringe of medical care into the mainstream. A recent study in the *New England Journal of Medicine* found that close to three-quarters of Americans have used some alternative therapies in the past year, most of which were not covered by their health insurance. These therapies include herbal medicines, massage, aromatherapy, meditation, yoga, acupuncture, and chiropractic manipulations. Indeed, the number of patient visits to such practitioners has now exceeded the total number of visits to family doctors, internists, and pediatricians combined. In other words, whether the medical profession likes it or not, the public is voting with their feet and leading their own health parade in an alternative direction.

The American and Canadian medical communities have long derided such treatments as being scientifically unprovable and, therefore, daft. However, the same practitioners have long recognized that those doctors with a good beside manner seem to have a positive effect on their patients' recovery, and that those who are rude or unsympathetic can hinder the recovery process. Medicine has also recognized that a patient's will to live can be a powerful ally in the recovery from serious illness. However, there are no pills that generate faith, no injections that create the will to live, and no operations that can impart bedside reassurance.

The biggest problem Western doctors have with the universe of alternative medicines is unfamiliarity. We lump them together, refusing to separate the beneficial from those that are useless, or even dangerous. But many doctors and patients are now questioning some practices in the universe of Western medicine. Our number-one prescription drug is a tranquilizer, given out by a male-dominated medical profession to a largely female patient base, to help them "handle" stress. We reach for pills to treat symptoms, then prescribe other pills to treat the side effects caused by the first ones. We encourage over-the-counter drugs such as iron pills, vitamin A supplements, and aspirin, that can all be lethal in small overdoses, with little or no warning to consumers. Our surgical knives have routinely ripped out millions of healthy children's tonsils without proof that we are helping any of them, and we have been quick to reach for the knife to do suspiciously high numbers of hysterectomies, breast tumor removals, and caesarean sections.

In other words, there are strengths and flaws in both the Western and alternative medical universes. We need to open our eyes to the limitations of any therapy. Meditation will not replace a chest X-ray in diagnosing a lung cancer, acupuncture will never treat an infection like tuberculosis, and brain surgery cannot correct the insomnia that leads to a stomach ulcer.

It has always been my view that we should seek to separate the good from the bad, and cherry-pick the best treatments from both worlds of medicine. So let's take a look at the best of the alternative treatments that can supplement our Western care, improve our health, and reduce our health-care costs.

## Acupuncture

This is one area of alternative medicine that I can address from personal experience. I first became intrigued by acupuncture after several years of family practice. It quickly became obvious that our "tool chest" of drugs had considerable limitations. One young woman in particular remains vivid in my memory because she had terminal breast cancer, with painful metastases to the spine and other bones. Her pain was excruciating and little reduced with maximal doses of our strongest painkillers. Her young children had for the last two years thought their mother was a drunk, because her medications made her speech slurred and her movements clumsy. When even two-hourly doses of morphine failed to help her, she asked me what to do.

That was all the impetus I needed to attend an introductory course put on by the Canadian Acupuncture Foundation, a group that teaches acupuncture to family doctors, anesthesiologists, and emergency MDs. Run by two medical doctors who specialize in using acupuncture for pain relief, Linda Rapson and Joe Wong of Toronto, the sessions link the science of today with the healing arts of yesterday. While I went with some skepticism, I was immediately impressed by acupuncture's effect on the patients presented to the group.

Upon my return, and after practising needle insertions on myself (as well as on classmates in seminars), I called in my terminal-cancer patients who suffered pain to ask if they would let me experiment on them. I asked each to come in without taking the usual pain medications, to let us both see whether a course of acupuncture was offering anything more than placebo value. The results were startling in all but one case, a man who felt no different (at least acupuncture had no side effects). As for the rest, most memorably the aforementioned young mother, the pain relief was almost immediate. A couple of patients experienced minor pain reductions in the office, but improved dramatically the next day. All the patients experienced a sharply decreased need for medications; in the case of the young mother the need dropped to zero.

While I make no pretence of lengthening the lives of terminal-cancer patients, there is no question that they could live their final days in peace, unclouded by a haze of pain and drugs. I have now done acupuncture as an adjunct to my regular medical treatments for over a dozen years. Having recently moved to Denver, where very few local MDs specialize in acupuncture, I have been kept busy by referrals from orthopedic surgeons (spinal injuries, sports injuries), neurosurgeons and neurologists (migraine and other headaches), anesthesiologists (nerve-root pains), general and cardiac surgeons (postoperative pains), family doctors (arthritis pains), ear, nose and throat specialists (TMJ, or temporo-mandibular joint/jaw pains, and acute sinusitis), podiatrists (heel spurs), and even obstetricians (for labor pains). Recently I've also begun seeing victims of motor-vehicle accidents who are referred by their lawyers, to help speed the recovery of neck and other injuries.

After more than 50,000 visits from such patients, I have found that acupuncture is effective in reducing symptoms (and the need for pills) in about 80% of uncomplicated pain cases like muscle injuries or tension headaches, although it works to lesser degrees in cases of rogue "cluster" headaches, or post-shingles neuritis pains, and other recalcitrant conditions that defy virtually all medical treatments. In most of my cases, prescription pain pills are not needed at all, apart from the occasional Tylenol or aspirin.While there are great variations, depending on underlying conditions, most people have four or five visits, at intervals of one to two weeks

Because of the combination of natural painkillers and cortisone released into the bloodstream, acupuncture is also dramatic in its improvement of range of movement in joints stiffened by arthritis or trauma. Treatments take about thirty minutes, and results can often be instantaneous and lasting. This is particularly dramatic in acute injuries such as whiplash, or a stiff shoulder or knee joint injured in sports. In no case are there any side effects, which, alas, cannot be said of Western drugs or surgery. That's why acupuncture can be invaluable if used initially, rather than as a last resort, after serial drugs and operations have failed. In many cases, a single treatment or two will suffice to let the body resume its normal movements, and once the pain cycle is broken, these movements serve to lubricate the joints and to build up surrounding muscles.

While insurance companies are slow to cover such claims (although they usually cover part of the visit fees if the practitioner is a medical doctor), they are quickly realizing that it is smarter to spend a couple of hundred dollars instead of several thousands required to follow our traditional lines of investigation and treatment; in those cases where acupuncture fails, there is no harm in falling back on our usual treatments.

## BREAKING THE MORPHINE HABIT

Back in the 1980s I was in Rochester, Minnesota, doing a few speeches for IBM. While there, I was invited to speak to the medical staff at the world-famous Mayo Clinic. After my presentation, I was invited to join them for ward rounds, which featured some challenging cases that had stumped doctors from around the world.

One recent admission was a thirty-nine-year-old woman who had suffered seven years of pain following cancer of the ovaries. Her problem was not from the cancer, but from the treatment; her doctors back home (not from the Mayo) had been overly aggressive with their radiation, and had scorched her entire lower abdomen, bowels and all. As a result, she suffered constant pain, which her doctors had treated with morphine. After a couple of years, she became a morphine addict. Then her doctors treated her addiction with methadone, following which she became —

surprise — a methadone addict. At no time had any of this Western medicine helped her original pain (which was, in fact, caused by Western medicine). Meanwhile her weight had plummeted, leaving her at only eighty-five pounds on a five-foot seven-inch frame.

After reviewing the details of this doctor-induced fiasco, the specialists at Mayo discussed treatment options, while the patient noted, as usual, that her pains while at rest were ten out of ten. After listening to the questions and suggestions from the doctors in attendance, all of which followed the usual lines of Western medical thinking, I asked the patient if anyone had ever tried acupuncture. As none had, I asked the nurse to bring me the smallest-gauge needle she had (I hadn't expected to be using my acupuncture needles and had left them in my hotel), so that I could try it on her. As I distracted the patient by asking her to describe her house and its new renovations, I inserted the needle into her right leg, just below the knee, and manually twiddled it. One of the doctors charged with the daily task of recording her pain levels could resist no longer, and asked her what level of pain she now had. With an astonished look on her face, she lifted her head from the pillow and said, "Two." I am told that the Mayo Clinic now recognizes acupuncture.

---

Acupuncture is one of the most senior of all alternative medicines, dating back to its origins as moxibustion in China, over two thousand years before the time of Christ. While the exact story is not recorded, it is supposed that sparks from prehistoric camp fires must have landed on certain spots of the human skin and helped relieve pains in other parts of the body. Moxibustion exists today, as a small pyramid of inflammable embers (much like incense or the material that makes up a "punk" for lighting firecrackers), but it's a little clumsy, somewhat uncomfortable, and not as efficient as a needle, which reaches directly into the deeper parts of the body.

Acupuncture needles come in various lengths, depending on the distance from the skin to the target nerve or muscle. The shortest is a half-inch long, and the longest in common use is four inches. There are needles that are a full six inches long, but these are used mainly to cure constipation. (For this condition, all we do is *show* the needle to the patient.) Each acupuncture needle is so fine it would fit through the bore of a flu-shot needle.

Bill Moyers recently published an excellent book on non-traditional medicine called *Healing and the Mind* and screened a TV special on national airwaves. In it he and Dr. David Eisenberg, an internist from Harvard, visited a Beijing operating room, and looked on as a patient underwent brain surgery, with three pairs of acupuncture needles as the main anesthetic. Small amounts of Western sedatives were also used, but the patient was fully awake. As the drill was boring through her skull, the patient responded to Moyer's questions, noting that she felt fine and was in no pain.

Up to this point, Western doctors are intrigued. However, when an acupuncturist starts explaining the phenomenon in terms of the mysterious inner energy flow the Chinese call *chi*, the masculine/feminine aspects of yin and yang, and "meridians," named after the large intestine or gallbladder, most Western doctors and scientists just roll their eyes.

Indeed, as recently as 1993, one boffin in the American Medical Association recently shrugged off the whole thing by saying he didn't believe acupuncture was any better than "just pinching the skin." Try operating on someone's brain (or fixing an NFL quarterback's frozen shoulder) by just pinching the skin, and you will quickly see the difference.

---

## CASE HISTORY

One measure of acupuncture's increasing respectability is illustrated by the fact that most of the patients in my new practice at Porter Hospital in Denver are referred by MDs, both family doctors and specialists. It seems doctors are open to new treatments, once they have seen them work on their own patients. One case in particular helped improve the view of acupuncture in our community.

A thirty-two-year-old man injured his right shoulder during a fall at work. He was able to lift his hand to almost touch his right ear and to move it forward from there, but was unable to draw his hand back any farther. Three weeks after his injury he was worse than ever and was greatly frustrated by his inability to return to work. He was referred to me by his orthopedic surgeon, and accompanied into my office by his boss and his therapist. They watched as I inserted one needle into his elbow and another into his shoulder tip, and stimulated both electrically. Within a few moments he could miraculously move his shoulder through its full range, with no pain at all. He could now get some meaningful results from the exercises designed by his surgeon and therapist. After ten days his atrophied muscles regained their bulk, and the strength of the arm returned to normal. All concerned were delighted that he was able to go back to work.

The significance of this case is that a few months later, he was able to use that arm to sign the biggest contract to date in the history of his profession. His boss praised him as the best in the business, and awarded him $20 million over four years. The Denver Broncos' star quarterback was the NFL's man of the year, and team owner Pat Bowlen calls him the hero of the future. But John Elway's 1992 season could only be completed because of a four-thousand-year-old Chinese treatment.

---

The reason acupuncture has had so little Western scientific attention is the usual one: lack of money. University budgets and hospital budgets are stretched to the limits, leaving little funding for pure research. Any research funding that is available comes from drug companies, which, by the merest coincidence, stand to sell some of their products in the process. Why would any drug company spend the required millions to demonstrate that acupuncture is a safer and more effective pain reliever than their expensive pills? Considering the money these same companies lavish on advertisements, promotions, and free dinners to encourage doctors to think of them every time they see a patient in pain, it's no wonder doctors are not exposed to the low-tech options.

So strongly does medical school train us to think in one scientific dimension that Western doctors have trouble seeing the sense in another. At least that was the story until the discovery of the connection between acupuncture and endorphine, first made at the University of Toronto and at Yale in 1976. At that time it was noted that acupuncture treatments caused a sustained elevation of endorphine, which is the body's own molecule of morphine. This strong painkiller occupies all the same receptor sites in the brain as does morphine from external sources.

Patients were tested for pain tolerance to a given stimulus, such as an electric current applied to dental nerves. After acupuncture, pain tolerance rose dramatically. After an intravenous shot of nalorphine, the antidote we use in hospitals to counter a morphine overdose, the patient's pain tolerance was immediately reversed, back to the same sensitivity as before the acupuncture treatment. This release of the body's own morphine also explains why acupuncture treatments are helpful for morphine addicts as they try to quit, and why it can help nicotine and ethanol addicts (smokers and alcoholics) to convert the object of their addictions to a harmless but potent opiate from their own body. Needless to say, the endorphine rationale finally gave Western doctors a scientific explanation, without which acupuncture was forever doomed to be called quackery.

As to the apparent mystery of the placement of the needles, often remote from the site of the pain, there is a sound medical explanation. Initially, the map of the body was defined by trial and error: ancient acupuncturists found success when they used some points, and none when they used others. At first glance, the arrangement of standard acupuncture points along invisible meridians in the body seems illogical; however, most make sense. For example, there is a spot in each hand that is so powerful a needle inserted there can be used as the only anesthetic for major surgery such as an appendectomy or thyroid removal. Known on the Chinese acupuncture map as *hoku*, or "large intestine 4," this spot is located in the fleshy part of the hand between the base of the thumb and index finger. A one-inch needle is inserted here, aimed at the base of the fifth finger.

## SOMETIMES NO NEED FOR DRUGS

Fibromyalgia, also known as fibromyositis, or fibrositis, is a common condition that causes pains similar to arthritis, except they occur between the joints, deep in the muscles and tendons. The condition was first described by Dr. Hugh Smythe and his colleagues at the Wellesley Hospital in Toronto. Smythe and his rheumatology colleagues (does this qualify as a "joint" venture?) noted that many patients have pains in the limbs, and in fact all through the body, that are exquisitely tender to direct pressure and together conspire to rack the body with agony. Smythe noted that these patients slept poorly and wondered if the lack of sleep was a cause or a result of the condition. He then turned to the most ready source of volunteers, the medical students in his hospital, and bribed them to stay awake for five days and nights. It turned out that when these sleep-deprived subjects were tested for pressure-point tenderness they exhibited all the same spots of pain as those found in his patients. That's why the standard drug for fibromyalgia is the anti-depressant amytryptaline (Elavil), which tends to give patients a better night's sleep and thus reduces muscle tenderness. Smythe and his colleagues set about documenting these pressure points, which I recorded at one of Smythe's lectures. They included the shoulder tips, a couple of inches above the inside of each knee, the points where the ribs met the cartilage of the breastbone, and other seemingly random spots. Several years later, when I was taking my acupuncture courses, I discovered the same spots again, on the ancient Chinese map of acupuncture points. Now, when I examine such patients, I not only palpate to see which of these points are tender, but I insert an acupuncture needle directly to make the area numb. In most such cases, there is no need for additional prescription drugs.

Anatomically this makes sense. There are two arteries in the wrist, the radial (which we use to feel our pulse) and the ulnar. The two join beneath the palm to form an arc, against which are plastered the sympathetic nerves that give immediate access to the spinal column and brain. When a needle hits this spot, the patient often feels flushed, and demonstrates the classic Horner's syndrome; they feel immediately hot and ask to open a window. This is not a sign of premature menopause (it happens to male patients as well), but it is a sign that the stimulation of a needle electronically or manually, which creates static electricity much like a Boy Scout rubbing a dry stick to start a fire, sends an electric current to the brain. The fact that the blood registers an immediate and measurable outpouring of endorphin adds to the medical explanation.

The second hormone released by acupuncture is ACTH, oradreno-cortico-tropic hormone. This is found at one end of a polypeptide chain, the other end of which carries the above-mentioned endorphin. So at the same time that endorphin is released to fight pain throughout the body, ACTH zeroes in on the adrenal glands, which are located above each kidney. These glands then pour their powerful anti-inflammatory hormone, cortisone, into the bloodstream. This process of cortisone release explains why acupuncture can be so useful in providing sustained pain relief in cases of arthritis and sports injuries, and so helpful in treating asthma.

Modern medical acupuncture also uses electricity, which is supplied by low-voltage machines similar to the TENS (TransCutaneous Nerve Stimulation) machines now in common use in hospital rehab centers. Western doctors know that electricity has therapeutic value, because we use it routinely for fractures that are not healing properly. When all else fails, surgeons sometimes open up the skin, cut through to the broken ends of the bone, and wrap a metal electrode around each end. The wires are then brought to the surface and connected to exactly the same machine that I use for acupuncture stimulation. Of course, it is much easier for the patient if the same "underground" current can be delivered without surgery, simply by inserting needles down to the precise depth of the trouble, bracketing the painful spot in a muscle, nerve, or bone. With a few seconds of such stimulation the patient can often demonstrate remarkable pain relief, and return to a full range of movements. Logic dictates that this is the reason that acupuncture needles work better than skin pads when stimulating both with a TENS current; the electricity can best heal deep-tissue injuries or inflammations when it is buzzing through the correct tissue plane and not restricted to the surface.

There are several other forms of therapy that use the same points or meridians on the body, but do not penetrate the skin:

### 1. Massage

As anyone who has had a professional massage will know, it is vastly different from an amateur back rub. A skilled massage therapist knows how to knead each of the acupuncture spots, probing deep into the muscles with skilled fingers. A good massage can release modest quantities of endorphin and ease a lot of mental tensions that aggravate the rest of the body. This tension release is as helpful to the sedentary person as to the professional athlete.

### 2. Shiatsu

A Japanese variation of massage, using static pressure upon acupuncture points, Shiatsu is fantastic for breaking down the painful "knots" in tense muscles and offers the sort of pain relief seen in massage.

### 3. TENS

As described earlier, TENS uses the same machines as in modern medical acupuncture, but instead attaches them to skin pads. This can be an excellent maintenance therapy for patients in between acupuncture treatments. The home machines are small, portable, and cheap.

### 4. Laser Acupuncture

Laser beams are used to stimulate the surface of the skin. Laser acupuncture works on all the principles of TENS and acupuncture, yet its results are limited because it cannot penetrate to the problem level. Also, the technology is very expensive.

### 5. Codetron

This is an expensive computerized machine that uses multiple skin electrodes. The machine stimulates two of these electrodes at a time, for a few seconds each, then switches to other random pairs, not letting the body get "used to" any one combination.

## Chiropractic

Chiropractic is a system of health care that emphasizes the relationship between structure and function in the body. To help maintain good function, chiropractors try to align the body's parts, especially the spine, through manipulation, massage, or therapeutic exercises. Often they use techniques common to physical therapy and many used in sports medicine. Chiropractors can be very useful for some pains and can manipulate or "crack" joints better than anyone. However, they have had some bad headlines when they transgress lines of logic; one recently was treating young children for earaches by discarding all antibiotics and replacing traditional treatments by simply manipulating the neck. Whenever possible, I recommend recognizing everyone's expertise, yet acknowledging their areas of ignorance. I have sent many of my patients with back spasms to skilled chiropractors (and indeed have had my own neck "cracked"), but I never ask them to cure cancer or infections. As consumers, I would recommend also asking about the age of the chiropractor's X-ray machines — many are old and produce poor pictures when compared with those available with modern hospital machines. I usually send my patients to our hospital for X-rays, then have them take them to the chiropractor.

## Other Alternative Therapies

Beyond the realm of therapies relating to acupuncture points, there are a host of other modalities that make use of the mind-body connection. These are starting to enter the mainstream of medical treatments, as Western doctors realize the limitations of purely drug- or surgery-based treatments.

## 1. Hypnosis

Feared by many to cause loss of control over the mind, hypnosis actually accomplishes the opposite, and helps the individual *gain* control. Professional hypnotists claim that over 85% of all people can be hypnotized (if they are willing). The mind-body connection is immediately apparent in hypnosis, because the subject undergoes an instant reduction in pulse rate, blood pressure, and galvanic skin resistance (a measure dependent on the amount of sweat produced by the skin). Shoulder muscles visibly relax and the jaw often becomes slack.

In skilled hands, post-hypnotic suggestion can be a useful tool in modifying habitual responses; for example, in getting smokers to stop lighting up each time they hear the phone ring. As the phone rings smokers are taught to take a slow breath as they focus on some other behavior, such as bending a thumb. This form of therapy can be taught to the individual, through the use of tapes (such as my own "Power Nap" tape), or simply through practice and imagery. Once learned, it is a powerful weapon against insomnia, anxiety, and stress. It is also helpful in treating pain.

## 2. Biofeedback

The brain is wired up to demonstrate its level of wave activity, either through an oscilloscope or through sound emission. The idea is that patients can learn to call up their own images to excite the brain waves, or to calm them down, depending on their needs. This can be helpful in treating pain cases, as well as cases of hives, ulcers, asthma, or epilepsy, where anxiety can lead to a chain reaction of disease symptoms.

While there are several kinds of machines, a simple one for demonstration purposes measures galvanic skin resistance. In the GSR II machine the patient holds two fingertips to the metal pads provided. If the patient conjures up an exciting or alarming image, the skin sweats, reducing the resistance to the flow of electricity. When the patient feels in a calm space, the skin becomes dry and does not conduct electricity very well. This change of resistance produces a change in sound, with agitation yielding a high-pitched noise, while tranquility generates a low note.

To illustrate this process to a live audience, I once asked for a volunteer to step forward and let me test her skin resistance on a GSR II machine. With her fingertips touching the two metal pads, I asked her a few inane questions without altering the dull, low note emitted by the machine. Then I asked her to describe her favorite movie star (Robert Redford, as it turned out). As she described his blond hair, square jaw, and "bedroom" eyes, the machine started to shriek an alarmingly high note. After the audience's laughter and our volunteer's embarrassment subsided, I asked her to describe her husband. She replied, "Well, to start with, he's overweight, bald, and a keen Rotarian..." As she spoke, the high-pitched sound left over from Redford sank to a basso profundo at an alarming rate, like a fighter plane being shot down from the sky. While the result was hilarious, it served to illustrate the immediate connection between what is on our mind and what is in our body. It is that simple to call up a calming image whenever you want to reassert control over your body's stress responses.

By practising with a biofeedback machine with a therapist, any patient can learn the skills of imagery to defuse at the outset crises that might have escalated into high blood pressure or chest pains. People suffering chronic pain can even teach their bodies to require less medication.

### 3. Relaxation Response

First described by cardiologist Dr. Craig Benson in his book of the same name, this tension-reducing technique is based on breathing. One of the first things to go in times of chronic or acute stress is the ability to breathe correctly. As we tense up, we tend to breathe shallow breaths, driven by the inefficient movements of the rib cage. Because new oxygen is not given full access to the depths of the lungs, carbon dioxide builds up in the bloodstream, where it is quickly converted to carbonic acid. As the blood's pH turns acid, muscles have more difficulty clearing out their lactic acid and they become stiff. In addition, the mind's sense of stress is heightened. The physical repercussions are often dramatic, throughout the heart, and indeed the whole body, including the immune system. Antibodies and "killer-T" white cells decline. Once the relaxation response is taught to the patient, these effects are immediately reversed. The immune system builds up its resistance to infection, the coronary arteries stop clogging up with sludge, the blood pressure drops, the pulse returns to normal, and the stomach stops its abnormal churnings.

### 4. Yoga/Tai Chi/Martial Arts/Meditation/Prayer

Any of these vehicles can carry the stormy mind to a safe harbor. All require discipline, and each has its disciples. Yoga combines mental calmness with breathing and stretching exercises, as does tai chi, which millions of Chinese do in public parks across China each morning. Meditation and prayer may not offer specific physical exercises, but each offers medically proven doses of stress reduction and, potentially, some disease prevention.

### 5. Homeopathy and Naturopathy

While this is a non-traditional field, one that is not much taught in medical schools, many good practices have emerged from the world of herbal medicines. After all, one of our oldest heart medicines comes from crushed foxglove plants (digitalis), and one of our newest treatments for ovarian cancer comes from the bark of the Pacific yew tree (tamoxifen). I recommended being very careful about the practitioner here, because there are a lot of charlatans about. Beware especially of those who discard all the known facts of Western medicine and who charge vast sums for meager results. This can be particularly tragic in the case of patients who suspend valid cancer treatments to invest in scam therapies, such as the apricot-pit derivative laetrile. If the herbal advice seems not to be working, or if it carries side effects, it would be wise to seek a quick second opinion before proceeding.

### 6. Peer Support

Without question, people who are lonely are more likely to die younger than those who have a good support system. We see this phenomenon when an elderly widow dies quietly within a few months of her spouse's demise, especially if she has few other friends around her. We also see how health can deteriorate in the case of the typical two-income family, balancing the demands of work and kids, but having no nearby family, nor time to cement strong bonds of friendship within the neighborhood. As a result, these parents are more likely to become patients, suffering mental or marital burnout, or a breakdown of some part of their body, such as early ulcers, or even heart attacks.

Dr. Dean Ornish reported in 1988 that his patients who had severe coronary-artery disease could reverse their conditions with the simple techniques of moderate exercise, a strictly controlled diet of 10 to 15% fat, and the support gained through group therapy and team-building. The therapeutic effects of having someone near to touch is likely why married people outlive singles and hermits, and why people living alone don't live as long as people with a pet. The same findings have been found with support groups of fellow sufferers of other diseases such as breast cancer, and have been seen in the success of well-publicised clinics like the Betty Ford clinic in California for alcoholism and substance abuse.

## Beware of Scams

A ny treatment is open to abuse, as has been well documented in cases of unnecessary surgery or overprescription of drugs. Alternative medical treatments also include some doubtful therapies, often pursued by unscrupulous practitioners. Indeed, some zealots become so distrustful of regular medicine and so enamored of their charismatic quack therapists that they neglect useful Western tests and end up with preventable tragedies like cervical cancer or strokes. Let the buyer beware, and remember that any medical symptom needs a diagnosis before it needs a treatment. Here are a few examples of popular alternative treatments that cross the line into the harmless hoax, or even into the dangerous scam.

### Chromium Hair Analysis

This form of "analysis" usually leads to a recommendation for an expensive course of chromium supplements. It turns out that these tests are useless, and that the amount of chromium the human body requires is so minuscule that it can be obtained by standing ten feet from a car bumper.

### Magnetic Therapy

Practitioners cover their patients in fine iron filings (under sheets of paper) and use large magnets under the body to "line the patient up." Assuming you already know which was is North, I can think of no other redeeming feature of this treatment other than placebo.

### Neural Injections

These are extremely painful injections of fluid into acupuncture points. I have seen patients with painful bruises all over their bodies (and even in the throat, following injections into the tonsils) that have had few benefits beyond the acupuncture itself.

### Megavitamin Treatment

Unless the patient suffers from scurvy, beriberi, or rickets, it is unlikely that megadoses of vitamins will do any good. I've seen patients who have had to take on extra part-time jobs just to pay for weekly urinalyses done by quack practitioners. However, there is a grain of truth in the megavitamin field, that of the role of vitamin C. Dr. Linus Pauling has long advocated large doses of vitamin C, especially when one has an infection. Assuming that these dosages do not cause any side effects (such as stomach upset, or in the case of some kidney patients, a propensity to stones) there seems to be no harm in trying this. However, this does not mean that the same doses of all vitamins can be toyed with. As we have already seen, vitamin A in mega-quantities can be fatal.

## Yeast Therapy

This has become a popular subtrade among quack practitioners. Yeast is supposed to grow in and on the body, which is why it can be cultured from the skin, mouth, vagina, and rectum. Indeed, it can become a true infection, such as is seen in *candida* infections in the vagina and throat. In such cases, treatment is usually a simple course of the appropriate anti-fungal agent, usually topically applied, but occasionally ingested. However, the yeast therapists go a little overboard here and put patients on a bizarre diet, treat them with expensive remedies and frequent visits, and admonish them to ignore all advice from their own internists, allergists, or pediatricans. After years of such nonsense, many come back to traditional practitioners only to find other causes for their symptoms that are treatable through more sensible means.

# 10

---

# Counterattack!
# Recipes

HERE IS NO SUCH THING AS EXPERTISE, only different areas of ignorance. That is why most diets fail. The doctor or scientist who contrives the lists of good foods may not have any expertise in making those foods palatable.

In my twenty years in practice, I have been impressed by how many people want changes in their health and, in spite of the glitz and excitement of the high-tech medical tools, prefer to choose low technology and high touch when given the option. After all, who wouldn't choose a bean burrito over a bypass? The theory is simple now that we know which foods are good and which are not.

The practical impediment is that people have, to borrow from Professor Henry Higgins, grown accustomed to the taste of all the wrong foods. Whether because of clever advertising campaigns, the omnipresent availability of bad foods, the good intentions of family and friends who share favorite old recipes, or simply because they like the flavor, people are in the wrong food habit and are toying with fate on their plate.

The reason for this is that there are two distinct universes of foods: the fat and the healthy. Each universe contains, say, a thousand food choices, only some of which may appeal to any given palate. The fat universe contains all our old favorites: the cheeseburgers, the bacon and eggs, the steak with béarnaise sauce, the french fries with gravy, the ice cream. From this universe there are probably three or four dozen meal choices that we rotate through the year. Certain items may even become forever associated with certain meals, such as the ham and eggs for Saturday breakfast, or the Sunday evening roast. We forget that there are all kinds of meals in this universe that we may not like, such as pork rinds, and some we may even despise, such as organ, or rattlesnake meat. With the help of recipes from our own and other cultures, we have spent years of trial and error, and have settled upon our most popular choices from the fat universe of foods.

Doctors encounter resistance when they tell patients they can no longer enjoy their favorite foods. This is especially true when patients reluctantly agree to try vegetarian food and stumble on some real duds from the healthy universe. Most common among my own patients is where the neophyte dieter tries kelp, bean curd, or raw tofu, and just about gags on the spot. *Yeccch.* "Hey, Henry, it's better to die young; let's go back and get some of those great-tasting chicken wings."

But this rejection of a few foods should not condemn the whole universe of healthy foods, any more than an inaugural taste of deep-fried offal should condemn the taste of the whole universe of fatty foods. All we need to do is find three or four dozen recipes from the healthy universe to replace the ones we now use from the fatty realm. Rather than risk having you put off by a couple of gustatory stinkers, I bring you the benefit of some tested recipes that are the product of years of work, from several prime sources.

In particular, I am grateful to Joelle Elliston, of Porter Hospital in Denver, for sharing her secrets. Our hospital happens to have a sixty-five-year tradition of vegetarianism (in this case, because of its Seventh-day Adventist origins), although it is in the middle of cattle country in the American West. We have a large and

renowned staff of cardiologists and heart surgeons and, in consequence, have many cardiac patients trying to get the hang of less
fattening foods. To appease both the hospital and the public,
Joelle has become expert in disguising good nutrition as tasty
food. Her meatless curry or her fake "meat" loaf have fooled the
most discerning gourmet. Her low-fat Black Forest cake tastes
sinfully rich, yet has a baffling low-fat level. When I invite guests
for lunch at our cafeteria, they cannot believe the quality or the
taste of the meal (especially because it's in a hospital). While
they may not always say they like it *better* than their usual
choices, virtually all say they enjoy it *as much* and feel great
about having avoided the fat (as well as the guilt and disease that
come with it).

I have also learned at the countertop, at the side of world-
class spa chefs such as Chris Klugman, then of the King Ranch
Spa outside Toronto, and Frank D. De Amicis, formerly of La
Costa Hotel and Spa in California and currently at the Doral
Hotel and Spa in Telluride. These gentlemen are true artists,
and bring some élan into the presentation of good foods. They
rise above the bland and invent some delightful combinations.
When a guest orders a vegetarian dish that is not on the menu,
these are the caliber of chefs who can make the diners wish
they had ordered the same thing.

In addition, I have been helped by my wife, Sharilyn, whose
efforts to prepare good daily meals that our three children will
actually eat has developed a great sense of what "sells."

Lastly, I am indebted to my patients, including those following our heart disease reversal program at Porter. They are the
ultimate test and have been quick to let us know which dishes
are winners, and which should be fed to the cat. The recipes
that follow are decidedly *not* in the latter category and have
accumulated the highest of rave reviews.

These meals will not only keep your stomach pleasantly full,
but they will help prevent and even reverse many diseases. It
has been said of the early Hawaiian missionaries, who arrived
as preachers yet ended up as land owners, that they set out to
do good *and* to do well. There is no reason we cannot accom-

plish similar dual objectives at the table: to serve good foods *and* to eat well.

The following recipes are ideal for all those who wish to stay healthy, and indeed, for all those who have strayed from the path and wish to return to improved health. Each meal is within the 10 to 15% fat level recommended by Drs. Pritikin, Ornish, and McDougall for reversing heart disease. Most are dairy-free, and thus suitable for those suffering from asthma, arthritis, or colitis. Some include low-fat milk, which in small quantities is a tolerable digression; however, for purists and those allergic to cow's milk, simply substitute low-fat soy milk when you encounter milk in a recipe. Each recipe is high in complex carbohydrates and is suitable for athletes training for the next Olympics. Each is high in fiber, to help young and old avoid bowel disorders, including constipation and cancers. Each has big enough portions to sustain energy all day long at the office. All are vegetarian. This keeps the costs down and appeals to those concerned about our fragile environment. Furthermore, they all taste good!

One of the biggest knocks against vegetarian food is that it is a pain to make. When a family is on the run, both parents racing home from work and trying to feed the kids before the soccer game or swim practice, it's all too easy to open the fridge and grab the high-fat weiners or pork chops. The idea of dirtying all the pots and pans to make a vegetarian meal seems as daunting as pounding millet to make bread. But vegetarian cooking doesn't have to be like that. All our recipes are simple to prepare, and several can be made in large batches and stored in the fridge or freezer, to be taken out and heated up with no fuss at all.

It is important to note that the recipes in any book, including this one, are only suggestions. I have had patients who are strongly allergic to almost any kind of foods, even good wholesome foods. Those with gluten intolerance, for example, will not be able to tolerate most breads. Some people break into terrible skin rashes, or develop acute asthma if they eat strawberries, peanuts, or tomatoes. Some develop diarrhea if they eat beans, or worsen their diverticulosis if they eat whole grapes. Still others have no physical allergy, but simply dislike certain foods, to the extent that they become nauseated at the very mention of their names. The point, then, is not to have everybody eat as one, but to have each individual experiment to find the right compromise that appeals to his or her palate, mindset, and body.

I'm not suggesting that every reader become a fanatic about foods, but simply to try to make most of each week's twenty-one meals from these criteria. That way it's not the end of the world if you are compelled by circumstances to transgress on occasion. *Bon appétit!*

# Counterattack! Recipes

## Appetizers

### Fat-Free Corn Chips

| 1 pkg | corn tortillas | 1 pkg |
|-------|----------------|-------|

*Preheat oven to 350°F (180°C). With a long, sharp knife cut a package of corn tortillas into triangles. Place in a single layer on cookie sheets and bake until golden and crisp, about 15 minutes. Because they are so thin, these chips have a tendency to burn, so watch them closely. Chips should be dry enough to snap — if underbaked they will be tough. Great with Bean Dip or Saucy Salsa (following).*

## Bean Dip

| | | |
|---|---|---|
| 19-oz can | refried beans | 540 mL |
| 8-oz can | tomato sauce | 227 mL |
| 1-2 | cloves garlic, minced | 1-2 |
| 1 tsp | chili powder | 5 mL |
| ¹/₂ tsp | dried basil | 2 mL |

*Place all ingredients in a blender and purée. Heat and serve as a dip with tortilla chips.*

*Yield: 3 cups (750 mL).*

## Saucy Salsa

| | | |
|---|---|---|
| 14-oz can | Italian plum tomatoes | 396 mL |
| 1 tbsp | dry minced onion, or | 15 mL |
| *¹/₂ cup* | *finely chopped fresh onion* | *125 mL* |
| 2 tbsp | fresh cilantro, finely minced | 25 mL |
| 1 | clove garlic, finely minced | 1 |
| 2-3 tsp | lemon juice | 10-15 mL |

*Place all ingredients in blender or food-processor container. Pulse machine on and off quickly several times to break up chunks of tomato. Do not purée. Let stand at least 2 hours before serving.*

*Yield: 2 cups (500 mL).*

# Soups

## Cold Apple Soup

| 6 | Granny Smith apples | 6 |
|---|---|---|
| 1 | juice of lemon | 1 |
| 2 qt | unsweetened apple juice | 2 L |
| 1 tsp | ground cinnamon | 5 mL |
| $1/2$ tsp | ground nutmeg | 2 mL |
| 1 tsp | vanilla extract | 5 mL |
| 3 tbsp | cornstarch | 45 mL |

Cut the unpeeled appealed apples into $1/2$-inch thick (5-cm) cubes, sprinkle with lemon juice and chill.

Combine apple juice with spices, vanilla, and cornstarch. Whisk liberally to break down lumps of starch. Allow mixture to sit for 1 hour, until remaining lumps dissolve.

Add apple cubes.

Yield: 2 quarts (2 L).

# Gazpacho

| | | |
|---|---|---|
| 3 | large tomatoes, peeled and finely chopped | 3 |
| 1 | green bell pepper, finely chopped | 1 |
| 1 | cucumber, peeled and finely chopped | 1 |
| 1 cup | cup celery, finely chopped | 250 mL |
| $^1/_2$ cup | green onion, finely chopped | 125 mL |
| 1 qt | tomato juice | 1 L |
| $^1/_4$ cup | red wine vinegar | 60 mL |
| 1 tbsp | olive oil | 15 mL |
| 2 tsp (or less) | salt | 20 mL |
| $^1/_2$ tsp | black pepper | 5 mL |

*Combine all ingredients in large non-metallic bowl and chill. Serve cold. You may garnish with a dollop of non-fat yogurt and croutons.*

*Serves 8.*

## Tofubaisse

| | | |
|---|---|---|
| 1 | large carrot, julienned | 1 |
| 3 | celery stalks, julienned | 3 |
| 2 | leeks, julienned | 2 |
| 3 | plum tomatoes, peeled and seeded | 3 |
| $2/_3$ cups | white wine | 200 mL |
| 6 cups | vegetable stock | 1.5 mL |
| 4 | cloves garlic, minced | 4 |
| pinch | saffron | pinch |
| $4^1/_2$ tsp | tapioca, dissolved in 8 tbsp (100 mL) water | 70 mL |
| 1 lb | fresh or thawed frozen tofu, cut into 1-inch (2.5 cm) cubes | |

*Sauté vegetables in a non-stick pan until tender. Remove and deglaze pan with white wine.*

*Add stock, garlic, and saffron. Simmer 30 minutes. Add tapioca mixture to thicken.*

*Return vegetables to pan.*

*Add tofu.*

*Serves 12.*

# Main Courses

## Savory French Garlic Stew

| | | |
|---|---|---|
| 4¹/₂ cups | cold water | 1 L |
| 18 | cloves garlic, or | 18 |
| 2¹/₂ tsp | *garlic powder* | *12 mL* |
| 4 cups | TVP chunks* | 1 L |
| ¹/₃ cup + 1 tbsp | lemon juice | 90 mL |
| 1 tbsp | vegetable broth mix | 15 mL |
| 1 | large onion, or | 1 |
| ¹/₄ cup | *dried onion flakes* | *50 mL* |
| 3 cups | canned Italian tomatoes | 750 mL |
| ¹/₂ tsp | dried basil | 2 mL |
| 1 tbsp | arrowroot or cornstarch | 15 mL |
| ¹/₂ cup | sliced stuffed green olives *(optional)* | 125 mL |

*In a food processor blend garlic and 1 cup (250 mL) water.*

*Combine garlic mixture, TVP chunks, 3 cups (750 mL) water, lemon juice, vegetable broth mix, and onion in a 3-4 qt (2 L) kettle and simmer 3-4 hours. (A Crockpot works well.)*

*Add tomatoes and basil. Bring to a boil.*

*Combine cornstarch and remaining water. Add to hot mixture. Cook 2-3 minutes.*

*Garnish with olives and serve with rice or noodles.*

*Serves 8-10.*

\* *TVP is textured vegetable protein*

## Barbecued Wheat "Ribs"

| 4 cups | instant gluten flour | 1 L |
| 1½ cups | rolled oats | 375 mL |
| 1 tsp | garlic powder | 5 mL |
| 1 tbsp | beef-like seasoning | 15 mL |
| 2 tbsp | onion powder | 25 mL |
| 1 tbsp | paprika | 15 mL |
| 3½ cups | cold water | 875 mL |

*Mix all dry ingredients together. Add most of the water and knead with a bread machine or by hand until smooth and elastic (like a stiff bread dough).*

*Cut into finger-shaped pieces about ½ inch (1 cm) square by 3-4 inches (7.5-10 cm) long. Put on an oiled cookie sheet about 1½ inches (4 cm) apart. Bake about 8 minutes at 400°F (200°C), just until slightly puffed.*

*Put in casserole and cover with Home-Style Barbecue Sauce\* (following). Bake at 225°F (120°C) for 1½ hours.*

*\*At this point the Barbecue Wheat "Ribs" may be frozen and baked later.*

*Serves 12.*

# Home-Style Barbecue Sauce

| | | |
|---|---|---|
| 4 cups | ketchup | 1 L |
| 4 cups | tomato purée | 1 L |
| 4 cups | water | 1 L |
| $^3/_4$ cup | cider vinegar | 175 mL |
| $^3/_4$ cup | brown sugar, or | 175 mL |
| $^2/_3$ *cup* | *honey* | *150 mL* |
| $^1/_2$ tsp | cayenne powder | 2 mL |
| 1 tsp | dry mustard | 5 mL |
| 1 tbsp | smoke flavoring (liquid) | 15 mL |
| 1 | onion, chopped, or | 1 |
| $^1/_3$ *cup* | *dried onion* | *75 mL* |
| $^1/_4$ tsp | coriander | 1 mL |
| $^1/_2$ tsp | dried basil | 2 mL |
| $^1/_3$ tsp | allspice | 3 mL |
| $1^1/_2$ tbsp | low-sodium soy sauce | 20 mL |

*Combine all ingredients and simmer until desired thickness is reached.*

*Yield: 3 qts (3 L).*

## Frozen Tofu

*Always keep frozen tofu on hand. Easy to defrost at room temperature, in a microwave, or by pouring hot water over the package, it soaks up marinades and has a chewy texture. It's good with vegetables in a won-ton wrapper as an "egg"-roll filling, in Chinese fried rice or a pot pie. Crumble onto pizza before baking or put in a pot of chili or curry sauce. Serve on rice or mashed potatoes, or enjoy it barbecued (see tofu recipes, following). Frozen tofu can be sliced, torn up or grated on the coarse side of a grater.*

## Barbecued Tofu

*Defrost 1 lb (450 g) of frozen tofu and press out excess water. Cut into thin slices or finger-size "ribs" and marinate in Home-Style Barbecue Sauce.*

*Place in a shallow oiled pan and bake at 375°F (190°C) for 10 minutes. Turn, baste with sauce, and cook 10 minutes more.*

*Serves 6.*

# Lemon-Thyme Tofu

| | | |
|---|---|---|
| 1 lb | tofu, defrosted, drained, rinsed, and cut into 8 equal-sized patties | 450 g |
| $\frac{1}{2}$ cup | lemon juice and zest | 125 mL |
| $\frac{1}{4}$ cup | lemon thyme leaves, bruised | 50 mL |
| 1 | shallot, peeled and minced | 1 |
| 1 tbsp | olive oil | 15 mL |
| | salt to taste | |

*Place tofu patties in a glass dish. Combine remaining ingredients and pour over tofu. Cover and marinate (marinade mixture should be blender-ized to crush leaves) at room temperature while you pre-heat hibachi.*

*Grill tofu patties over medium coals until golden on both sides, no more than 5 - 7 minutes on each side, basting periodically but turning only once.*

*Serves 4.*

**TIP**

*Simmer tofu patties in water while assembling rest of ingredients. Freshly drained, they will soak up the marinade.*

*Lemon thyme is a low-growing ground cover plant with tiny, bright green leaves bounded in yellow. Not only does it look great in flower beds but it also flavors foods with a lemon tang. If you don't have any in the garden, substitute standard thyme in this recipe. Great served with stir-fried broccoli and pearl onions, and grilled potatoes.*

## Scrambled Tofu

| 1 lb | tofu, defrosted, drained and rinsed | 450 g |
| 1½ tsp, or to taste | vegetable-broth-powder seasoning | 7 mL |
| dash | turmeric | dash |
| ½ tsp | dried basil | 1 mL |
| pinch | garlic powder | pinch |

*Place tofu in a non-stick skillet and mash until crumbly with a wooden spoon.*

*Add seasonings and cook until heated through and water is evaporated. The turmeric is for color only, not for taste, so sprinkle it sparingly. The mixture will turn more yellow as the tofu warms up.*

*Additional ingredients may be added if desired, such as green onions, mushrooms, and bell peppers.*

*Scrambled tofu may be eaten with toast and/or hash browns for breakfast, in a pita pocket as a sandwich filling, in a tortilla with salsa, or it may be used to make Tofu Eggless Salad.*

*Serves 4 - 6.*

# Savory Black Beans with Zesty Tomatoes

| | | |
|---|---|---|
| 2 cups | dried black beans | 500 mL |
| 6 cups | water | 1.5 L |
| 2 | large garlic cloves | 2 |
| 2 | onions, chopped | 2 |
| 1 | large green pepper, chopped | 1 |
| 1 tsp | cumin | 5 mL |
| 1 tsp | dried basil | 5 mL |
| 6 | tomatoes, chopped | 6 |
| 1 | bunch green onions, chopped | 1 |
| 1 | garlic clove, crushed | 1 |
| 3 tbsp | lemon juice | 45 mL |
| 4-5 dashes | Tabasco sauce | 4-5 dashes |
| 2 tbsp | fresh cilantro or parsley | 25 mL |

*Place beans and water in large pot. Add garlic cloves. Cook over low heat about 2 hours.*

*Remove the garlic. Add chopped onions and green pepper, cumin and basil. Cook an additional hour until beans are tender.*

*Combine tomatoes, green onions, crushed garlic, lemon juice, Tabasco, and cilantro in a bowl. Refrigerate until ready to serve, at least 1 hour. Serve the beans over brown rice, garnished with some of the tomato mixture.*

*Serves 6 - 8.*

## Fajitas Margarita

| | | |
|---|---|---|
| 4 cups | TVP chunks | 1 L |
| 8$\frac{1}{2}$ cups | cold water | 2 L |
| 1 cup | low-sodium soy sauce | 250 mL |
| 1 tbsp | garlic granules | 15 mL |
| 3 tbsp | minced onion | 45 mL |
| 1 tsp | dried red pepper, crushed | 5 mL |
| $\frac{3}{4}$ cup | lime (or lemon) juice | 175 mL |
| 1 tsp | cumin | 5 mL |
| $\frac{1}{2}$ cup | honey | 125 mL |
| 2 tbsp | cilantro, chopped, or | 25 mL |
| *1 tbsp* | *dried cilantro* | *15 mL* |
| 1 tsp | chili powder | 5 mL |
| 3 tbsp | cornstarch | 45 mL |

*Put all ingredients except cornstarch and $\frac{1}{2}$ cup (125 mL) water into a 2-3 quart (2-3L) kettle. Bring to a boil, cover and simmer for 2 hours to rehydrate and blend flavors.*

*Combine cornstarch with $\frac{1}{2}$ cup (125 mL) water and stir. Add all at once to hot TVP chunk mixture. More water may be added if "saucier" chunks are desired, or if mixture looks a little dry.*

*Serve with warmed tortillas, fresh tomato wedges, sautéed (or steamed) onions and peppers, finely shredded lettuce, and grated Parmesan cheese (if desired).*

*Serves 8 - 10, generously.*

# Perfect Pancit

| | | |
|---|---|---|
| 2 pkg | rice-stick noodles | 2 |
| | vegetable oil spray *(optional)* | |
| 8 | large cloves garlic, chopped | 8 |
| | or crushed | |
| 1 lb | tofu, cubed and drained | 450 g |
| | for about 1 hour *(optional)* | |
| $^1/_4$ cup | low-sodium soy sauce | 50 mL |
| 1 tsp | seasoning | 5 mL |
| $^3/_4$ cup | shredded onions | 175 mL |
| 1 cup | shredded carrots | 250 mL |
| 3 cups | shredded bok choy | 750 mL |
| $^1/_2$ cup | shredded celery | 125 mL |
| 1 cup | water | 250 mL |
| 1 tsp | sugar | 5 mL |
| $^1/_4$ cup | green onions, finely chopped | 50 mL |

It's best to use a Chinese wok for cooking this dish, but if you don't have one, use a non-stick pot.

*Soak noodles in a large bowl of hot water for approximately 5-10 minutes and drain. Set aside.*

*Spray wok with vegetable oil and brown $^1/_2$ of garlic for about 1 minute.*

*Add tofu and continue to mix while adding 2 tsp (10 mL) of soy sauce and $^1/_2$ tsp (2 mL) seasoning. If you want to omit the tofu, use all the garlic, the soy sauce, and the seasoning, and add all remaining ingredients except green onions.*

*Cover until vegetables are half-cooked, then add noodles.*

*Keep mixing while adding water until water is absorbed and noodles are cooked. You may add a little more water and soy sauce according to your taste.*

*Garnish with green onions before serving.*

*Serves 10 - 12.*

# Barley and Brown Rice Pilaf

| | | |
|---|---|---|
| 2 | large onions | 2 |
| $4^1/_2$ cups | chicken-style broth | $1^1/_4$ L |
| 1 cup | long-grain brown rice | 250 mL |
| 1 cup | pearl barley | 250 mL |
| $^1/_2$ tsp | dried thyme leaves | 2 mL |
| 2 tbsp | lemon juice | 25 mL |
| | salt | |

*In a 3-4 quart (3-4 L) pan, braise-deglaze onions until richly browned; start with $^1/_2$ cup broth, then use water. With last addition of water, scrape onions from pan. Rinse and dry pan.*

*Rinse and drain rice and barley. Add to pan and stir over medium-high heat until grains are dry and smell toasted.*

*Add remaining 4 cups (1 L) broth, onion and thyme. Bring to boil on high heat, then cover and simmer gently until grains are tender to bite, 40 to 50 minutes.*

*Stir in lemon juice and heat until boiling. Season with salt to taste.*

*Serve or, if making ahead, cover and chill until next day; to reheat, use the following directions. Add salt to taste.*

*To reheat: pour rice into a microwave-safe bowl and heat in a microwave oven on full power (100%) for 3 minutes. Continue to heat and stir 1 minute at a time until hot. Or add about $^1/_2$ cup (125 mL) broth to pan and stir over medium heat until hot, about 15 minutes.*

*Serves 6 - 8.*

# Mosaic of Rice and Vegetables

| | | |
|---|---|---|
| 2 | celery stalks, diced | 2 |
| 2 | large onions, diced | 2 |
| 1 | carrot, diced | 1 |
| 4 cups | uncooked rice | 1 L |
| 6 cups | water | 1.5 L |
| 3/4 cup | low-sodium soy sauce | 175 mL |
| 1/2 lb | tofu | 250 g |
| pinch | chicken-style seasoning | pinch |
| pinch | turmeric | pinch |
| 1 1/2 cups | green onion, sliced diagonally | 375 mL |
| 1/4 cup | toasted almonds, slivered, or *sesame seeds* | 50 mL |

*Sauté celery and onion with non-stick spray until onion is soft, about 10 minutes.*

*Add rice, water, carrot, and soy sauce and bring to a boil. Reduce heat to low, cover and cook until all liquid is absorbed.*

*Thinly slice or scramble tofu and brown in a skillet, sprinkling with chicken-style seasoning and a light dusting of turmeric to make it yellow. Can be made ahead and cut into strips or slivers when cooled.*

*Spoon rice onto oval platter. Arrange band of tofu slivers down the center of the rice. Sprinkle green onions and toasted almonds or sesame seeds over the top and serve.*

*Serves 12 - 16.*

## Polenta

| | | |
|---|---|---|
| 4 cups | water | 1 L |
| 2$\frac{1}{2}$ tbsp | broth mix | 30 mL |
| 1-2 | bay leaves | 1-2 |
| 1 cup | cornmeal or instant polenta | 250 mL |

*Bring water to a boil. Add broth mix and bay leaves.*

*Stir cornmeal into hot mixture, reduce heat and stir with a whisk until it thickens. Turn to low heat and cover while it cooks for 10-15 minutes more.*

*Spray a 9 x 12 inch (3L) pan with non-stick spray and pour cornmeal into pan. Spread out. Chill until firm. Cut into squares.*

*Grill squares until heated through (about 3 minutes on each side). Serve with Spicy Marinara Sauce.*

*Serves 6 - 8.*

# Vegetable Curry

| | | |
|---|---|---|
| 2 tsp | vegetable broth | 10 mL |
| 4$\frac{1}{4}$ cups | water | 1 L |
| 1 tbsp | curry powder | 15 mL |
| 1-2 | cloves garlic | 1-2 |
| $\frac{1}{4}$-$\frac{1}{2}$ tsp | cumin | 1-2 mL |
| $\frac{1}{2}$ lb | carrots, sliced | 250 g |
| 1 cup | green pepper, cut into 1-inch (2.5-cm) strips | 250 mL |
| 1 | onion, sliced | 1 |
| $\frac{1}{2}$ lb | cauliflower, cut into bite-size pieces, or | 250 g |
| 10-oz pkg | frozen cauliflower | 284 g |
| 1 | small zucchini, sliced | 1 |
| 19-oz can | tomatoes, diced | 540 mL |
| 19-oz can | garbanzo beans | 540 mL |
| $\frac{1}{3}$ cup | raisins | 75 mL |
| $\frac{1}{3}$ cup | red peppers, diced (optional) | 75 mL |
| 1 cup | green cabbage, chopped | 250 mL |
| 2 tbsp | cornstarch | 25 mL |

*Combine all ingredients except cornstarch and $\frac{1}{4}$ cup (60 mL) water, in suitable pan. Bring to a boil, turn down heat and simmer 1 hour.*

*Combine remaining water and corn starch (use more corn starch if you want thicker sauce). Add to boiling vegetable mixture. Cool until thickened. Seve over rice or couscous.*

*Serves 8 - 12.*

## Spinach Pasta Pie

| | | |
|---|---|---|
| 1¹/₂ cups | orzo (uncooked) | 375 mL |
| ¹/₄ cup | brewer's yeast flakes | 50 mL |
| 2 tbsp | instant gluten flour | 25 mL |
| 20-oz can | spaghetti sauce *(optional)* | 566 mL |
| 10-oz pkg | frozen spinach, chopped | 300 g |
| ¹/₂ cup | non-fat or soy yogurt | 125 mL |
| 1 | egg white | 1 |
| ¹/₂ tsp | nutmeg | 2 mL |
| 2¹/₂ oz | fat-free cheese alternative, shredded | 70 g |

*Cook orzo al dente. Drain in colander about 1 minute only, then put in a 2-quart (2-L) mixing bowl.*

*Mix together brewer's yeast and flour and sprinkle over cooked orzo, folding in immediately with a spatula. Add ¹/₂ cup (125 mL) spaghetti sauce. Fold into mix thoroughly.*

*Spray a 9- or 10-inch (22- or 25-cm) pie pan with non-stick spray. Put orzo mixture over bottom and up the sides of pan to form a shell.*

*Cook spinach and drain well.*

*Combine yogurt, egg white, and nutmeg. Mix thoroughly. Add spinach and spoon into the bottom of pasta-lined pie shell.*

*Spread remaining spaghetti sauce atop filling.*

*Cover edge of pie with foil.*

*Bake in 350°F (180°C) oven for 30 minutes and remove.*

*Top with shredded "cheese." Return to oven and bake 3-5 minutes more or till cheese is melted. Cool 5 minutes before serving.*

*Serves 6 - 8.*

# Seitan (Wheat Meat)

### Dough:

| | | |
|---|---|---|
| 3 cups | instant gluten flour | 750 mL |
| 1/2 cup | whole-wheat flour | 125 mL |
| 1/2 cup | rolled oats | 125 mL |
| 3/4 tsp | garlic powder | 4 mL |
| 2 cups | cold water | 500 mL |

### Broth:

| | | |
|---|---|---|
| 6 cups | water | 1.5 L |
| 1 tbsp | olive oil | 15 mL |
| 3/4 cup | low-sodium soy sauce | 175 mL |
| 1 | celery stalk with leaves | 1 |
| 1 tbsp | molasses | 15 mL |
| 1/4 cup | honey | 60 mL |
| 1 tsp | dried basil | 5 mL |
| 2 | medium onions, quartered | 2 |
| 1 | garlic clove, minced | 1 |

*Mix together flours, oats, and garlic powder.*

*Add cold water all at once.*

*Knead 5–6 mins into a smooth elastic ball. Let sit a few minutes to "relax." Then shape into a log.*

*Seitan is cooked in 2 steps: (1) Put shaped dough piece into a large pot with 3 qts (3 L) boiling water. Boil dough 20–30 minutes or until it floats. Drain and chill. (May refrigerate overnight.) Remove from fridge and cut into thin slices.*

*(2) Combine all broth ingredients in large pot. Stir well. Bring to a boil, add seitan slices, then lower heat and simmer about 45 minutes, or 12 minutes in a pressure cooker.*

*The seitan is now ready to serve in a variety of ways. Delicious served as Hawaiian Barbecue Seitan (following), or with Plum Fancy Sauce (see Sauces). It's also the basis for Wheat-Meat Loaf and Cashew Herb Loaf (following Hawaiian Barbecue Seitan).*

*Serves 12.*

# Hawaiian Barbecue Seitan

| | | |
|---|---|---|
| $^3/_4$ cup | low-sodium soy sauce | 175 mL |
| 2 tbsp | lemon juice | 25 mL |
| $^1/_2$ cup | brown sugar, or | 125 mL |
| $^1/_3$ cup | honey | 85 mL |
| 3 | cloves garlic, minced | 3 |
| 2 tsp | fresh gingerroot, grated | 10 mL |
| 1 tbsp | ketchup | 15 mL |
| 12 | seitan slices | 12 |
| | (see recipe preceding) | |

*Mix all ingredients except seitan together in bowl to make approx. 1 cup Hawaiian Barbecue sauce.*

*Put Seitan slices, however many you choose, into bowl and pour sauce over. Cover and rotate bowl occasionally to make sure all slices are marinated — about 30 minutes or longer.*

*To finish, remove slices from marinade and sauté in heavy non-stick fry pan. Pour a little of marinade into fry pan to help provide a nice caramelized finish to seitan pieces.*

*Serves 4 - 8.*

# Wheat-Meat Loaf

| | | |
|---|---|---|
| 1½ cups | instant gluten flour | 375 mL |
| ½ cup | oatmeal or other grain | 125 mL |
| ½ cup | nuts, finely chopped *(optional)* | 125 mL |
| 1½ cups | vegetables,* finely chopped | 375 mL |
| ½ tsp each | dried basil and rosemary | 2 mL |
| 1 - 2 tbsp | low-sodium soy sauce | 15-25 mL |
| 2 cups | liquid** | 500 mL |
| 1 cup | hot water | 250 mL |

*Mix together in a bowl flour, oatmeal, and nuts. Add chopped vegetables and toss with seasonings.*

*Add soy sauce to liquid and stir to blend. Add liquids to dry ingredients all at once and mix well.*

*Pack into an oiled loaf pan, pressing down till top is firm.*

*Pour hot water on top of loaf and put in oven. Bake 30 minutes at 400°F (200°C) till top has browned. Cover with foil and turn oven down to 300°F (150°C). Bake 1 more hour. Let stand 30 minutes before cutting.*

*Make ahead and refrigerate or freeze for quick meals.*

*Serves 6.*

**TIP**
*Serve with Fat-Free Brown Gravy for a "comfort-food" meal!*

*Use 2 of the following: celery, onion, green or red pepper, grated carrot, mushrooms.
**Liquid may be: water, tomato juice, vegetable juice, or salt-free broth.

## Cashew-Herb Loaf

| | | |
|---|---|---|
| 1/2 cup | raw cashews | 125 mL |
| 3/4 cup | onion, chopped | 175 mL |
| 2-3 tbsp | low-sodium soy sauce | 25-45 mL |
| 1/2 cup | almond or soya milk | 125 mL |
| 1/2 cup | water | 125 mL |
| 1 tbsp | cornstarch | 15 mL |
| 1 tbsp | gelatin | 15 mL |
| 1 1/2 cups | seitan, ground* | 375 mL |
| 1 tbsp | parsley, dry | 15 mL |
| 1 tsp | paprika | 5 mL |
| 1/2 tsp | garlic powder | 2 mL |
| 1/4 tsp each | dried basil, marjoram, rosemary | 1 mL |
| 1 tsp | brewer's yeast flakes | 5 mL |
| 2/3 cup | bread crumbs | 150 mL |
| 1/2 tsp | celery seeds | 2 mL |
| 3/4 tsp | sage | 3 mL |

*Wash and toast cashews (under broiler). Chop. Put in 2-3 quart (2-3 L) bowl.*

*Add all remaining ingredients and mix well.*

*Spoon into 9x9-inch (2L) baking dish sprayed with non-stick spray.*

*Bake at 350°F (180°C) for 45-60 minutes. Cool 10 minutes before slicing. Can be made ahead and reheated.*

*Serve with peas or corn and your salad of choice.*

*Serves 8 - 10.*

* See Seitan (Wheat Meat) recipe.

# Oatmeal Wheatgerm Burger

| | | |
|---|---|---|
| $^1/_4$ cup | warm water | 60 mL |
| 1 tbsp | dry yeast | 15 mL |
| $1^1/_2$ cups | oatmeal | 325 mL |
| 1 cup | toasted wheatgerm | 250 mL |
| 2 | egg whites | 2 |
| $14^1/_2$ oz | non-fat evaporated milk | 225 mL |
| $^1/_4$ cup | low-sodium soy sauce | 60 mL |
| 1 tsp | sage | 10 mL |
| 1 | large onion, minced | 1 |

*In large bowl, add warm water and sprinkle with yeast to soften. Add remaining ingredients and blend.*

*Preheat (medium heat) non-stick fry pan. Measure approx. $^1/_4$ cup (60 mL) of mixture and drop onto pan. Cook until browned and "set" on one side, then turn and set other side. (If patty browns too much before it's set, turn heat down and cook a little longer before turning.)*

*May be served with Creamy Mushroom Sauce, Fat-Free Brown Gravy, ketchup, or in a whole-wheat hamburger bun.*

*Serves 10-12.*

# Roasted Corn-and-Barley Croquettes

| | | |
|---|---|---|
| 1 cup | corn kernels, roasted | 250 mL |
| 1 cup | barley, cooked (by boiling in water) | 250 mL |
| $^1/_2$ cup | water from cooked barley | 125 mL |
| 1 cup | potatoes, peeled and boiled | 250 mL |
| 1 tbsp | garlic, minced | 15 mL |
| 1 tsp | canola oil | 5 mL |
| $^1/_4$ cup | green onion, finely chopped | 60 mL |
| $^1/_2$ cup | green pepper, finely diced | 125 mL |
| 1 tsp | chili powder | 5 mL |
| 1 tsp | cumin | 5 mL |
| $^1/_2$ tsp | salt | 3 mL |
| dash | pepper | dash |
| 2 | egg whites | 2 |

*Roast whole fresh corn with husk on in 375 °F (190 °C) oven for 1$^1/_2$ hours. Cool and peel away husk. Cut kernels from cob.*

*Drain boiled barley, reserving $^1/_2$ cup water.*

*Boil potatoes until well done.*

*Sauté garlic in oil over low heat for 2 minutes. Add green onion and green pepper. Increase heat and sauté for 1 minute.*

*Add half of reserved barley water and remove from heat. Stir to release flavor.*

*Rice or mash boiled potatoes and add to mixture.*

*Add egg whites and mix well. If necessary, add more barley water to make a pasty consistency.*

*Shape into 8 patties and grill under broiler or sauté on non-stick fry pan.*

*Delicious served with Creamy Mushroom Sauce or Fat-Free Brown Gravy.*

*Serves 4.*

# Haystack (Quick Nourishing Meal)

| | | |
|---|---|---|
| 32-oz can | pinto beans in chili gravy | 500 g |
| 8-oz bag | no-fat (baked) corn chips* | 200 g |
| $^1/_2$ head | shredded lettuce | $^1/_2$ head |
| 3 | medium tomatoes, diced | 3 |
| 1 | medium onion, minced | 1 |
| 1 cup | salsa | 250 mL |

*Heat beans while putting remaining items in separate serving dishes.*
*Let everyone make his or her own "haystack." Put corn chips on bottom of plate, then a layer of beans, followed by lettuce, tomatoes, onion, and salsa. Enjoy!*

*Serves 4-5.*

*\*See recipe for Fat-Free Corn Chips, page 164.*

# Vegetables

## Teriyaki Corn

| | | |
|---|---|---|
| $^1/_4$ cup | low-sodium soy sauce | 50 mL |
| 2 tsp | vegetable oil | 10 mL |
| 2 | cloves garlic, finely minced | 2 |
| 1 tbsp | light-colored molasses | 15 mL |
| 1 tsp | grated gingerroot | 5 mL |
| 6 | ears fresh corn on the cob, shucked | 6 |

*Preheat grill. In small bowl, combine soy sauce, oil, garlic, molasses, and gingerroot. Place corn in a shallow pan and brush with sauce.*

*Grill, turning and basting frequently with sauce, until evenly browned, about 8 minutes.*

*Serves 6.*

## Baked Hash Browns

| | | |
|---|---|---|
| 2 | medium potatoes, peeled | 2 |
| 1 tsp | onion powder | 5 mL |

*Preheat waffle iron on high temperature. Shred freshly washed potatoes. Add onion powder.*

*Spray iron with non-stick spray. Spread potato mixture over iron, no more than 1-in. (2-cm) thick. Close iron cover.*

*Cook 15 - 20 minutes. Do not open cover while cooking.*

*Serves 2.*

# Spicy Mountain Potatoes

| | | |
|---|---|---|
| 6 | medium potatoes | 6 |
| 1 | large onion, cut in rings | 1 |
| 2 tbsp | lemon juice | 25 mL |
| $^3/_4$ tsp | pimento, chopped | 3 mL |
| 16-20 | olives, halved *(optional)* | 16-20 |
| $^1/_2$ cup | mild green chilies | 125 mL |

This is an adaptation of a traditional dish that comes from the native peoples of Peru. Supposedly the poorer the family, the less cheese and the more chilies the mixture contained.

*Quarter potatoes and steam until tender, but not mushy, about 20 minutes. Cut into bite-size pieces.*

*Mix together onions, lemon juice, and pimento, and marinate at room temperature while potatoes cook.*

*Mix potatoes with Melty "Cheese" Sauce (following). Drain onions and stir in. Add olives and chilies. Place in a serving dish and garnish.*

*Serve this with a crusty bread and two vegetable dishes from the following list: squash, pan-fried cabbage or other greens, fresh sliced tomatoes.*

*Serves 5 - 6.*

## Melty "Cheese" Sauce

| | | |
|---|---|---|
| 2 cups | water | 500 mL |
| 1/2 cup | pimentos | 125 mL |
| 1/4 cup | brewer's yeast flakes | 50 mL |
| 1 1/2 tsp | salt | 7 mL |
| 1/2 tsp | onion powder | 2 mL |
| 1/4 tsp | garlic powder | 1 mL |
| 3 tbsp | cornstarch | 45 mL |
| 1/4 cup | cashews, or | 50 mL |
| *1/4 cup* | *cooked potato* | *50 mL* |
| 1-2 tbsp | lemon juice | 15-25 mL |
| 1-2 tbsp | butter flavoring (liquid) | 15-25 mL |

*Purée in blender until smooth.*

*Cook in heavy saucepan, stirring constantly until thick, about 5-6 minutes. Great as a dip or sauce.*

*Yield: approx. 3 cups (750 mL).*

# Mushrooms Supreme

| 2 cups | water | 500 mL |
|---|---|---|
| 1 | onion, chopped | 1 |
| 2 | bay leaves | 2 |
| $1/_2$ tsp | dried basil | 1 mL |
| 1 | green pepper | 1 |
| | cut in medium chunks | |
| $1^1/_2$ lbs | mushrooms, quartered | 750 g |
| 1 tbsp | low-sodium tamari | 15 mL |
| 1 cup | white grape juice | 250 mL |
| $1/_2$ cup | tomato sauce | 125 mL |
| 1 tbsp | parsley flakes | 15 mL |
| 1 | clove garlic, chopped | 1 |

*Put $1/_2$ cup (125 mL) water in a large cooking pot. Add the chopped onion, bay leaves, and basil. Sauté about 5 minutes. Add chopped green pepper and mushrooms. Continue cooking for about 10 minutes.*

*Add the remaining water, tamari, grape juice, tomato sauce, garlic, and parsley. Add a little fresh-ground pepper, if desired. Simmer slowly over low heat for at least 1 hour until the liquid becomes thick and glossy. Remove bay leaves.*

*Serve very hot over brown rice or baked potatoes.*

*Serves 4.*

# Sauces

## Plum Fancy Sauce

| | | |
|---|---|---|
| ²/₃ cup | dry black beans, or | 150 mL |
| *16-oz* | *can, drained* | *475 mL* |
| 1 cup | oriental plum sauce | 250 mL |
| 2 tbsp | lemon juice | 25 mL |
| ¹/₄ tsp | garlic powder *(optional)* | 1 mL |
| 1 | bay leaf | 1 |
| 1 tsp | dry minced onion | 5 mL |
| 1 tbsp | soy sauce | 15 mL |

*Wash beans and cook as directed; drain off most of the liquid. Add all remaining ingredients. Heat slowly to blend flavors.*

*Yield: 2 cups (500 mL).*

# Spicy Marinara Sauce

| | | |
|---|---|---|
| 1 | clove garlic | 1 |
| 1 | onion, chopped | 1 |
| 2 cups | tomatoes, fresh or canned, chopped | 500 mL |
| 2 cups | canned tomato sauce | 500 mL |
| 1 tbsp | molasses or honey | 15 mL |
| 1/4 cup | fresh parsley, chopped, or | 60 mL |
| 2 tbsp | *dried parsley* | *30 mL* |
| 1/2 tsp | dry mustard | 2 mL |
| 1 tsp | oregano | 5 mL |
| 1/4 tsp | chili powder *(optional)* | 1 mL |
| 1/2 tsp | paprika | 2 mL |
| 1/8 tsp | cayenne *(optional)* | .5 mL |
| 1 tsp (or less) | salt | 5 mL |
| 1/4 cup | fat-free parmesan cheese *(optional)* | 60 mL |

*Put onion and garlic into a 2-qt (2-L) pot with just enough water to cover — about 1/4 cup (60 mL). Cook 3-4 minutes.*

*Add remaining ingredients, bring to a boil, then cover and simmer for 30 minutes, or till ready to eat.*

*Great with polenta or pasta!*

*Yield: 4 1/2 cups.*

## Garbanzo-Rosemary Sauce

| | | |
|---|---|---|
| 2 15-oz cans | garbanzo beans | 850 mL |
| ¹/₂ cup | liquid from drained beans | 125 mL |
| 1 | large onion, sliced or diced | 1 |
| 4 | large cloves garlic | 4 |
| 1 15-oz can | tomatoes, cut up | 425 mL |
| ¹/₂ tsp | dried basil | 2 mL |
| 1 tsp | dried rosemary, or | 5 mL |
| 1 tbsp | *fresh rosemary, chopped* | *15 mL* |
| ¹/₄ cup | fresh parsley, minced | 50 mL |

*Drain beans, saving ¹/₂ cup (125 mL) of liquid.*

*Purée 1 can of garbanzos with ¹/₂ cup (125 mL) liquid. Set aside.*

*Cook onion and garlic in enough water to cover until soft. Drain.*

*Add tomatoes and second can of garbanzos to onion and garlic in heavy 3-quart (3-L) kettle. Add puréed garbanzos, basil, and rosemary. Simmer 15 minutes.*

*Add fresh parsley.*

*Serve over baked potatoes, rice, or pasta. Add vegetables and/or salad for a complete meal.*

*Yield: 6 cups (1.5 L).*

# Cilantro Fruit Salsa

| | | |
|---|---|---|
| ¹/₄ cup | green onion, minced | 60 mL |
| ¹/₂ tsp | garlic clove, minced | 2 mL |
| ¹/₂ cup | papaya or mango, diced | 125 mL |
| ¹/₂ cup | pineapple, diced | 125 mL |
| ¹/₂ cup | honeydew melon, diced | 125 mL |
| ¹/₄ cup | unsweetened pineapple, or other fruit juice | 60 mL |
| ¹/₂ cup | strawberries, quartered | 125 mL |
| 2 tbsp | cilantro, minced | 30 mL |

*Spray pan with non-stick spray. Cook onion and garlic for 2 minutes.*

*Add payaya, pineapple, and melon. Cook 1-2 minutes.*

*Add juice and cook until just warmed. Remove from heat.*

*Add strawberries and cilantro. Cool to room temperature or chill to serve.*

*Perfect with Wheat-Meat Loaf and Oatmeal Wheatgerm Burger.*

*Yield: 3 cups (750 mL).*

## Creamy Mushroom Sauce

| | | |
|---|---|---|
| 1 | onion, chopped | 1 |
| ¹/₂ lb | mushrooms, sliced | 250 g |
| ¹/₂ cup | cold water | 125 mL |
| 2 cups | skim milk (may use nut, soy, or rice milk instead) | 500 mL |
| 1 tbsp | low-sodium soy sauce | 15 mL |
| pinch | garlic powder | pinch |
| 2 tbsp | cornstarch or arrowroot | 25 mL |

*Sauté onion and mushrooms in ¹/₄ cup (60 mL) water for 10 minutes. Add milk, soy sauce, and garlic powder.*

*Mix cornstarch in remaining water. Add to mushroom mixture. Cook and stir over medium heat until mixture thickens.*

*Serve with Wheat-Meat Loaf or Roasted Corn and Barley Croquettes.*

*Yield: 3 cups (750 mL).*

# Fat-Free Brown Gravy

| | | |
|---|---|---|
| 4 cups | water | 1 L |
| 1 | small onion | 1 |
| 2 | cloves garlic | 2 |
| $1/_8$ cup | low-sodium soy sauce | 25 mL |
| pinch | dried basil | pinch |
| pinch | dried sage | pinch |
| 1 | bay leaf | 1 |
| $1/_2$ cup | flour | 125 mL |

*Combine all ingredients in saucepan except flour. Bring to a boil and simmer for 30-40 minutes. (This broth may be refrigerated for later use.)*

*Put flour in a dry skillet over medium heat to brown. Keep stirring to prevent burning. When flour is a medium brown color, start adding the broth in stages, stirring constantly to prevent lumping. If gravy is too thin, a little cornstarch mixed with water may be used to thicken it. If it is too thick, thin it with water. If it is lumpy, it may be puréed in a blender until smooth.*

*Yield: 4 cups (1L).*

## Corn Butter

| | | |
|---|---|---|
| 2 tsp | gelatin | 10 mL |
| $^1/_4$ cup | cold water | 50 mL |
| 1 cup | boiling water | 250 mL |
| 1 cup | cornmeal mush | 250 mL |
| $^1/_4$ cup | raw cashews or cooked potato | 50 mL |
| $^1/_2$ tsp | salt (if mush unsalted) | 2 mL |
| 2 tsp | lemon juice | 10 mL |
| 1 tbsp | finely grated raw carrot | 15 mL |
| 1 tsp | butter flavoring | 5 mL |

*This golden spread looks like butter and even melts on warm bread, vegetables, and other foods.*

*Soak gelatin in cold water for several minutes. (This can be done in the blender.) Pour boiling water over gelatin, and whiz to dissolve. Add remaining ingredients and liquefy thoroughly until smooth as cream. Pour into attractive serving jar, cover, and refrigerate.*

*For a smoother cornmeal mush, soak cornmeal overnight in its cooking water before cooking. Keeps two weeks in refrigerator.*

*Corn butter can be used on hot pasta tossed with assorted braised vegetables for a quick meal.*

*Yield: $2^1/_2$ cups (625 mL).*

# Salads

## Party Potato Salad

| | | |
|---|---|---|
| 3½ cups | cooked potatoes with skins, ¾-inch *(2-cm)* cubes | 875 mL |
| 1 cup | finely chopped celery | 250 mL |
| ½ cup | finely chopped onions | 125 mL |
| 2 tbsp | chopped fresh parsley | 25 mL |
| 1 cup | non-fat mayonnaise | 250 mL |
| 1 tbsp | lemon juice | 15 mL |
| 1 tsp or less | salt | 5 mL |
| ¼ tsp | garlic powder | 1 mL |
| 1½ tsp | fresh dill chopped *(optional)* | 7 mL |
| pinch | turmeric *(optional)* | pinch |

*Put all ingredients into bowl and mix together well. Serve warm or cold.*

*Serves 8 - 10.*

## Tofu Eggless Salad

| | | |
|---|---|---|
| 1 | recipe Scrambled Tofu*, cooled | 1 |
| 3 tbsp | non-fat mayonnaise | 45 mL |
| 1 tsp | mustard | 5 mL |
| 1 | clove garlic, peeled | 1 |

*Combine half of the Scrambled Tofu with the non-fat mayonnaise, mustard, and garlic in a blender or small food processor, and purée.*

*Mix in a small bowl with the other half of the Scrambled Tofu (for texture).*

*Use as is for sandwich filling, or add finely diced celery, chives, or other herbs.*

*Serves 6.*

*\*See page 174.*

# Broccoli Salad

| | | |
|---|---|---|
| 4 cups | fresh broccoli spears | 1 L |
| 1 tbsp | garlic, finely chopped | 15 mL |
| 1 cup | onions, thinly sliced | 250 mL |
| $^1/_2$ cup | pimentos, chopped | 125 mL |
| 1 tbsp | onion powder | 15 mL |
| $1^1/_2$ tsp | dried basil | 7 mL |
| $1^1/_2$ tsp | salt | 7 mL |
| 2 tbsp | toasted sesame seeds | 25 mL |
| $1^1/_2$ tsp | fresh lemon juice (optional) | 7 mL |

Steam broccoli until crisp-tender (about 5 minutes). Drain and put into bowl.

In skillet sauté garlic and pimentos until garlic is slightly browned. Add onions and sauté until just soft (about 10 minutes).

Add mixture to broccoli, mix in remaining ingredients, then cover and chill.

Serves 8 - 10.

# Red, White, and Green Slaw

| | | |
|---|---|---|
| 3 cups | greens (romaine or spinach) | 750 mL |
| 3 cups | cabbage, shredded | 750 mL |
| 1 cup | carrots, beets, or turnips, julienned | 250 mL |
| 2 | small tomatoes, chopped | 2 |
| $^1/_2$ cup | dry roasted peanuts | 125 mL |
| $1^1/_2$ cups | kidney beans | 375 mL |

Prepare vegetables. Drain beans.

Combine all ingredients and toss with Yogurt-Poppy Seed Dressing.

Yield: approx. 10 cups (2.5 L).

**TIP**

Serve with whole-grain bread as a complete meal for 4 or 5.

# Yogurt-Poppy Seed Dressing

| | | |
|---|---|---|
| $^1/_2$ cup | non-fat mayonnaise | 125 mL |
| $^1/_2$ cup | non-fat plain yogurt | 125 mL |
| 1 tsp | poppy seeds | 5 mL |
| $^1/_4$ tsp | dried dill | 1 mL |
| 2 tsp | red wine vinegar | 10 mL |

*Combine dressing ingredients in small bowl.*

*Yield: 1 cup (250 mL)*

## Cucumber-Almond Bulgur Salad

| | | |
|---|---|---|
| 2 cups | water | 500 mL |
| 1 tsp (or less) | salt | 5 mL |
| 1 cup | uncooked bulgur wheat | 250 mL |
| 1 cup | slivered almonds | 250 mL |
| 1 tbsp | canola or olive oil | 15 mL |
| 4 tbsp | olive oil | 60 mL |
| 3 cups | cucumbers peeled, seeded and diced | 750 mL |
| $1/2$ cup | green onions thinly sliced | 125 mL |
| 4 tbsp | lemon juice | 60 mL |
| 2 tsp | dried oregano | 10 mL |
| $1/2$ tsp | dried basil | 2 mL |
| $1/4$ tsp | pepper | 1 mL |

*Bring water to a simmer in small saucepan. Add $1/2$ tsp (2 mL) salt and the bulgur wheat. Cover and let stand 4-5 minutes. Then remove from heat and set aside. (If you want to serve the salad right away, transfer the cooked bulgur wheat to a bowl and set that bowl inside a pan of ice. This will cool the grains quickly.)*

*Sauté the almonds in 1 tbsp (15 mL) olive oil until lightly browned, stirring constantly to prevent burning. Immediately transfer to a dish to stop their cooking. Set aside.*

*In a large bowl, combine cucumber, green onions, remaining olive oil, lemon juice, oregano, basil, pepper, and remaining salt. Add the cooked bulgur and almonds. Chill and serve.*

*Serves 6.*

# Desserts

## Jewel Tapioca

| | | |
|---|---|---|
| 6$\frac{1}{2}$ tbsp | quick-cooking tapioca | 100 mL |
| 4 cups | orange juice | 1 L |
| $\frac{1}{2}$ cup | honey | 125 mL |
| 20-oz can | pineapple chunks | 570 mL |
| 2 8-oz cans | mandarin oranges | 224 mL |
| 3 | bananas | 3 |
| 1 pkg | frozen boysenberries (optional) | 1 pkg |

*Mix tapioca with honey, juice and let stand five minutes.*

*Bring to a boil over medium heat, stirring constantly. Cool 20 minutes.*

*Stir again and refrigerate several hours or overnight.*

*Just before serving mix in canned fruit, slice in bananas, and add frozen berries last. Delicious to top off a substantial summer meal!*

*Serves 4.*

# Frozen Fresh Pineapple Slices

| | | |
|---|---|---|
| 2 cups | fresh raspberries | 500 mL |
| 2 cups | unsweetened apple juice | 500 mL |
| 2 tbsp | cornstarch | 15 mL |
| 1 | medium-ripe pineapple, halved lengthwise, cored, cut into $^1/_4$-inch (1-cm) slices. | 1 |

*In a blender, purée raspberries with apple juice. Strain purée and put in mixing bowl.*

*Whisk in cornstarch, breaking up as many lumps as possible. Allow sauce to sit for an hour to dissolve lumps further.*

*On salad plates, ladle 1 oz (25 mL) of raspberry sauce and spread over plate. Arrange 3 - 4 slices of pineapple on each plate and freeze.*

*Serves 10.*

# Fruit and Rice Pudding

| | | |
|---|---|---|
| 2 cups | brown rice, cooked | 500 mL |
| $^1/_4$ cup | raisins | 60 mL |
| 1 cup | tinned of fresh pineapple, crushed | 250 mL |
| $^1/_2$ tsp | almond extract | 2 mL |
| 2 tsp | vanilla | 10 mL |
| $^3/_4$ cup | hot water | 175 mL |
| 3 tbsp | orange-juice concentrate | 45 mL |
| 1 | banana | 1 |

*Mix together rice, raisins, and pineapple in a glass baking dish. Set aside.*

*Blend remaining ingredients until creamy, then pour over rice mixture and stir.*

*Bake uncovered at 350°F (180°C) for 45 minutes. May be served hot or cold.*

*Serves 6.*

## Grilled Apple Quarters

| 4 | firm green apples (pippin or Granny Smith), unpeeled, cored, and quartered | 4 |
| 1 | juice of 1 lime | 1 |
| $^1/_2$ cup | brown sugar | 125 mL |
| 1 tsp | butter flavoring *(optional)* | 5 mL |

Once the barbecue fire has burned down and the dinner is almost done, one of the simplest ways to do dessert is to offer each diner a skewered apple and let him or her cook it.

*Dip apples in lime juice (and butter flavor, if desired) to prevent darkening. Place brown sugar on a piece of waxed paper and press apple quarters into sugar to coat. Thread onto bamboo skewers sideways.*

*On a well-burned-down fire, grill apples, turning, until just beginning to brown. Depending on the fire, this will probably take less than 10 minutes.*

*Serves 4.*

## Grilled Bananas with Coconut

| 4 | bananas | 4 |
| 1 | juice of 1 lime | 1 |
| $^1/_2$ cup | coconut, grated | 125 mL |

*Don't peel the bananas until you're ready to grill. Cook them over a barbecue fire that's well burned down.*

*Peel bananas and squeeze lime juice over them to prevent darkening. Thread lengthwise onto skewers. Roll in grated coconut.*

*Place on coolest part of the grill, wbeing careful that bananas don't burn. Grill and turn, just until coconut begins to brown, no more than 10 minutes.*

*Serves 4.*

## Hot Apricot Compote

| 16 | dried apricot halves | 16 |
| 2 cups | unsweetened apple juice | 448 mL |
| $^1/_4$ tsp | cinnamon | 1 mL |
| $^1/_4$ tsp | ground cloves | 1 mL |

*Place apricots in a stainless-steel pan. Add apple juice, cinnamon, and cloves and refrigerate overnight so that apricots will reconstitute. Bake apricots, covered, at 350°F (180°C) for 15 minutes. Serve hot.*

*Serves 4.*

## Apple Crisp

| 4 | apples (spy, Idaho red, Granny Smith), cored and cut into $^1/_2$-in (1-cm) slices | 4 |
| 1 | lemon | 1 |
| $^1/_3$ cup | honey or maple syrup *(optional)* | 40 mL |
| $^1/_4$ cup | whole-wheat flour | 60 mL |
| $^1/_4$ cup | oatmeal | 60 mL |
| 1 tsp | cinnamon | 10 mL |
| $^1/_2$ tsp | nutmeg | 5 mL |

*Line shallow baking dish with apples.*
   *Squeeze juice of lemon over apples, then pour honey over.*
   *Combine flour, oatmeal, cinnamon and nutmeg, and sprinkle over apples.*
   *Bake in oven at 400°F (200°C) for 30 minutes, or in microwave for 10 minutes. Presto! Low-fat apple crisp, delicious hot or cold.*

*Serves 6.*

*Note: The same mix of apples, honey, oatmeal, cinnamon, and nutmeg can be rolled in soft tortillas and baked in 400°F (200°C) oven for 15 minutes. (They go soggy in microwave.)*

# Breads, Cookies, and Cakes

## Whole-Wheat Bread

| | | |
|---|---|---|
| 5³⁄₄ cups | warm water | 1.5 L |
| 2 tbsp | active dry yeast | 25 mL |
| 2 tbsp | salt | 25 mL |
| ¹⁄₂ cup | honey | 125 mL |
| 13-16 cups | whole-wheat flour | 3.25-4 L |

*Combine warm water, yeast, salt, honey, and 5 cups (1.25 L) flour in mixing bowl and let stand for 3 - 4 minutes.*

*Add flour while mixing with dough hook until sides of the bowl are clean. Knead for 12 minutes.*

*Brush counter lightly with oil. Place bread dough on counter.*

*Divide into 4 equal portions and form into loaves.*

*Spray 4 large bread pans with non-stick spray and add loaves.*

*Let rise until doubled in size and bake at 350°F (180°C) for 35 minutes.*

*Place on cooling rack until cool.*

*Yield: 4 loaves.*

## Carrot-Raisin Squares

| | | |
|---|---|---|
| 2¹/₂ cups | whole-wheat pastry flour | 625 mL |
| 1¹/₂ tsp | baking soda | 7 mL |
| 1¹/₂ tsp | cream of tartar | 7 mL |
| 2 tsp | cinnamon | 10 mL |
| ¹/₂ tsp | nutmeg | 2 mL |
| 1 tsp | salt *(optional)* | 5 mL |
| 3 tbsp | flax seeds | 45 mL |
| ¹/₂ cup | water | 125 mL |
| 1 cup | cooked carrots, puréed | 250 mL |
| 1 tbsp | vanilla extract | 15 mL |
| 1¹/₂ cups | maple syrup | 375 mL |
| ¹/₄ cup | juice concentrate: apple or pineapple | 50 mL |
| 1³/₄ cups | carrots, grated, packed | 425 mL |
| 1 cup | raisins or currants | 250 mL |

*Spray bottom of 2 9-inch (22-cm) baking pans, or 1 12-inch (30x40 cm) cookie sheet, with non-stick spray and line with paper cut to fit.*

*Sift first six ingredients together into 2-quart (2-L) bowl.*

*Put flax seeds and water in blender and blend till very finely ground and smooth.*

*Add cooked carrots, vanilla, syrup, and juice concentrate. Blend thoroughly. Pour mixture into ³/₄-qt (.75 L) bowl.*

*Add grated carrots and raisins at once. Fold in very quickly and immediately pour into prepared pans. Do not overmix or "stir out" air.*

*Bake at 350°F (180°C) for 30 - 40 minutes. Cut into squares while still warm.*

*Yield: 40-60 squares.*

# Summer Fruit Cake

| | | |
|---|---|---|
| 2¼ cups | whole-wheat pastry flour | 500 mL |
| 1½ tsp | baking soda | 7 mL |
| 2 tsp | baking powder | 10 mL |
| 2¼ tsp | cinnamon | 11 mL |
| ½ tsp | allspice | 2 mL |
| 2 | egg whites | 2 |
| ½ cup | water | 125 mL |
| ¾ cup | honey | 175 mL |
| 1¼ cup | applesauce | 300 mL |
| 1 cup | mashed bananas | 250 mL |
| 2 cups | pitted sour cherries, chopped (fresh or canned) | 500 mL |
| 1 cup | fresh pineapple, chopped, or | 250 mL |
| *8 oz* | *canned and drained pineapple* | *224 g* |
| 1 cup | raisins | 250 mL |
| 1 cup | coconut, grated *(optional)* | 250 mL |
| ¾ cup | walnuts chopped *(optional)* | 175 mL |
| 2 doz | pitted sour cherries, whole | 2 doz |

*Mix together flour, baking soda, baking powder, cinnamon, and allspice in large bowl.*

*Mix together egg white and water in small bowl and add along with honey, and applesauce to flour mixture. Mix in.*

*Combine bananas, chopped cherries, pineapple, raisins, coconut, and walnuts, and add to mixture. Stir together.*

*Turn into a 13 x 9 x 2 inch (3-L) non-stick baking pan. (Lightly oil and flour if you do not have a non-stick pan.)*

*Before baking decorate with whole pitted sour cherries. Bake at 350°F (180°C) for 1 hour.*

## Black Forest Cake

| | | |
|---|---|---|
| 2 cups | whole-wheat pastry flour | 500 mL |
| $\frac{1}{2}$ cup | cocoa powder or carob | 125 mL |
| $1\frac{1}{2}$ tsp | baking powder | 7 mL |
| 1 tsp | baking soda | 5 mL |
| $\frac{3}{4}$ tsp | salt *(optional)* | 4 mL |
| 1 tsp | cinnamon | 5 mL |
| 3 tbsp | flax seeds | 45 mL |
| $\frac{1}{2}$ cup | water | 125 mL |
| $1\frac{1}{2}$ cups | plain yogurt (non-fat or soy) | 375 mL |
| 2 tsp | vanilla extract | 10 mL |
| 1 cup | honey | 250 mL |
| 1 quart | cherry pie filling | 1 L |

*Spray bottom of 2 9-inch (22-cm) baking pans with non-stick spray and line with parchment paper cut to fit. Press down.*

*Sift first six ingredients together into $1\frac{1}{2}$-quart (1.5-L) bowl.*

*Put flax seeds and water in blender and run until very finely ground and smooth.*

*Add yogurt, vanilla, and honey. Mix thoroughly.*

*Put liquid mixture into a 3-4 quart (3-4 L) mixing bowl. Add sifted dry ingredients all at once and fold in. Immediately pour into prepared pans. Do not overmix or "stir out" air.*

*Bake at 350°F (180°C) 30-40 minutes.*

*When cool, remove from pans and place one layer over the other.*

# Blueberry Topping

| 4 cups | fresh or frozen blueberries | 1 L |
| 1½ cups | apple juice | 375 mL |
| ½ tsp | cinnamon | 2 mL |
| 2 tbsp | cornstarch | 25 mL |

*Mix ingredients together and cook until thickened.*
*Serve over whole-wheat pancakes or waffles, and top with non-fat vanilla yogurt.*

*Yield: 4 cups (1 L).*

VARIATION: *Whole-wheat pancakes are also good topped with natural-style peanut butter and sliced bananas before adding blueberry topping and yogurt.*

# Fruit Butter

| 1 cup | dried fruit (apricots, raisins, pears, prunes, dates, apples, figs) | 250 mL |
| 1 cup | water | 250 mL |

*Cook dried fruit with water until of jam consistency.*
*Serve chunky or whiz in blender until smooth. Serve warm or cold as a spread on breads, pancakes, and waffles, or in crepes.*
*Keeps 1 week in refrigerator.*

*Yield: approximately 2 cups (500 mL).*

# Drinks

## Almond Milk

| | | |
|---|---|---|
| $^1/_2$ cup | almonds (may be blanched for whiter color) | 125 mL |
| 1 tsp | vanilla | 5 mL |
| 2 tbsp | sesame seeds *(optional)* | 25 mL |
| pinch | salt | pinch |
| 2 | dates, or | 2 |
| $^1/_4$-$^1/_2$ *cup* | *honey* | *75-125 mL* |

*Blend with enough water to cover until nice and smooth.*
*Add 2 - 2$^1/_2$ cups (500-625 mL) more water while blending.*

*Yield: 3 cups (750 mL).*

## Breakfast Smoothie

| | | |
|---|---|---|
| 1 cup | orange juice | 250 mL |
| 1 cup | apricot nectar | 250 mL |
| 2 cups | pineapple juice | 500 mL |
| 1 | banana | 1 |
| $^1/_2$ | lemon, juiced | $^1/_2$ |

*Blend all ingredients until smooth. Makes 6 small servings. You may have to double recipe if your family members are hearty breakfast eaters.*

*Serves 6.*

# 1

---

# Fifty Ways to Help
# Your Heart

Recent studies have shown that heart disease can actually be reversed without drugs or surgery, through a number of lifestyle changes. For those who wish to prevent heart disease, the same lifestyle modifications apply. Hear are 50 ways to help your heart if you are recovering from a heart attack, have high blood pressure, or are simply interested in staying healthy.

Of course when making any major lifestyle changes, please consult your physician.

## Decrease Your Fat Intake

Fat is the number-one culprit in heart disease. It clogs the arteries, a condition that ultimately can lead to heart attacks. The good news is that the body has the capacity to heal itself if the constant "fat assault" is eliminated. Here are a few tips to help you on the road to fat reduction.

**1. Avoid fatty foods like hot dogs, bacon, sausage, chicken wings, and french fries.**

**2. In place of oil, use water or oil-free vegetable stock to sauté.**

**3. Beware the salad bar.**

Salad bars can offer a great low-fat alternative — but pass on the cheese, eggs, and fat-filled dressings.

**4. Avoid Caesar salads.**

The standard dressing contains egg yolks and oil (and often anchovies). The total fat content is the same as a bowl of ice cream! And any time you use eggs, throw out the yolks and use the whites only.

**5. Try balsamic vinegar on your salads, or as a topping on fresh fruit desserts.**

Its bittersweet taste is a great substitute for high-fat salad dressings or for dessert toppings.

**6. Order your pizzas loaded, but hold the anchovies, meats, and cheeses.**

The vegetables and tomato sauce make a great topping, and you can eat all you want.

**7. Remember that whole milk is labeled as only 3.5% fat, and yet with all the water removed, more than half the calories come from fat.**

Even 2% milk is high in fat. If you choose to drink milk, make it skim.

**8. Try unsweetened applesauce on your toast or bagels.**

It's a great-tasting substitute for cream cheese, butter or margarine.

**9. Avoid most muffins, unless they specify LOW FAT.**

The ones that say only LOW CHOLESTEROL often have high-fat levels.

**10. Try fruit butter (see page 213) as a substitute spread for bread.**

# Eat a Starch-based, Fiber-rich Diet

Shifting your focus from a protein-based diet to a starch-based one helps you reduce your fat intake while allowing you to enjoy large, tasty helpings of foods.

## 1. Instead of traditional meals centered on beef, poultry, or fish, try making egg-free pasta, rice, potatoes, or legumes the main focus.

Many of your favorite sauces, with minor fat-reducing modifications, can be used to top these foods. Black-bean burritos and spaghetti with marinara sauce are two delicious options.

## 2. Eat baked beans or other legumes in tomato or barbecue sauce.

They are a great source of fiber and can be served hot or cold.

## 3. Make your own popcorn.

Another great source of fiber, popcorn is filling and has hardly any fat if butter and oil are not used.

## 4. The next time you are at a salad bar, add some chick peas, peas and corn to your lettuce and tomato.

## 5. Beware the juicers.

Fruit juice is the fruit with all the fiber thrown away. Most juices are high in calories, and no more filling than plain water. It's much better to eat the whole fruit, and quench your thirst with water.

## 6. Substitute whole-grain bread for white bread and eat at least five slices a day.

Check the fine print to make sure the bread is not made with egg yolks.

## 7. For breakfast enjoy oatmeal, whole-wheat toast, egg-free waffles, and pancakes with syrup.

Another tasty option is hash-brown potatoes made in the microwave or in a non-stick frying pan. Look for pre-cut frozen hash browns that have no fat and lots of fiber.

### 8. Oatmeal is great, but avoid fat-filled oatmeal cookies.

Oat bran is also a good source of fiber.

### 9. Treat yourself to a microwaved apple with cinnamon.

Whole apples can punctured or sliced in a bowl. They taste sweet like the filling in an apple pie, but have none of the pastry fat.

### 10. Slice vegetables such as carrots, zucchini, and other favorites and keep in a bowl of water in the front of the fridge.

And if you like to have "zing," use non-fat dips, such as Dijon mustard or salsa.

## Improve Your Stress Management

We all face stress; it's unavoidable in the high-pressure, fast-paced world we live in. How we react to stress is definitely an important key to a healthier body and more content state of mind.

### 1. Learn to breathe correctly.

Loosen the clothes and belt around the waistline and put your hands over your stomach. Puff out your stomach as you inhale. Breathe out slowly through your lungs, and continue to blow out some more. Repeat a couple of these breaths on the hour and on the half hour, and again just before picking up the phone or entering a stressful meeting.

### 2. Learn to say no.

Practise this the next time you are asked to take on an extra volunteer job, or any extracurricular work that will take you away from productive time with your family, friends or customers.

### 3. Say no to cigarettes — even if you are a nonsmoker.

Be truthful when someone asks, "Do you mind if I smoke?" Secondhand smoke increases anxiety and can cause coronary arteries to constrict (to the point of chest pain for some).

### 4. Try taking a bath instead of a shower.

While time may not permit it in the mornings, an evening bath can ease a lot of aches and encourage a good night's sleep. Aromatic essences and quiet music also soothe the senses.

### 5. Avoid reading work papers in bed.

Once you turn your night table into an extra office desk, you will never sleep as soundly. If you routinely work in bed, you are likely to end up sleeping at the office.

### 6. Use fashion to set your moods.

As soon as you come home from work, change into another costume. If you work all day in a suit, then old paint clothes will help you feel at ease. If you are a painter, more dressy attire might do the trick.

### 7. Have an agenda for traffic.

If you drive to work, keep audio tapes handy. You can listen to your favorite novels, be inspired by world-class speakers, or learn a new language in the time most people consider wasted.

### 8. Develop a hobby or outside interest to take your mind off work.

True workaholics rarely win the long-distance race. Winston Churchill would never have achieved wartime excellence unless he'd been able to paint during his few spare hours.

### 9. Manage your time.

Take ten minutes before bedtime to plot your next day's activities. Write down the things you want to accomplish and how long they will take. There is no point trying to fit twenty-five hours of tasks into an eight- or ten-hour work day.

### 10. Manage your priorities.

Remember, you are the boss of your own department of one, so be a kind boss. Give yourself recess, time to exercise, and the benefits of good nutrition.

## Exercise

Y ou don't have to be an athlete to benefit from exercise. Moderate exercise for thirty minutes at least three times a week can help reverse and prevent heart disease, and improve your overall outlook on life.

**1. Before embarking on a new sport or activity, especially if you are over thirty-five, see your doctor for a physical checkup.**

**2. Pick a sport, any sport.**

With thousands of activities to choose from, pick something that suits your attention span and your physical limitations. If you can interest your family in the same sport, the activity will strengthen bonding and lessen stress at home.

**3. Buy a pair of comfortable walking shoes and take them to work.**

Most dress shoes have the same heel design as if you were wearing the boxes they came in. Proper heel padding and sufficiently wide forefoot make for good shoes that encourage you to walk.

**4. If your home or office is reached by elevator, try getting off at a lower floor and doing some stair climbing.**

**5. If you have a bike, fit it with a basket for local errands.**

That trip to the store doesn't burn up any calories if you take your car.

**6. Never take an escalator when a flight of stairs is available.**

**7. Park your car in the farthest corner of the parking lot to guarantee you'll do some walking.**

**8. Turn off the television for at least a half-hour every evening and go for a walk.**

The combination of fresh air and modest exercise helps get you off to sleep.

### 9. Check your pulse regularly when pursuing vigorous activities.

This applies to racquet sports or running, and also to shoveling snow, walking in hot weather, or sitting in a hot tub or sauna. When you reach your physician-recommended target zone, it's time to slow down.

### 10. If you are feeling stiff, especially when getting out of bed the next morning, do a few stretching and bending exercises while still under the covers.

That will encourage the joints to have more lubricating fluid and will save you from the "old-man shuffle" when you rise.

## Make Some Good Choices

### 1. Consider becoming a vegetarian, if not full-time, at least for one or two meals a day to start.

It is well documented that vegetarians (like Seventh-day Adventists, and people in societies that enjoy plentiful supplies of vegetables and grains) have fewer heart attacks.

### 2. Don't be influenced by advertising brainwash.

Food ads are not aimed to improve your heart's health; they are designed to sell products. If we had real truth in advertising, beer ads would be full of beer bellies, candy ads would feature facial pimples,and burger ads would use overweight people.

### 3. Check your favorite bookstore or library for resources to help you on the road to good health.

There's a host of books containing recipes and cooking tips, stress-management resources, and exercise hints.

### 4. Drink at least eight glasses of water a day.

If your tap water has an unpleasant taste, try bottled or filtered water. Enhance its appeal by using a good glass, a few ice cubes or a lemon slice. Keep a carafe on your desk at work.

### 5. Be a smart consumer.

Carefully read labels on the products you buy, and don't be afraid to ask for special orders at restaurants to keep you on your low-fat diet.

### 6. If you drink coffee, consider drinking less, but spending more per cup.

The higher-priced arabica beans have only half the caffeine of the cheaper robusta beans. Also, coffee made in drip coffeemakers or espresso machines contains less caffeine than coffee made in a conventional percolator.

### 7. If you are overweight, lose it.

Following a low-fat diet can help you shed unwanted pounds and get you off the yo-yo diet syndrome.

### 8. Make better use of spare time.

Most Americans get nothing out of their weekends because they spend time doing chores with little time left for fun. Try to create memories by taking day trips, overnight expeditions, or occasional weekend retreats — it will do your heart good.

### 9. Consider having a pet or at least borrowing one for a while.

When your cat comes up for a cuddle, your own blood pressure and stress levels drop measurably. That's why many post-heart attack patients are benefiting from pet visitation programs.

### 10. Reserve treats for special occasions.

It's okay to indulge in a piece of cake or pumpkin pie every once in a while, but don't overdo. Your heart will thank you!

# Nutrient Analysis of Common Foods

| Food | Unit | Weight (g) | Cal | CHO (g) | Prot (g) | Fat (g) |
|---|---|---|---|---|---|---|
| Almonds: dried, shelled, slivered (not packed) | 1 tbsp (15 mL) | 7 | 43 | 1.4 | 1.3 | 3.9 |
| Anchovy: 1–4" (.5–10 cm) flat | 1 whole | 4 | 5 | 0 | 0.8 | 0.3 |
| Angle food cake: see Cake | | | | | | |
| Apple: raw with skin | 1 whole | 150 | 80 | 20.0 | 0.3 | 0.8 |
| Apple: raw, pared, diced | 1 cup (250 mL) | 110 | 59 | 15.5 | 0.2 | 0.3 |
| Apple butter | 1 tbsp (15 mL) | 18 | 33 | 8.2 | 0.1 | 0.1 |
| Apple juice: canned or bottled | 1 cup 250 mL) | 248 | 117 | 29.5 | 0.2 | 0 |
| Applesauce: canned, sweetened | 1 cup (250 mL) | 255 | 232 | 60.7 | 0.5 | 0.3 |
| Apricots: raw | 3 whole | 14 | 55 | 13.7 | 1.1 | 0.2 |
| Apricot nectar: canned or bottled | 1 cup (250 mL) | 251 | 143 | 36.6 | 0.8 | 0.3 |
| Artichoke: frozen, cooked, bud or globe | 1 whole | 300 | 52 | 11.9 | 3.4 | 0.2 |
| Asparagus: canned spears, $\frac{1}{2}$" (1 cm) diameter | 4 spears | 80 | 27 | 2.7 | 1.9 | 0.3 |
| Asparagus: canned spears, low sodium | 1 cup (250 mL) | 235 | 47 | 7.3 | 6.1 | 0.7 |
| Avocado: California, raw, $3\frac{1}{2}$" (7 cm) diameter (unpeeled) | 1 whole | 284 | 369 | 12.9 | 4.7 | 36.7 |
| Avocado: California, raw, pureed, mashed, or sieved | 1 tbsp (15 mL) | 14 | 25 | 0.9 | 0.3 | 2.4 |
| Bacon: Canadian, cooked | 1 oz (30 mL) | 28 | 78 | 0.1 | 7.7 | 5.0 |
| Bacon: cooked [approximately 1 lb (450 g)] raw | 2 slices | 15 | 86 | 0.5 | 3.8 | 7.8 |
| Bacon bits: with coconut oil | 1 tsp (5 mL) | 3 | 15 | 0.9 | 1.3 | 0.6 |
| Bacon bits: with soy oil | 1 tsp (5 mL) | 3 | 14 | 0.9 | 1.4 | 0.6 |
| Bagel: water | 1 whole | 73 | 212 | 41.1 | 7.9 | 1.3 |
| Baking powder: double acting | 1 tsp (5 mL) | 3 | 3 | 0.7 | 0 | 0 |
| Baking powder: low sodium | 1 tsp (5 mL) | 4 | 7 | 1.8 | 0 | 0 |
| Baking soda | $\frac{1}{4}$ tsp (2 mL) | 4 | 0 | 0 | 0 | 0 |
| Banana, raw, medium | 1 whole | 175 | 101 | 26.4 | 1.3 | 0.2 |
| Barbecue sauce: commercial (corn oil) | 1 tbsp | 16 | 14 | 1.3 | 0.2 | 1.1 |

| Food | Unit | Weight (g) | Cal | CHO (g) | Prot (g) | Fat (g) |
|---|---|---|---|---|---|---|
| Beans: garbanzos or chick-peas | 1 cup (250 mL) | 185 | 248 | 42.1 | 14.1 | 3.3 |
| Beans: pork and beans in tomato sauce, canned | 1 cup (250 mL) | 255 | 311 | 48.5 | 15.6 | 6.6 |
| Beans: kidney | 1 cup (250 mL) | 185 | 218 | 39.6 | 14.4 | 0.9 |
| Beans: lentils | 1 cup (250 mL) | 200 | 212 | 38.6 | 15.6 | 0 |
| Beans: lima, frozen, cooked | 1 cup (250 mL) | 170 | 168 | 32.5 | 10.2 | 0.2 |
| Beans: lima, canned | 1 cup (250 mL) | 170 | 163 | 31.1 | 9.2 | 0.5 |
| Beans: lima, canned, low sodium | 1 cup (250 mL) | 170 | 162 | 30.1 | 9.9 | 0.5 |
| Beans: pinto, calico, red Mexican | 1 cup (250 mL) | 185 | 218 | 39.6 | 14.4 | 0.9 |
| Beans: mung, sprouts, cooked and drained | 1 cup (250 mL) | 125 | 35 | 6.5 | 4.0 | 0.3 |
| Beans: mung, sprouts, uncooked | 1 cup (250 mL) | 105 | 37 | 6.9 | 4.0 | 0.2 |
| Bans: green, snap, fresh, frozen, cooked | 1 cup (250 mL) | 130 | 34 | 7.8 | 2.1 | 0.1 |
| Beans: green, snap, canned | 1 cup (250 mL) | 135 | 32 | 7.0 | 1.9 | 0.3 |
| Beans: green, snap, canned, low sodium | 1 cup (250 mL) | 135 | 30 | 6.5 | 2.0 | 0.1 |
| Beans: white, Great Northern, navy, cooked | 1 cup (250 mL) | 180 | 212 | 38.2 | 14.0 | 1.1 |
| Beans: yellow or wax, frozen, cooked | 1 cup (250 mL) | 125 | 28 | 5.8 | 1.8 | 0.3 |
| Beans: yellow or wax, canned | 1 cup (250 mL) | 135 | 32 | 7.0 | 1.9 | 0.4 |
| Beans: yellow or wax, canned, low sodium | 1 cup (250 mL) | 135 | 28 | 6.3 | 1.6 | 0.1 |
| Beef: dried, chipped, uncooked | 1 oz (30 mL) | 28 | 58 | 0 | 9.7 | 1.8 |
| Beef: <6% fat; flank, round (lean only) | 1 oz (30 mL) | 28 | 53 | 0 | 8.9 | 1.7 |
| Beef: 10% fat, chuck, filet mignon, New York strip, porterhouse, T-bone, tenderloin, ground round, choice grade (lean only) | 1 oz (30 mL) | 28 | 61 | 0 | 8.5 | 2.7 |
| Beef: 15% fat; club, rib eye roast (lean only) | 1 oz (30 mL) | 28 | 74 | 0 | 8.1 | 4.4 |
| Beef: 20% fat; ground chuck | 1 oz (30 mL) | 28 | 82 | 0 | 7.7 | 5.5 |
| Beef: 25% fat; ground beef (hamburger), chuck, steak, pot roast (lean and fat) | 1 oz (30 mL) | 28 | 93 | 0 | 7.4 | 6.8 |
| Beef: >30% fat; brisket, rib eye steak, standing rib roast, spareribs (lean and fat) | 1 oz (30 mL) | 28 | 110 | 0 | 6.5 | 9.1 |
| Beef: corned | 1 oz (30 mL) | 28 | 110 | 0 | 6.5 | 9.1 |
| Beef tongue: medium-fat, cooked, 3 x 2 x ¹/₈" (5 x 1 x .25 cm) | 1 slice | 20 | 49 | 0.1 | 4.3 | 3.3 |
| Beef: kidney, cooked ¹/₂ x ¹/₂ x ¹/₄" (1 x 1 x .5 cm) | 1 oz (30 mL) | 140 | 353 | 1.1 | 46.2 | 16.8 |
| Beef: liver | 1 oz (30 mL) | 28 | 40 | 1.5 | 5.7 | 1.1 |
| Beef tallow: suet | 1 tbsp (15 mL) | 14 | 120 | 0 | 0.2 | 13.2 |
| Beef regular | 12 oz (150 mL) | 360 | 151 | 13.7 | 1.1 | 0 |
| Beets: red, canned, diced, sliced, or whole | 1 cup (250 mL) | 170 | 63 | 15.0 | 1.7 | 0.2 |
| Beets: red, canned, diced, sliced, or whole, low sodium | 1 cup (250 mL) | 170 | 63 | 14.8 | 1.5 | 0.2 |
| Biscuit: made with shortening | 1 whole | 28 | 103 | 12.8 | 2.1 | 4.8 |
| Blackberries: raw (also boysenberries, dewberries) | 1 cup (250 mL) | 144 | 84 | 18.6 | 1.7 | 1.3 |
| Bologna: 1 slice | 1 oz (30 mL) | 28 | 86 | 0.3 | 3.4 | 8.3 |
| Bouillon cube: all kinds (1 tsp instant bouillon) | 1 cube | 4 | 5 | 0.2 | 0.8 | 0.1 |
| Braunschweiger (liver sausage) | 1 oz (30 mL) | 28 | 90 | 0.7 | 4.2 | 9.2 |
| Bread: cracked wheat | 1 slice | 25 | 66 | 13.0 | 2.2 | 0.6 |
| Bread: English muffin | 1 whole | 57 | 133 | 25.5 | 4.4 | 1.4 |
| Bread: French, enriched, 2 ¹/₂ x 2 x ¹/₂" (5 x 5 oz 1 cm) | 1 slice | 15 | 44 | 8.3 | 1.4 | 0.5 |
| Bread: pita, pocket | 1 large | 52 | 145 | 30.0 | 5.0 | 1.0 |
| Bread: pumpernickel (dark rye) | 1 slice | 32 | 79 | 17.0 | 2.9 | 0.4 |
| Bread: raisin | 1 slice | 25 | 66 | 13.4 | 1.7 | 0.7 |
| Bread: rye (light) | 1 slice | 25 | 61 | 13.0 | 2.3 | 0.3 |

| Food | Unit | Weight (g) | Cal | CHO (g) | Prot (g) | Fat (g) |
|---|---|---|---|---|---|---|
| Bread: white, enriched | 1 slice | 25 | 68 | 12.6 | 2.2 | 0.8 |
| Bread: whole wheat, firm crumb | 1 slice | 25 | 61 | 11.9 | 2.6 | 0.8 |
| Bread: white, low sodium | 1 slice | 28 | 76 | 14.1 | 2.4 | 0.9 |
| Broccoli: medium stalk, fresh, cooked, and drained | 1 stalk | 180 | 47 | 8.1 | 5.6 | 0.5 |
| Brussels sprouts: frozen, cooked, and drained | 1 cup (250 mL) | 155 | 51 | 10.1 | 5.0 | 0.3 |
| Butter: 1 pat | 1 tsp (5 mL) | 5 | 36 | 0 | 0 | 4.1 |
| Buttermilk: made from skim milk | 1 cup (250 mL) | 245 | 88 | 12.5 | 8.8 | 0.2 |
| Buttermilk: made from low-fat milk | 1 cup (250 mL) | 245 | 99 | 11.7 | 8.1 | 2.2 |
| Cabbage: common or Chinese, shredded, cooked, drained | 1 cup (250 mL) | 145 | 29 | 6.2 | 1.6 | 0.3 |
| Cabbage: common or Chinese varieties, raw, shredded | 1 cup (250 mL) | 90 | 22 | 4.9 | 1.2 | 0.2 |
| Cake: angel food, $\frac{1}{12}$ of 10" (25 cm) tube cake | 1 slice | 60 | 161 | 36.1 | 4.3 | 0.1 |
| Cake: coffee cake (mix), $2\frac{5}{8}$ x $2\frac{3}{4}$ x $1\frac{1}{4}$ " (4 x 4 x 3 cm) | 1 slice | 72 | 232 | 37.7 | 4.5 | 6.9 |
| Cake: cream cheese, without crust or topping | 1 slice | 85 | 368 | 25.7 | 7.6 | 26.8 |
| Cake: devil's food (frozen) $\frac{1}{8}$ of $7\frac{1}{2}$" (18 cm) cake | 1 slice | 85 | 323 | 47.3 | 3.7 | 15.0 |
| Cake: devil's food cupcake with icing (mix), $2\frac{1}{2}$" (7 cm) diameter | 1 whole | 35 | 119 | 20.4 | 1.5 | 4.3 |
| Cake: gingerbread (mix), $2\frac{3}{4}$ x $2\frac{3}{4}$ x $1\frac{3}{8}$" (4 x 4 x 3 cm) | 1 slice | 63 | 174 | 32.2 | 2.0 | 4.3 |
| Cake: marble with white icing (mix), $\frac{1}{12}$ of layer cake | 1 slice | 87 | 288 | 53.9 | 3.8 | 7.6 |
| Cake: yellow with chocolate icing (mix) $\frac{1}{12}$ of layer cake | 1 slice | 92 | 310 | 53.0 | 3.8 | 10.4 |
| Candy: candy corn, approximately 72 pieces | $\frac{1}{4}$ cup (60 mL) | 50 | 182 | 44.8 | 0 | 1.0 |
| Candy*: chocolate, bittersweet | 1 oz (30 mL) | 28 | 135 | 13.3 | 2.2 | 11.3 |
| Candy*: chocolate, sweet | 1 oz (30 mL) | 28 | 150 | 16.4 | 1.2 | 10.0 |
| Candy: chocolate covered mint, $1\frac{3}{8}$ x $\frac{3}{8}$" (3 x 1 cm) | 1 small | 11 | 45 | 8.9 | 0.2 | 1.2 |
| Candy: chocolate covered raisins | 1 cup | 190 | 808 | 134.0 | 10.3 | 32.5 |
| Candy: chocolate covered vanilla ice cream | 1 piece | 13 | 56 | 9.1 | 0.5 | 2.2 |
| Candy: fudge, plain, 2 cubic inch | 1 piece | 21 | 84 | 15.8 | 0.6 | 2.6 |
| Candy: gum drops, 1 large or 8 small | 1 large | 10 | 34 | 8.7 | 0.01 | |
| Candy: jellybeans | 10 pieces | 28 | 104 | 26.4 | 0 | 0.1 |
| Candy: M & M® type | $\frac{1}{4}$ cup (60 mL) | 49 | 230 | 35.8 | 2.6 | 9.7 |
| Candy: peanut brittle, $2\frac{1}{2}$ x $2\frac{1}{2}$ x $\frac{1}{3}$" (4 x 4 x .5 cm) piece | 1 oz (30 mL) | 28 | 119 | 23.0 | 1.6 | 2.9 |
| Candy: chocolate-flavored roll (Tootsie Roll®) | 1 piece | 7 | 28 | 5.8 | 0.2 | 0.6 |
| Candy bar*: chocolate coated almonds, or peanut bar (Mr. Goodbar®) | 1 oz (30 mL) | 28 | 161 | 11.2 | 3.5 | 12.4 |
| Candy bar*: chocolate coated with coconut center (Mound®) | 1 oz (30 mL) | 28 | 124 | 20.4 | 0.8 | 5.0 |
| Candy bar*: fudge, peanut, caramel (O'Henry®, Snicker®, Rally®, Baby Ruth®) | 1 oz (30 mL) | 28 | 130 | 16.6 | 2.7 | 6.5 |
| Candy bar*: Hershey Krackel® or Nestlés Crunch® | 1 oz (30 mL) | 28 | 144 | 15.0 | 2.3 | 8.3 |
| Candy bar*: milk chocolate bar or 7 chocolate kisses | 1 oz (30 mL) | 28 | 147 | 16.1 | 2.2 | 9.2 |
| Cantaloupe: 5" (12 cm) diameter | 1 whole | 91 | 159 | 39.8 | 3.7 | 0.5 |
| Cantaloupe: cubed or diced, approximately 20/cup | 1 cup (250 mL) | 160 | 48 | 12.0 | 1.1 | 0.2 |
| Carbonated beverage: Coco-Cola® | 12 oz (150 mL) | 369 | 144 | 37.2 | 0 | 0 |

* The weight of candy bars often changes. The analysis here is given for 1 ounce and can be calculated for the total unit (1 piece of candy)

| Food | Unit | Weight (g) | Cal | CHO (g) | Prot (g) | Fat (g) |
|---|---|---|---|---|---|---|
| Carbonated beverage: ginger ale | 12 oz (150 mL) | 366 | 108 | 28.8 | 0 | 0 |
| Carbonated beverage: Sprite® | 12 oz (150 mL) | 366 | 143 | 36.0 | 0 | 0 |
| Carbonated beverage: Sprite® without sugar | 12 oz (150 mL) | 366 | 5 | 0 | 0 | 0 |
| Carbonated beverage: Fresca® | 12 oz (150 mL) | 366 | 3 | 0 | 0 | 0 |
| Carbonated beverage: Tab® | 12 oz (150 mL) | 366 | 1 | 0.1 | 0 | 0 |
| Carrot: raw, approximately $1^1/_8$ x $7^1/_2$ (3 x 18 cm) | 1 whole | 81 | 30 | 7.0 | 0.8 | 0.1 |
| Carrots: fresh, cooked, sliced | 1 cup (250 mL) | 155 | 48 | 11.0 | 1.4 | 0.3 |
| Carrots: canned solids, sliced | 1 cup (250 mL) | 155 | 47 | 10.4 | 1.2 | 0.5 |
| Carrots: canned solids, sliced, low sodium | 1 cup (250 mL) | 155 | 39 | 8.7 | 1.2 | 0.2 |
| Cashews: roasted in oil, unsalted (14 large, 18 medium, or 26 small) | 1 oz (30 mL) | 28 | 159 | 8.3 | 4.9 | 12.8 |
| Catfish: freshwater, raw | 1 oz (30 mL) | 28 | 29 | 0 | 5.0 | 1.0 |
| Cauliflower: frozen, cooked, approximately 7 florets | 1 cup (250 mL) | 180 | 32 | 5.9 | 3.4 | 0.4 |
| Caviar: sturgeon, granular | 1 tbsp (15 mL) | 16 | 42 | 0.5 | 4.3 | 2.4 |
| Celery: green, raw | 1 stalk | 40 | 7 | 1.6 | 0.4 | 0 |
| Cereal: bran, unprocessed | 1 oz (30 mL) | 28 | 91 | 12.3 | 3.9 | 0.4 |
| Cereal: bran buds | 1 cup (250 mL) | 60 | 144 | 44.6 | 7.6 | 1.8 |
| Cereal: 40% bran flakes | 1 cup (250 mL) | 35 | 106 | 28.2 | 3.6 | 0.6 |
| Cereal: Cheerios® or puffed oats | 1 cup (250 mL) | 25 | 99 | 18.8 | 3.0 | 1.4 |
| Cereal: corn flakes | 1 cup (250 mL) | 25 | 97 | 21.3 | 2.0 | 0.1 |
| Cereal: corn grits, enriched, cooked without salt | 1 cup (250 mL) | 245 | 125 | 27.0 | 2.9 | 0.2 |
| Cereal: cream of rice, cooked without salt | 1 cup (250 mL) | 245 | 123 | 27.4 | 2.0 | 0 |
| Cereal: cream of wheat, cooked without salt | 1 cup (250 mL) | 240 | 180 | 40.6 | 5.3 | 1.0 |
| Cereal: farina, enriched, regular, cooked without salt | 1 cup (250 mL) | 245 | 103 | 21.3 | 3.2 | 0.5 |
| Cereal: farina, enriched, quick-cooking, cooked with salt | 1 cup (250 mL) | 245 | 105 | 21.8 | 3.2 | 0.5 |
| Cereal: farina, enriched, instant-cooking, cooked without salt | 1 cup (250 mL) | 245 | 135 | 27.9 | 4.2 | 0.5 |
| Cereal: granola, without coconut or other saturated fat | $^1/_4$ cup (60 mL) | 28 | 139 | 16.9 | 2.9 | 6.7 |
| Cereal: granola, cooked [$^1/_4$ cup (60 mL) dry = $^1/_2$ cup (125 mL) cooked] | $^1/_2$ cup (125 mL) | 120 | 100 | 21.0 | 3.0 | 1.0 |
| Cereal: Grape = Nuts® | 1 cup (250 mL) | 110 | 430 | 92.8 | 11.0 | 0.7 |
| Cereal: oatmeal, cooked without salt | 1 cup (250 mL) | 240 | 132 | 23.3 | 4.8 | 2.4 |
| Cereal: puffed rice | 1 cup (250 mL) | 15 | 60 | 13.4 | 0.9 | 0.1 |
| Cereal: puffed wheat | 1 cup (250 mL) | 15 | 54 | 11.8 | 2.3 | 0.2 |
| Cereal: raisin bran | 1 cup (250 mL) | 50 | 144 | 39.7 | 4.2 | 0.7 |
| Cereal: Rice Krispies® | 1 cup (250 mL) | 30 | 117 | 26.3 | 1.8 | 0.1 |
| Cereal: Spoon Size Shredded Wheat®, approximately 50 biscuits per cup | 1 cup (250 mL) | 50 | 180 | 40.0 | 5.0 | 1.3 |
| Cereal: Shredded Wheat® biscuits | 1 whole | 25 | 90 | 20.0 | 2.5 | 0.6 |
| Cereal: sugar-coated corn flakes | 1 cup (250 mL) | 40 | 154 | 36.5 | 1.8 | 0.1 |
| Cereal: Wheat Chex® | $^1/_3$ cup (80 mL) | 28 | 110 | 23.0 | 2.0 | 1.0 |
| Cereal: wheat germ | 1 tbsp (15 mL) | 6 | 23 | 3.0 | 1.8 | 0.7 |
| Cereal: Wheaties® or Total® | 1 cup (250 mL) | 30 | 104 | 24.2 | 3.1 | 0.7 |
| Cheese: American | 1 oz (30 mL) | 28 | 106 | 0.5 | 6.3 | 8.9 |
| Cheese: blue | 1 oz (30 mL) | 28 | 100 | 0.7 | 6.1 | 8.2 |
| Cheese: brick | 1 oz (30 mL) | 28 | 105 | 0.8 | 6.6 | 8.4 |
| Cheese: brie | 1 oz (30 mL) | 28 | 95 | 0.1 | 5.9 | 7.9 |
| Cheese: camembert | 1 oz (30 mL) | 28 | 85 | 0.1 | 5.6 | 6.9 |
| Cheese: cheddar | 1 oz (30 mL) | 28 | 114 | 0.4 | 7.1 | 9.4 |

| Food | Unit | Weight (g) | Cal | CHO (g) | Prot (g) | Fat (g) |
|---|---|---|---|---|---|---|
| Cheese: colby | 1 oz (30 mL) | 28 | 112 | 0.4 | 6.7 | 9.1 |
| Cheese: cottage, creamed (4% fat) | $^1/_4$ cup (60 mL) | 53 | 54 | 1.4 | 6.6 | 2.4 |
| Cheese: cottage, low-fat (2% fat) | $^1/_4$ cup (60 mL) | 57 | 51 | 2.1 | 7.8 | 1.1 |
| Cheese: cottage, dry curd | $^1/_4$ cup (60 mL) | 36 | 31 | 0.7 | 6.3 | 0.2 |
| Cheese: cream cheese, 2 tbsp | 1 oz (30 mL) | 28 | 99 | 0.8 | 2.1 | 9.9 |
| Cheese: edam | 1 oz (30 mL) | 28 | 101 | 0.4 | 7.1 | 7.9 |
| Cheese: feta | 1 oz (30 mL) | 28 | 75 | 1.2 | 4.0 | 6.0 |
| Cheese: gouda | 1 oz (30 mL) | 28 | 11 | 0.6 | 7.1 | 7.8 |
| Cheese: gruyère | 1 oz (30 mL) | 28 | 117 | 0.1 | 8.5 | 9.2 |
| Cheese: monterey | 1 oz (30 mL) | 28 | 106 | 0.2 | 6.9 | 8.6 |
| Cheese: mozzarella, part-skim, low moisture | 1 oz (30 mL) | 28 | 79 | 0.9 | 7.8 | 4.9 |
| Cheese: mozzarella, whole milk | 1 oz (30 mL) | 28 | 80 | 0.6 | 5.5 | 6.1 |
| Cheese: muenster | 1 oz (30 mL) | 28 | 104 | 0.3 | 6.6 | 8.5 |
| Cheese: neufchatel | 1 oz (30 mL) | 28 | 74 | 0.8 | 2.8 | 6.6 |
| Cheese: parmesan, grated | 1 tbsp (15 mL) | 5 | 23 | 0.2 | 2.1 | 1.5 |
| Cheese: provolone | 1 oz (30 mL) | 28 | 100 | 0.6 | 7.3 | 7.6 |
| Cheese: ricotta, whole milk (13% fat) | $^1/_4$ cup (60 mL) | 62 | 108 | 1.9 | 7.0 | 8.1 |
| Cheese: ricotta, part skim milk (8% fat) | $^1/_4$ cup (60 mL) | 62 | 86 | 3.2 | 7.1 | 4.9 |
| Cheese: romano | 1 oz )30 mL) | 28 | 110 | 1.0 | 9.0 | 7.6 |
| Cheese: roquefort | 1 oz (30 mL) | 28 | 105 | 0.6 | 6.1 | 8.7 |
| Cheese: Swiss | 1 oz (30 mL) | 28 | 95 | 0.6 | 7.0 | 7.1 |
| Cheese: Velveeta® (cheese spread) | 1 oz (30 mL) | 28 | 82 | 2.5 | 4.7 | 6.0 |
| Cheese: 1% butterfat (Countdown®) | 1 oz (30 mL) | 28 | 40 | 3.6 | 6.6 | 0.3 |
| Cheese: 4-8% butterfat, processed (Breeze®, Chefs Delight®, Country Club®, Mellow Age®, Tasty®, Lite-Line®, low-fat DI-ET®) | 1 oz (30 mL) | 28 | 50 | 2.8 | 5.8 | 1.7 |
| Cheese: 5% butterfat, natural (St. Otho) | 1 oz (30 mL) | 28 | 49 | 3.1 | 9.1 | 1.1 |
| Cheese: 19-32% polyunsaturated fat (Golden®, Image®, Cheez-ola®, Dorman®, Nutrend®, Scandi®, Unique®) | 1 oz (30 mL) | 28 | 98 | 1.1 | 6.2 | 7.5 |
| Cheese: 23% polyunsaturated fat, low sodium, (Cheez-ola®) | 1 oz (30 mL) | 28 | 90 | 0.6 | 6.8 | 6.3 |
| Cherries: raw, sweet, unpitted | 10 whole | 75 | 47 | 11.7 | 0.9 | 0.2 |
| Cherries: canned, sweet, syrup-packed, pitted | 1 cup (250 mL) | 257 | 208 | 52.7 | 2.3 | 0.5 |
| Chicken: gizzard, all classes, cooked, chopped | 1 cup (250 mL) | 145 | 215 | 1.0 | 39.2 | 4.8 |
| Chicken: light meat, no skin | 1 oz (30 mL) | 28 | 51 | 0 | 9.2 | 1.4 |
| Chicken: dark meat, no skin | 1 oz (30 mL) | 28 | 52 | 0 | 8.3 | 1.8 |
| Chicken: dark and light meat, with skin | 1 oz (30 mL) | 28 | 70 | 0 | 7.7 | 4.2 |
| Chicken fat | 1 tbsp (15 mL) | 14 | 125 | 0 | 0 | 14.0 |
| Chicken liver: cooked, whole 2 x 2 x $^5/_8$" (5 x 5 x 2 cm) | 1 liver | 25 | 41 | 0.2 | 6.6 | 1.1 |
| Chick-peas: see Beans | | | | | | |
| Chocolate: bitter or baking | 1 oz. (30 mL) | 28 | 143 | 8.2 | 3.0 | 15.0 |
| Chocolate syrup (or topping): fudge type | 2 tbsp (30 mL) | 38 | 124 | 20.3 | 1.9 | 5.1 |
| Clams: canned solids (chopped or minced) | 1 cup (250 mL) | 160 | 143 | 3.0 | 25.3 | 2.4 |
| Cocoa: dry powder, medium fat, plain | 1 tbsp (15 mL) | 5 | 14 | 2.8 | 0.9 | 1.0 |
| Cocoa mix: 1 oz package | 1 pkg | 28 | 102 | 20.1 | 5.3 | 0.8 |
| Coconut: shredded, fresh, meat only | 1 cup (250 mL) | 80 | 277 | 7.5 | 2.8 | 28.2 |
| Cookie: commercial, chocolate chip, $2^1/_4$ x $^3/_8$" (3 x 1 cm) | 1 cookie | 11 | 50 | 7.3 | 0.6 | 2.2 |
| Cookie: commercial, fig bar, $1^5/_8$ x $1^5/_8$ (4 x 4 cm) | 1 cookie | 14 | 50 | 10.6 | 0.6 | 0.8 |
| Cookie: commercial, gingersnap, 2 x 1/4" (5 x .5 cm) | 1 cookie | 7 | 29 | 5.6 | 0.4 | 0.6 |
| Cookie: commercial, macaroon, 2 3/4 x 1/4" (6 x .5 cm) | 1 cookie | 19 | 91 | 12.5 | 1.0 | 4.4 |
| Cookie: commercial, marshmallow, chocolate-coated | 1 cookie | 13 | 53 | 9.4 | 0.5 | 1.7 |

| Food | Unit | Weight (g) | Cal | CHO (g) | Prot (g) | Fat (g) |
|---|---|---|---|---|---|---|
| Cookie: commercial, oatmeal with raisins, 2 $^5/_8$ x $^1/_4$" (6 x .5 cm) | 1 cookie | 13 | 59 | 9.6 | 0.8 | 2.0 |
| Cookie: commercial, peanut butter sandwich, 1$^3/_4$ x $^1/_2$" (4 x 1 cm) | 1 cookie | 12 | 58 | 8.2 | 1.2 | 2.4 |
| Cookie: commercial, sandwich, round 1$^3/_4$ x $^3/_8$" (4 x 1 cm) | 1 cookie | 10 | 50 | 6.9 | 0.5 | 2.3 |
| Cookie: commercial, vanilla wafer, 1$^3/_4$ x $^1/_4$" (4 x .5 cm) | 1 wafer | 4 | 19 | 2.9 | 0.2 | 0.6 |
| Cookie: prepared mix, brownies, 1$^3/_4$ x 1$^3/_4$ x $^7/_8$" (4 x 4 x 2 cm) | 1 piece | 20 | 86 | 12.6 | 1.0 | 4.0 |
| Cordial: apricot brandy, benedictine, anisette, crème de menthe, or curaçao | 4 tsp (20 mL) | 20 | 66 | 6.3 | 0 | 0 |
| Corn: canned, whole kernel | 1 cup (250 mL) | 165 | 139 | 32.7 | 4.3 | 1.3 |
| Corn: canned, whole kernel, low sodium | 1 cup (250 mL) | 165 | 152 | 29.7 | 4.1 | 1.2 |
| Corn: canned, cream style, low sodium | 1 cup (250 mL) | 256 | 210 | 47.4 | 6.7 | 2.8 |
| Corn chips | 1$^1/_4$ cup (300 mL) | 43 | 239 | 22.7 | 2.9 | 15.8 |
| Corn meal: white and yellow, enriched, degermed | 1 cup (250 mL) | 138 | 502 | 108.2 | 10.9 | 1.7 |
| Corned beef: see Beef | | | | | | |
| Cornstarch: not packed | 1 tbsp (15 mL) | 8 | 29 | 7.0 | 0 | 0 |
| Cottage cheese: see Cheese | | | | | | |
| Crab: fresh, cooked, not packed | 1 cup (250 mL) | 125 | 106 | 0.6 | 21.6 | 1.3 |
| Crab: canned solids, packed | 1 cup (250 mL) | 160 | 149 | 1.8 | 27.8 | 2.6 |
| Crackers: animal | 10 whole | 26 | 112 | 20.8 | 1.7 | 2.4 |
| Cracker: graham, chocolate-coated | 1 whole | 13 | 62 | 8.8 | 0.7 | 3.1 |
| Crackers: graham, sugar honey, 2 squares, 2$^1/_2$" (6 cm) each | 2 whole | 14 | 58 | 10.8 | 1.0 | 1.6 |
| Cracker: matzo | 1 whole | 30 | 118 | 26.1 | 3.2 | 0.3 |
| Crackers: melba toast | 3 whole | 12 | 60 | 9.0 | 2.0 | 2.0 |
| Crackers: melba toast, low sodium | 3 whole | 12 | 60 | 9.0 | 2.0 | 2.0 |
| Crackers: saltines, single crackers | 4 whole | 11 | 48 | 8.0 | 1.0 | 1.3 |
| Crackers: sandwich, cheese and peanut butter [1-oz (28 g) pack] | 4 whole | 28 | 139 | 15.9 | 4.3 | 6.8 |
| Crackers: Triscuit® | 1 whole | 4 | 21 | 3.0 | 0.4 | 0.8 |
| Cranberries: raw, chopped | 1 cup (250 mL) | 110 | 51 | 11.9 | 0.4 | 0.8 |
| Cranberry juice: cocktail, sweetened | 1 cup (250 mL) | 253 | 164 | 41.7 | 0.3 | 0.3 |
| Cranberry sauce: sweetened, canned | 1 cup (250 mL) | 277 | 404 | 103.9 | 0.3 | 0.6 |
| Cream: fluid, half and half (11.7% fat) | 1 tbsp (15 mL) | 15 | 20 | 0.7 | 0.5 | 1.7 |
| Cream: fluid, light (20.6% fat) | 1 tbsp (15 mL) | 15 | 29 | 0.6 | 0.4 | 2.9 |
| Cream: fluid, light, whipping (31.3% fat), approximately 2 cups (500 mL) | 1 cup (250 mL) | 239 | 699 | 7.1 | 5.2 | 73.9 |
| Cream: fluid, heavy or whipping (37.6% fat), approximately 2 cups (500 mL) whipped | 1 cup (250 mL) | 238 | 821 | 6.6 | 4.9 | 88.1 |
| Cream: sour | 1 tbsp (15 mL) | 14 | 31 | 0.6 | 0.5 | 3.0 |
| Cream: sour, imitation (IMO®, Wonder®) | 1 tbsp (15 mL) | 15 | 26 | 0.7 | 0.5 | 2.4 |
| Creamer: nondairy, powder, containing saturated fat (Creamora® and Coffee-Mate®) | 1 tbsp (15 mL) | 6 | 33 | 3.3 | 0.3 | 2.1 |
| Creamer: nondairy, liquid, containing saturated fat (Coffee Rich®) | 1 tbsp (15 mL) | 15 | 20 | 1.7 | 0.2 | 1.5 |
| Creamer: nondairy, liquid, containing polyunsaturated fat (Poly Perx® and Mocha Mix®) | 1 tbsp (15 mL) | 15 | 20 | 1.8 | 0.1 | 1.5 |

| Food | Unit | Weight (g) | Cal | CHO (g) | Prot (g) | Fat (g) |
|---|---|---|---|---|---|---|
| Cucumbers: raw, pared, whole | 1 whole | 280 | 39 | 9.0 | 1.7 | 0.3 |
| Dates: hydrated, without pits | 10 whole | 80 | 219 | 58.3 | 1.8 | 0.4 |
| Dessert topping: frozen, semisolid (Cool Whip®) | 1 tbsp (15 mL) | 4 | 13 | 0.9 | 0.1 | 1.0 |
| Dessert topping: nondairy, pressurized | 1 tbsp (15 mL) | 4 | 11 | 0.6 | 0 | 0.9 |
| Doughnut: cake type, plain | 1 whole | 14 | 55 | 7.2 | 0.6 | 2.6 |
| Doughnut: yeast leavened, plain | 1 whole | 42 | 176 | 16.0 | 2.7 | 11.3 |
| Duck: flesh only, raw, domesticated | 1 oz (30 mL) | 28 | 47 | 0 | 6.1 | 2.3 |
| Duck: flesh and skin, raw, domesticated | 1 oz (30 mL) | 28 | 92 | 0 | 4.5 | 8.1 |
| Eclair: custard filling with chocolate, 5 x 2 x 1¾" (12 x 5 x 4 cm) | 1 whole | 100 | 239 | 23.2 | 6.2 | 13.6 |
| Egg: chicken, fresh, medium | 1 whole | 50 | 79 | 0.6 | 6.1 | 5.6 |
| Egg: chicken, white, fresh | 1 white | 33 | 16 | 0.4 | 3.4 | tr |
| Egg: chicken, yolk, fresh | 1 yolk | 17 | 63 | 0 | 2.8 | 5.6 |
| Eggnog: commercial | 1 cup (250 mL) | 254 | 342 | 34.4 | 9.7 | 19.0 |
| Egg substitute: Egg Beaters®, 1 egg equivalent | ¼ cup (60 mL) | 60 | 40 | 3.0 | 7.0 | 0 |
| Egg substitute: Second Nature®, 1 egg equivalent | 3 tbsp (50 mL) | 47 | 35 | 0.5 | 4.7 | 1.6 |
| Egg substitute: Lucern®, 1 egg equivalent | ¼ cup (60 mL) | 60 | 50 | 2.0 | 6.0 | 2.0 |
| Eggplant: cooked, diced | 1 cup (250 mL) | 200 | 38 | 8.2 | 2.0 | 0.4 |
| English muffin: see Bread | | | | | | |
| Fig: raw, whole 1½" (4 cm) diameter | 1 small | 40 | 32 | 8.1 | 0.5 | 0.1 |
| Fish: see Catfish, Haddock, Halibut, Herring, Snapper, Flounder, Sole | | | | | | |
| Fish sticks: breaded, cooked, frozen | 1 oz (30 mL) | 28 | 50 | 1.0 | 4.7 | 2.5 |
| Flounder: raw | 1 oz (30 mL) | 28 | 22 | 0 | 4.7 | 0.2 |
| Flour: white, all purpose, enriched, unsifted | 1 cup (250 mL) | 125 | 455 | 95.1 | 13.1 | 1.3 |
| Flour: white, self-rising, enriched, unsifted | 1 cup (250 mL) | 125 | 440 | 92.8 | 11.6 | 1.3 |
| Flour: whole wheat | 1 cup (250 mL) | 120 | 400 | 85.2 | 16.0 | 2.4 |
| Frankfurter: 5 x ¾" (12 x 2 cm) | 1 whole | 45 | 139 | 0.8 | 5.6 | 12.4 |
| Frosting mix: prepared | 1 tbsp (15 mL) | 15 | 61 | 13.2 | 0.3 | 1.5 |
| Frosting: ready to spread (with animal or vegetable shortening) | 1 tbsp (15 mL) | 15 | 55 | 10.8 | 0.1 | 1.6 |
| Fruit cocktail: canned, solids and liquid, water-packed | 1 cup (250 mL) | 245 | 91 | 23.8 | 1.0 | 0.2 |
| Garbanzos: see Beans | | | | | | |
| Gelatin: dry, unflavored, 1 envelope | 1 pkg | 7 | 23 | 0 | 6.0 | 0 |
| Gelatin: sweetened dessert powder (JELL-O®) prepared with water, plain | ½ cup (125 mL) | 120 | 71 | 16.9 | 1.8 | 0 |
| Gelatin: low calorie, prepared with water | ½ cup (125 mL) | 120 | 8 | 0 | 2.0 | 0 |
| Gin: see Liquor | | | | | | |
| Gizzard: chicken, all classes, cooked, chopped | ¼ cup (60 mL) | 36 | 54 | 0.3 | 9.8 | 1.2 |
| Goose: flesh only, raw | 1 oz (30 mL) | 28 | 45 | 0 | 6.3 | 2.0 |
| Grapes: raw, seedless (Thompson) | 10 grapes | 50 | 34 | 8.7 | 0.3 | 0.2 |
| Grape juice: frozen concentrate, sweetened, diluted | 1 cup (250 mL) | 250 | 133 | 33.3 | 0.5 | 0 |
| Grapefruit: all varieties | 1 whole | 400 | 80 | 20.8 | 1.0 | 0.2 |
| Grapefruit juice: unsweetened, frozen concentrate, diluted | 1 cup (250 mL) | 247 | 101 | 24.2 | 1.2 | 0.2 |
| Greens, collard: frozen, cooked | 1 cup (250 mL) | 170 | 51 | 9.5 | 4.9 | 0.7 |
| Haddock: raw | 1 oz (30 mL) | 28 | 29 | 0 | 6.6 | 0.1 |
| Halibut: Atlantic or Pacific, broiled | 1 oz (30 mL) | 28 | 28 | 0 | 5.9 | 0.3 |
| Ham: see Pork | | | | | | |
| Hamburger: see Beef | | | | | | |

| Food | Unit | Weight (g) | Cal | CHO (g) | Prot (g) | Fat (g) |
|------|------|-----------:|----:|--------:|---------:|--------:|
| Herring: canned, solids and liquid, plain | 1 oz (30 mL) | 28 | 59 | 0 | 5.6 | 3.1 |
| Honey: strained | 1 tbsp (15 mL) | 21 | 64 | 17.3 | 0.1 | 0 |
| Honeydew: 7 x 2" (18 x 5 cm) wedge, $^1/_{10}$ of melon | 1 slice | 226 | 49 | 11.5 | 1.2 | 0.4 |
| Horseradish: prepared | 1 tbsp (15 mL) | 15 | 6 | 1.4 | 0.2 | 0 |
| Ice cream: rich, approximately 16% fat, hardened | 1 cup (250 mL) | 148 | 349 | 32.0 | 4.1 | 23.7 |
| Ice cream: regular, approximately 10% fat, hardened | 1 cup (250 mL) | 133 | 269 | 31.7 | 4.8 | 14.3 |
| Ice cream bar: chocolate-covered (Eskimo Pie) | 1 bar | 85 | 270 | 22.0 | 2.9 | 19.1 |
| Ice cream sandwich: 3 oz size | 1 whole | 85 | 238 | 35.8 | 4.3 | 8.5 |
| Ice cream cone | 1 cone | 3 | 11 | 2.3 | 0.3 | 0.1 |
| Ice milk: 5.1% fat, soft serve | 1 cup (250 mL) | 175 | 223 | 38.4 | 8.0 | 4.6 |
| Ice milk: 5.1% fat, hardened | 1 cup (250 mL) | 131 | 184 | 29.0 | 5.2 | 5.6 |
| Instant breakfast: dry powder, all flavors except eggnog | $1^1/_4$ oz (40 mL) | 36 | 130 | 23.4 | 7.2 | 0.9 |
| Jelly: sweetened | 1 tbsp (15 mL) | 18 | 49 | 12.7 | 0 | 0 |
| Knockwurst link: 4 x $1^1/_8$ (10 x 3 cm) | 1 link | 68 | 165 | 1.5 | 9.6 | 18.5 |
| Ladyfingers | 1 whole | 11 | 40 | 7.1 | 0.9 | 0.9 |
| Lamb: <7% fat, chop, leg, roast, sirloin chop (lean only) | 1 oz (30 mL) | 28 | 53 | 0 | 8.2 | 2.0 |
| Lamb: 10% fat, shank, shoulder (lean only) | 1 oz (30 mL) | 28 | 58 | 0 | 7.6 | 2.8 |
| Lamb: 20% fat, leg, roast, sirloin chop (lean and fat) | 1 oz (30 mL) | 28 | 79 | 0 | 7.2 | 5.4 |
| Lamb: 30% fat, breast, chop, rib (lean and fat) | 1 oz (30 mL) | 28 | 96 | 0 | 6.2 | 7.7 |
| Lard | 1 tbsp (15 mL) | 13 | 117 | 0 | 0 | 12.8 |
| Lemon: raw, 1 wedge | 1 slice | 18 | 3 | 1.0 | 0.1 | 0 |
| Lemon juice: canned, unsweetened | 1 tbsp (15 mL) | 15 | 4 | 1.2 | 0.1 | tr |
| Lemonade: concentrate, frozen, diluted | 1 cup (250 mL) | 248 | 88 | 22.9 | 0.2 | 0 |
| Lentils: see Beans | | | | | | |
| Lettuce: raw, crisp head varieties, chopped or shredded | 1 cup (250 mL) | 55 | 7 | 1.6 | 0.5 | 0.1 |
| Liquor: gin, rum, vodka, whiskey | 1 oz (30 mL) | 28 | 70 | 0 | 0 | 0 |
| Liver: see Beef or Chicken | | | | | | |
| Lobster: northern, cooked, $^1/_2$" (1 cm) cubes | 1 cup (250 mL) | 145 | 138 | 0.4 | 27.1 | 1.5 |
| Luncheon meal: see Salami, Bologna, Braunschweiger, Sausage, Turkey | | | | | | |
| Macadamia nuts: 15 whole nuts | 1 oz (30 mL) | 28 | 196 | 4.5 | 2.2 | 20.3 |
| Macaroni: enriched, cooked, hot | 1 cup (250 mL) | 140 | 155 | 32.2 | 4.8 | 0.6 |
| Mackerel: canned, solids and liquids | $^1/_4$ cup (60 mL) | 35 | 64 | 0 | 7.5 | 3.5 |
| Mango: raw | 1 whole | 300 | 152 | 38.8 | 1.6 | 0.9 |
| Margarine P/S > 3.1 (Promise® soft, Parkay® soft safflower, Hains® soft, Saffola® soft) | 1 tbsp (15 mL) | 14 | 102 | 0.1 | 0.1 | 11.5 |
| Margarine: P/S 2.6 to 3.0 (Mrs. Filbert's® soft corn oil, Promise® stick, Parkay® liquid squeeze) | 1 tbsp (15 mL) | 14 | 102 | 0.1 | 0.1 | 11.5 |
| Margarine: P/S 2.0 to 2.5 (Fleischmann's® soft, Chiffon® soft, Parkay® corn oil soft) | 1 tbsp (15 mL) | 14 | 102 | 0.1 | 0.1 | 11.5 |
| Margarine: P/S 1.6 to 1.9 (Fleischmann's® stick, Chiffon® stick, Meadow gold® stick) | 1 tbsp (15 mL) | 14 | 102 | 0.1 | 0.1 | 11.5 |
| Margarine: P/S 1.0 to 1.5 (Mazola® stick, Parkay® corn oil stick, Imperial® stick) | 1 tbsp (15 mL) | 14 | 100 | 0.1 | 0.1 | 11.3 |
| Margarine: low sodium, P/S 1.7 (Fleischmann's®, Mazola®) | 1 tbsp (15 mL) | 14 | 100 | 0.1 | 0.1 | 11.2 |
| Margarine: P/S <0.5, all vegetable fat (Kraft® all purpose stick, Swift all purpose stick) | 1 tbsp (15 mL) | 14 | 102 | 0.1 | 0.1 | 11.5 |
| Margarine: P/S <0.5, vegetable and animal or all animal (Gaylord® stick, Meadowlake® stick) | 1 tbsp (15 mL) | 14 | 102 | 0.1 | 0.1 | 11.5 |

| Food | Unit | Weight (g) | Cal | CHO (g) | Prot (g) | Fat (g) |
|---|---|---|---|---|---|---|
| Margarine: P/S 2.4, (diet tub Fleischmann's ® soft, Imperial® soft | 1 tbsp (15 mL) | 14 | 50 | 0.1 | 0 | 5.6 |
| Mellorine | 1 cup (250 mL) | 131 | 244 | 30.8 | 5.9 | 11.1 |
| Milk: skim (less than 1% fat) | 1 cup (250 mL) | 245 | 86 | 11.9 | 8.4 | 0.4 |
| Milk: low fat (1% to 2% fat) | 1 cup (250 mL) | 244 | 102 | 11.7 | 8.0 | 2.6 |
| Milk: whole (3.3% fat) | 1 cup (250 mL) | 244 | 150 | 11.4 | 8.0 | 8.2 |
| Milk, canned, evaporated, whole | 1 cup(250 mL) | 252 | 338 | 25.3 | 17.2 | 19.1 |
| Milk: canned, evaporated, skim | 1 cup (250 mL) | 256 | 200 | 29.0 | 19.4 | 0.6 |
| Milk: nonfat, dry powder, approximately 1 cup reconstituted | $^1/_3$ cup (80 mL) | 23 | 81 | 11.8 | 8.0 | 0.2 |
| Milk: canned, condensed, sweetened | 1 cup (250 mL) | 306 | 982 | 166.2 | 24.2 | 26.6 |
| Milk: chocolate drink, fluid, commercial made with whole milk | 1 cup (250 mL) | 250 | 213 | 27.5 | 8.5 | 8.5 |
| Milk: low sodium (whole) | 1 cup (250 mL) | 244 | 149 | 10.9 | 7.6 | 8.4 |
| Milkshake: chocolate | 11 oz (45 mL) | 311 | 369 | 65.9 | 9.5 | 8.4 |
| Milkshake: vanilla | 11 oz (45 mL) | 313 | 350 | 55.6 | 12.1 | 9.5 |
| Molasses: light | 1 tbsp (15 mL) | 21 | 52 | 13.3 | 0 | 0 |
| Mushrooms: raw, sliced, chopped, or diced | 1 cup (250 mL) | 70 | 20 | 3.1 | 1.9 | 0.2 |
| Mustard: prepared, yellow | 1 tsp (5 mL) | 5 | 4 | 0.3 | 0.2 | 0.2 |
| Nectarine: raw, $2^1/_2$ (5 cm) diameter | 1 whole | 150 | 88 | 23.6 | 0.8 | 0 |
| Noodles: egg, enriched, cooked | 1 cup (250 mL) | 160 | 200 | 37.3 | 6.6 | 2.4 |
| Noodles: chow mein, canned | 1 cup (250 mL) | 45 | 220 | 26.1 | 5.9 | 10.6 |
| Oil: coconut | 1 tbsp (15 mL) | 14 | 120 | 0 | 0 | 13.6 |
| Oil: cod liver | 1 tbsp (15 mL) | 14 | 120 | 0 | 0 | 13.6 |
| Oil: corn | 1 tbsp (15 mL) | 14 | 120 | 0 | 0 | 13.6 |
| Oil: cottonseed | 1 tbsp (15 mL) | 14 | 120 | 0 | 0 | 13.6 |
| Oil: olive | 1 tbsp (15 mL) | 14 | 119 | 0 | 0 | 13.5 |
| Oil: palm kernel | 1 tbsp (15 mL) | 14 | 120 | 0 | 0 | 13.6 |
| Oil: peanut | 1 tbsp (15 mL) | 14 | 119 | 0 | 0 | 13.5 |
| Oil: safflower | 1 tbsp (15 mL) | 14 | 120 | 0 | 0 | 13.6 |
| Oil: soybean | 1 tbsp (15 mL) | 14 | 120 | 0 | 0 | 13.6 |
| Oil: soybean-cottonseed blend | 1 tbsp (15 mL) | 14 | 120 | 0 | 0 | 13.6 |
| Oil: sunflower | 1 tbsp (15 mL) | 14 | 120 | 0 | 0 | 13.6 |
| Okra: frozen, cooked, cuts | 1 cup (250 mL) | 185 | 70 | 16.3 | 4.1 | 0.2 |
| Olives: ripe, whole, extra large | 10 whole | 55 | 61 | 1.2 | 0.5 | 6.5 |
| Olives: green, whole, large | 10 whole | 46 | 45 | 0.5 | 0.5 | 4.9 |
| Onions: green, raw | 2 med | 30 | 14 | 3.2 | 0.3 | 0.1 |
| Onions: mature, raw, chopped | 1 cup (250 mL) | 170 | 65 | 14.8 | 2.6 | 0.2 |
| Onions: mature, cooked, whole or sliced | 1 cup (250 mL) | 210 | 61 | 13.7 | 2.5 | 0.2 |
| Orange: Florida, medium | 1 whole | 204 | 71 | 18.1 | 1.1 | 0.3 |
| Orange juice: concentrate, frozen, unsweetened, diluted | 1 cup (250 mL) | 249 | 122 | 28.9 | 1.7 | 0.2 |
| Oysters: canned, 18 to 27 medium or 27 to 44 small | 12 oz (375 mL) | 340 | 224 | 11.6 | 28.6 | 6.1 |
| Oysters: raw, 13 to 19 medium or 19 to 31 small | 1 cup (250 mL) | 240 | 158 | 8.2 | 20.2 | 4.3 |
| Pancake: made from mix, 6 x $^1/_2$" (7 x 1 cm) | 1 cake | 73 | 164 | 23.7 | 5.3 | 5.3 |
| Peach: raw, pared, $2^3/_4$" (6 cm) diameter, approximately $2^1/_2$ per lb (450 g) | 1 whole | 175 | 51 | 12.9 | 0.8 | 0.1 |
| Peaches: canned, syrup-packed, halves, slices, or chunks | 1 cup (250 mL) | 256 | 200 | 51.5 | 1.0 | 0.3 |
| Peanut butter | 1 cup (250 mL) | 258 | 1,520 | 48.5 | 65.0 | 130.5 |

| Food | Unit | Weight (g) | Cal | CHO (g) | Prot (g) | Fat (g) |
|---|---|---|---|---|---|---|
| Peanuts: roasted, salted, 10 Virginia, 20 Spanish, or 1 tbsp chopped | 10 nuts | 9 | 53 | 1.7 | 2.3 | 4.5 |
| Pear: raw, Bartletts, 2½ x 3½" (6 x 8 cm) | 1 whole | 180 | 100 | 25.1 | 1.1 | 0.7 |
| Pear: canned, syrup-packed, with 1⅔ tsp (25 mL) liquid | 1 half | 76 | 58 | 14.9 | 0.2 | 0.2 |
| Pear nectar: canned | 1 cup (250 mL) | 250 | 130 | 33.0 | 0.8 | 0.5 |
| Peas: cow or black-eyed, canned, cooked | 1 cup (250 mL) | 255 | 179 | 31.6 | 12.8 | 0.8 |
| Peas: green, immature, canned solids | 1 cup (250 mL) | 170 | 150 | 28.6 | 8.0 | 0.7 |
| Peas: green, immature, canned solids, low sodium | 1 cup (250 mL) | 170 | 122 | 22.1 | 7.5 | 0.7 |
| Pecans: chopped or pieces | 1 tbsp (15 mL) | 7 | 51 | 1.1 | 0.7 | 5.2 |
| Pepper: immature, green, raw | 1 whole | 200 | 36 | 7.9 | 2.0 | 0.3 |
| Pepper: jalapeño, canned | 1 whole | 18 | 5 | 1.1 | 0.2 | 0 |
| Pepper: jalapeño, fresh | 1 whole | 18 | 7 | 1.6 | 0.2 | 0 |
| Pheasant: flesh only, raw | 1 oz (30 mL) | 28 | 46 | 0 | 6.7 | 1.9 |
| Pickle: dill or sour, large, 4 x 1¾" (10 x 2 cm) | 1 whole | 135 | 15 | 3.0 | 0.9 | 0.3 |
| Pickle: dill or sour, 3¾ x 1¼" (8 x 3 cm), low sodium | 1 whole | 65 | 7 | 1.4 | 0.5 | 0.1 |
| Pickles: fresh, sweetened (bread and butter), 1½ x ¼" (2 x .5 cm) | 2 slices | 15 | 11 | 2.7 | 0.1 | 0 |
| Pickle: sweet, gherkins, large, 3 x 1" (8 x 2 cm) | 1 whole | 35 | 51 | 12.8 | 0.2 | 0.1 |
| Pickle relish: finely chopped, sweet | 1 tbsp (15 mL) | 15 | 21 | 5.1 | 0.1 | 0.1 |
| Pie: frozen, baked apple, 8" (20 cm) diameter | 1 pie | 550 | 1,386 | 219.0 | 10.6 | 54.8 |
| Pie: frozen, baked, cherry, 8" (20 cm) diameter | 1 pie | 580 | 1,690 | 257.4 | 12.5 | 70.0 |
| Pie: mix, baked, coconut custard (eggs and milk), 8" (20 cm) diameter | 1 pie | 797 | 1,618 | 231.9 | 34.3 | 63.0 |
| Pineapple: raw, diced pieces | 1 cup (250 mL) | 155 | 81 | 21.2 | 0.6 | 0.3 |
| Pineapple: canned, syrup-packed, chunk, tidbit, or crushed | 1 cup (250 mL) | 255 | 189 | 49.5 | 0.8 | 0.3 |
| Pineapple: canned, water-packed, tidbits | 1 cup (250 mL) | 246 | 96 | 25.1 | 0.7 | 0.2 |
| Pineapple: in its own juice (no sugar added), 4 slices with juice or 1 cup (250 mL) with juice | 1 cup (250 mL) | 227 | 140 | 35.0 | 1.0 | 1.0 |
| Pineapple juice: canned, unsweetened | 1 cup (250 mL) | 250 | 138 | 33.8 | 1.0 | 0.3 |
| Plum: hybrid, fresh, 2⅛" (2.5 cm) diameter | 1 whole | 70 | 32 | 8.1 | 0.3 | 0.1 |
| Plums: canned, served with 2¾ tbsp (40 mL) syrup | 3 whole | 140 | 110 | 28.7 | 0.5 | 0.1 |
| Popcorn: no salt or fat added to popped corn | 1 cup (250 mL) | 6 | 23 | 4.6 | 0.8 | 0.3 |
| Pork: fresh, 10% fat, ham or picnic ham (lean only) | 1 oz (30 mL) | 28 | 61 | 0 | 8.4 | 2.8 |
| Pork: fresh, 13-20% fat, Boston butt roast, chop, loin, shoulder (lean only) | 1 oz (30 mL) | 28 | 71 | 0 | 8.0 | 3.9 |
| Pork: fresh, 23-30% fat, Boston butt, ground pork, ham, loin picnic, shoulder (lean and fat) | 1 oz (30 mL) | 28 | 103 | 0 | 6.6 | 8.3 |
| Pork: spareribs, 37% fat (lean and fat) | 1 oz (30 mL) | 28 | 125 | 0 | 5.9 | 11.0 |
| Pork: cured, 7-10% fat, ham or picnic ham (lean only) | 1 oz (30 mL) | 28 | 56 | 0 | 7.6 | 2.7 |
| Pork: cured, 13-20% fat, Boston butt, shoulder (lean only) | 1 oz (30 mL) | 28 | 75 | 0 | 6.9 | 5.1 |
| Pork: cured, 23-30% fat, ham, picnic, shoulder (lean and fat) | 1 oz (30 mL) | 28 | 93 | 0 | 6.4 | 7.2 |
| Pork: cured, 23-30% fat, ham, picnic, shoulder (lean and fat) | 1 oz (30 mL) | 28 | 93 | 0 | 6.4 | 7.2 |
| Pork: deviled ham, canned | ¼ cup (60 mL) | 56 | 198 | 0 | 7.8 | 18.2 |
| Potato chips | 10 chips | 20 | 114 | 10.0 | 1.1 | 8.0 |

| Food | Unit | Weight (g) | Cal | CHO (g) | Prot (g) | Fat (g) |
|---|---|---|---|---|---|---|
| Potatoes: fresh, boiled, diced, or sliced | 1 cup (250 mL) | 155 | 101 | 22.5 | 2.9 | 0.2 |
| Potato: fresh, baked in skin, 2⅓ x 4¾" (3 x 6 cm) | 1 whole | 202 | 145 | 32.8 | 4.0 | 0.2 |
| Potato: frozen, french fried, 4" (5 cm) strips (oven-heated) | 10 strips | 78 | 172 | 26.3 | 2.8 | 6.6 |
| Potato, sweet: fresh, baked, 5 x 2" (12 x 5 cm) | 1 whole | 146 | 161 | 37.0 | 2.4 | 0.6 |
| Potatoes, sweet: pieces, canned in syrup | 1 cup (250 mL) | 200 | 216 | 49.8 | 4.0 | 0.4 |
| Pretzels: extruded type, rods, 7½ x ½" (18 x 1 cm) | 1 whole | 14 | 55 | 10.6 | 1.4 | 0.6 |
| Pretzels: twisted type | 10 whole | 30 | 117 | 22.8 | 2.9 | 1.4 |
| Prunes: dried, uncooked, without pits | 10 whole | 102 | 260 | 68.7 | 2.1 | 0.6 |
| Prunes: dried, cooked, no added sugar | 1 cup (250 mL) | 250 | 253 | 66.7 | 2.1 | 0.6 |
| Prune juice: canned or bottled | 1 cup (250 mL) | 256 | 197 | 48.6 | 1.0 | 0.3 |
| Pudding mix: chocolate, regular, prepared with whole milk | 1 cup (250 mL) | 260 | 322 | 59.3 | 8.8 | 7.8 |
| Pudding mix: chocolate, instant, prepared with whole milk | 1 cup (250 mL) | 260 | 325 | 63.4 | 7.8 | 6.5 |
| Pudding mix: low calorie, dry form, 1 package (all kinds) | 4 oz (125 mL) | 128 | 100 | 24.0 | 0 | 0 |
| Pumpkin: canned | 1 cup (250 mL) | 245 | 81 | 19.4 | 2.5 | 0.7 |
| Quail: flesh and skin, raw | 1 oz (30 mL) | 28 | 48 | 0 | 7.2 | 2.0 |
| Raisins: natural, seedless, uncooked, whole, not packed | 1 tbsp (15 mL) | 9 | 26 | 7.0 | 0.2 | tr |
| Raspberries: raw, red | 1 cup (250 mL) | 123 | 70 | 16.7 | 1.5 | 0.6 |
| Rhubarb: frozen, sweetened | 1 cup (250 mL) | 270 | 381 | 97.2 | 1.4 | 0.3 |
| Rice: brown, cooked without salt | 1 cup (250 mL) | 195 | 232 | 49.7 | 4.9 | 1.2 |
| Rice: white, enriched, cooked without salt | 1 cup (250 mL) | 205 | 221 | 49.6 | 4.1 | 0.4 |
| Roll: hard, enriched | 1 roll | 25 | 78 | 14.9 | 2.5 | 0.8 |
| Roll: soft, enriched, brown and serve, or Parker House | 1 roll | 28 | 83 | 14.8 | 2.3 | 1.6 |
| Roll: enriched, hotdog, 6 x 2" (15 x 5 cm) or hamburger, 3½ x 1½" (8 x 3 cm) | 1 whole | 40 | 119 | 21.2 | 3.3 | 2.2 |
| Rum: see Liquor | | | | | | |
| Salad dressing: blue or roquefort | 1 tbsp (15 mL) | 15 | 76 | 1.1 | 0.7 | 8.0 |
| Salad dressing: blue or roquefort, low calorie | 1 tbsp (15 mL) | 16 | 12 | 0.7 | 0.5 | 0.9 |
| Salad dressing: French | 1 tbsp (15 mL) | 16 | 66 | 2.8 | 0.1 | 6.2 |
| Salad dressing: French, low calorie | 1 tbsp (15 mL) | 16 | 15 | 2.5 | 0.1 | 0.7 |
| Salad dressing: Italian | 1 tbsp (15 mL) | 15 | 83 | 1.0 | tr | 9.0 |
| Salad dressing: Italian, low calorie | 1 tbsp (15 mL) | 15 | 8 | 0.4 | tr | 0.7 |
| Salad dressing: mayonnaise | 1 tbsp (15 mL) | 15 | 101 | 0.3 | 0.2 | 11.2 |
| Salad dressing: mayonnaise, low sodium | 1 tbsp (15 mL) | 14 | 99 | 0.3 | 0.2 | 11.0 |
| Salad dressing: mayonnaise type (Miracle Whip®) | 1 tbsp (15 mL) | 15 | 65 | 2.2 | 0.2 | 6.3 |
| Salad dressing: mayonnaise type, low calorie | 1 tbsp (15 mL) | 16 | 22 | 0.8 | 0.2 | 2.0 |
| Salad dressing: Russian | 1 tbsp (15 mL) | 15 | 74 | 1.6 | 0.2 | 7.6 |
| Salad dressing: Thousand Island | 1 tbsp (15 mL) | 16 | 80 | 2.5 | 0.1 | 8.0 |
| Salad dressing: Thousand Island, low calorie | 1 tbsp (15 mL) | 15 | 27 | 2.3 | 0.1 | 2.1 |
| Salami: cooked, 4½" (10 cm) diameter slice | 1 oz (30 mL) | 28 | 73 | 0.4 | 5.0 | 5.8 |
| Salmon: fresh, broiled or baked, no added fat | 1 oz (30 mL) | 28 | 48 | 0 | 7.7 | 1.6 |
| Salmon: canned, drained, pink | 1 oz (30 mL) | 28 | 49 | 0 | 5.7 | 1.9 |
| Salmon: smoked (Lox) | 1 oz (30 mL) | 28 | 50 | 0 | 6.1 | 2.6 |
| Salt: table | 1 tsp (5 mL) | 6 | 0 | 0 | 0 | 0 |
| Salt pork | 1 oz (30 mL) | 28 | 219 | 0 | 1.1 | 24.0 |
| Sandwich spread: with chopped pickle | 1 tbsp (15 mL) | 15 | 58 | 2.4 | 0.1 | 5.5 |
| Sandwich spread: low calorie | 1 tbsp (15 mL) | 15 | 17 | 1.2 | 0.2 | 1.4 |

| Food | Unit | Weight (g) | Cal | CHO (g) | Prot (g) | Fat (g) |
|------|------|-----------:|----:|--------:|---------:|--------:|
| Sardine: canned in oil | 1 whole | 12 | 24 | 0 | 2.9 | 0.5 |
| Sauerkraut: canned, solids and liquid | 1 cup (250 mL) | 235 | 42 | 9.4 | 2.4 | 0.5 |
| Sausage, Polish | 1 link | 76 | 231 | 0.9 | 11.9 | 19.6 |
| Sausage, pork (uncooked) | 1 link | 13 | 49 | 0 | 2.4 | 4.2 |
| Sausage, Vienna: canned | 1 whole | 16 | 56 | 0 | 2.2 | 5.2 |
| Scallops: fresh, cooked, steamed | 1 oz (30 mL) | 28 | 32 | — | 6.6 | 0.3 |
| Sesame seeds: dry, hulled | 1 tbsp (15 mL) | 8 | 47 | 1.4 | 1.5 | 4.4 |
| Sherbet: orange | 1 cup (250 mL) | 193 | 270 | 58.7 | 2.2 | 3.8 |
| Shortening: animal | 1 tbsp (15 mL) | 13 | 111 | 0 | 0 | 12.5 |
| Shortening: animal-vegetable | 1 tbsp (15 mL) | 13 | 111 | 0 | 0 | 12.5 |
| Shortening: vegetable | 1 tbsp (15 mL) | 13 | 111 | 0 | 0 | 12.5 |
| Shrimp: 4½ oz (100 g) can drained | 1 cup (250 mL) | 128 | 148 | 0.8 | 31.0 | 1.5 |
| Shrimp: canned, small | 10 whole | 17 | 20 | 0.1 | 4.1 | 0.2 |
| Shrimp: fresh, cooked, 8 shrimp, each 3¼" (8 cm) long | 2 oz (60 mL) | 58 | 67 | 0.4 | 14.0 | 0.7 |
| Snapper: red or gray, raw | 1 oz (30 mL) | 28 | 26 | 0 | 5.6 | 0.3 |
| Sole: raw | 1 oz (30 mL) | 28 | 22 | 0 | 4.7 | 0.2 |
| Soup: canned, bean with pork, prepared with with equal volume of water | 1 cup (250 mL) | 250 | 170 | 21.8 | 8.0 | 6.0 |
| Soup: canned, beef broth, prepared with equal volume of water | 1 cup (250 mL) | 240 | 31 | 2.6 | 5.0 | 0 |
| Soup: canned, cream of celery, prepared with equal volume of water | 1 cup (250 mL) | 240 | 86 | 8.9 | 1.7 | 5.5 |
| Soup: canned, cream of chicken, prepared with equal volume of water | 1 cup (250 mL) | 240 | 94 | 7.9 | 2.9 | 5.8 |
| Soup: canned, cream of mushroom, prepared with equal volume of water | 1 cup (250 mL) | 240 | 132 | 10.1 | 2.4 | 9.4 |
| Soup: canned, chicken noodle, prepared with equal volume of water | 1 cup (250 mL) | 240 | 67 | 7.9 | 3.4 | 2.4 |
| Soup: canned, clam chowder, Manhattan style, prepared with equal volume of water | 1 cup (250 mL) | 245 | 78 | 12.3 | 2.2 | 2.2 |
| Soup: canned, minestrone, prepared with equal volume of water | 1 cup (250 mL) | 245 | 105 | 14.2 | 4.9 | 2.7 |
| Soup: canned, onion, prepared with equal volume of water | 1 cup (250 mL) | 240 | 65 | 5.3 | 5.3 | 2.4 |
| Soup: canned, split pea, prepared with equal volume of water | 1 cup (250 mL) | 245 | 145 | 20.6 | 8.6 | 3.2 |
| Soup: canned, tomato, prepared with equal volume of water | 1 cup (250 mL) | 245 | 88 | 15.7 | 2.0 | 2.0 |
| Soup: canned, vegetable beef, prepared with equal volume of water | 1 cup (250 mL) | 245 | 89 | 9.6 | 5.3 | 3.4 |
| Soup: canned, vegetarian vegetable, prepared with equal volume of water | 1 cup (250 mL) | 245 | 80 | 13.2 | 2.2 | 2.2 |
| Soup: dehydrated, onion, 1 package | ½ oz (45 mL) | 43 | 150 | 23.2 | 6.0 | 4.6 |
| Sour cream: see Cream | | | | | | |
| Soy sauce | 1 tbsp (15 mL) | 18 | 12 | 1.7 | 1.0 | 0.2 |
| Soybeans: mature seeds, cooked | 1 cup (250 mL) | 180 | 234 | 19.4 | 19.8 | 10.3 |
| Soybean curd (tofu): 2½ x 2¾ x 1" (5 x 5 x 1 cm) | 1 piece | 120 | 86 | 2.9 | 9.4 | 5.0 |
| Soybean seeds: sprouted, raw | 1 cup (250 mL) | 105 | 48 | 5.6 | 6.5 | 1.5 |
| Soybean seeds: sprouted, cooked | 1 cup (250 mL) | 125 | 48 | 4.6 | 6.6 | 1.8 |

| Food | Unit | Weight (g) | Cal | CHO (g) | Prot (g) | Fat (g) |
|---|---|---|---|---|---|---|
| Spaghetti: enriched, cooked with salt | 1 cup (250 mL) | 140 | 155 | 32.2 | 4.8 | 0.6 |
| Spaghetti with meat balls and tomato sauce: canned, rings | 1 cup (250 mL) | 250 | 258 | 28.5 | 12.3 | 10.3 |
| Spinach: frozen, cooked | 1 cup (250 mL) | 205 | 47 | 7.6 | 6.2 | 0.6 |
| Spinach: canned, low sodium | 1 cup (250 mL) | 205 | 53 | 8.2 | 6.6 | 1.0 |
| Squash, summer: fresh, cooked, sliced | 1 cup (250 mL) | 180 | 25 | 5.6 | 1.6 | 0.2 |
| Squash, winter: frozen, cooked | 1 cup (250 mL) | 240 | 91 | 22.1 | 2.9 | 0.7 |
| Steak: see Beef | | | | | | |
| Stew: beef and vegetable, canned | 1 cup (250 mL) | 245 | 194 | 17.4 | 14.2 | 7.6 |
| Strawberries: fresh, whole | 1 cup (250 mL) | 149 | 55 | 12.5 | 1.0 | 0.7 |
| Sugar: brown, packed | 1 cup (250 mL) | 220 | 821 | 212.1 | 0 | 0 |
| Sugar: granulated | 1 tbsp (15 mL) | 12 | 46 | 11.9 | 0 | 0 |
| Sugar: powdered (confectioners'), unsifted | 1 tbsp (15 mL) | 8 | 31 | 8.0 | 0 | 0 |
| Sunflower seed kernels: dry, hulled | 1 tbsp (15 mL) | 9 | 51 | 1.8 | 2.2 | 4.3 |
| Sweet roll: Danish pastry, without nuts or fruit, 4$\frac{1}{2}$ x 1" (10 x .5 cm) | 1 whole | 65 | 274 | 29.6 | 4.8 | 15.3 |
| Sweetbreads (thymus), beef | 1 oz (30 mL) | 28 | 90 | 0 | 7.3 | 6.6 |
| Syrup: cane and maple | 1 tbsp (15 mL) | 20 | 50 | 12.8 | 0 | 0 |
| Taco shell: fried tortilla | 1 whole | 30 | 146 | 19.7 | 2.6 | 5.6 |
| Tangerine: large, 2$\frac{1}{2}$" (5 cm) diameter | 1 whole | 136 | 46 | 11.7 | 0.8 | 0.2 |
| Tapioca: dry | 1 tbsp (15 mL) | 10 | 33 | 8.2 | 0.1 | tr |
| Tartar sauce | 1 tbsp (15 mL) | 14 | 76 | 0.6 | 0.2 | 8.3 |
| Tofu: see Soybean curd | | | | | | |
| Tomatoes: canned, solids and liquid | 1 cup (250 mL) | 241 | 51 | 10.4 | 2.4 | 0.5 |
| Tomatoes: medium, fresh, raw | 1 whole | 200 | 40 | 8.6 | 2.0 | 0.4 |
| Tomatoes: fresh, cooked | 1 cup (250 mL) | 241 | 3 | 13.3 | 3.1 | 0.5 |
| Tomatoes: canned, solids and liquid, low sodium | 1 cup (250 mL) | 241 | 48 | 10.1 | 2.4 | 0.5 |
| Tomato catsup: canned or bottled | 1 cup (250 mL) | 273 | 289 | 69.3 | 5.5 | 1.1 |
| Tomato chili sauce: bottled | 1 cup (250 mL) | 273 | 284 | 67.7 | 6.8 | 0.8 |
| Tomato juice: canned or bottled | 1 cup (250 mL) | 243 | 46 | 10.4 | 2.2 | 0.2 |
| Tomato juice: canned or bottled, low sodium | 1 cup (250 mL) | 242 | 46 | 10.4 | 1.9 | 0.2 |
| Tomato paste: canned | 1 cup (250 mL) | 262 | 215 | 48.7 | 8.9 | 1.0 |
| Tomato paste: low sodium | 1 cup (250 mL) | 262 | 215 | 48.7 | 8.9 | 1.0 |
| Tomato sauce | 1 cup (250 mL) | 240 | 80 | 18.0 | 3.0 | 0 |
| Tomato sauce: low sodium | 1 cup (250 mL) | 240 | 80 | 18.0 | 3.0 | 0 |
| Tortilla: corn 6" (15 cm) diameter | 1 whole | 30 | 70 | 13.4 | 1.6 | 0.6 |
| Tortilla: flour | 1 whole | 30 | 108 | 22.4 | 2.9 | 1.2 |
| Tuna: water-packed, canned, chunk style, solids and liquid, low sodium | 6$\frac{1}{2}$ oz (200 mL) | 184 | 234 | 0 | 51.5 | 1.5 |
| Tuna: oil-packed, canned (drained) | 4$\frac{1}{2}$ oz (135 mL) | 127 | 295 | 0 | 46.1 | 10.9 |
| Turkey: light meat, without skin | 1 oz (30 mL) | 28 | 45 | 0 | 9.3 | 0.7 |
| Turkey: dark meat, without skin | 1 oz (30 mL) | 28 | 48 | 0 | 8.5 | 1.5 |
| Turkey: light and dark with skin | 1 oz (30 mL) | 28 | 63 | 0 | 9.0 | 2.9 |
| Turkey bologna or franks | 1 oz (30 mL) | 28 | 71 | 2.1 | 3.5 | 5.4 |
| Turkey ham | 1 oz (30 mL) | 28 | 40 | 0.5 | 5.5 | 1.5 |
| Turkey pastrami | 1 oz (30 mL) | 28 | 34 | 0.8 | 5.2 | 1.6 |
| Turkey salami: with skin | 1 oz (30 mL) | 28 | 50 | 0.5 | 4.6 | 3.6 |
| Turnip greens: frozen, chopped, cooked | 1 cup (250 mL) | 165 | 38 | 6.4 | 4.1 | 0.5 |
| Turnips: fresh, cooked, cubes | 1 cup (250 mL) | 155 | 36 | 7.6 | 1.2 | 0.3 |

| Food | Unit | Weight (g) | Cal | CHO (g) | Prot (g) | Fat (g) |
|---|---|---|---|---|---|---|
| Veal: <6% fat, breast riblet, cutlet, leg, loin, rump, shank, shoulder steak (lean only) | 1 oz. (30 mL) | 28 | 40 | 0 | 5.7 | 1.7 |
| Veal: 10% fat, cutlet, leg, rump, shank, shoulder, steak (lean and fat) | 1 oz (30 mL) | 28 | 61 | 0 | 8.2 | 3.0 |
| Veal: 15% fat, loin (lean and fat) | 1 oz (30 mL) | 28 | 67 | 0 | 7.5 | 3.8 |
| Veal: 20% fat, rib (lean and fat) | 1 oz (30 mL) | 28 | 86 | 0 | 7.4 | 6.0 |
| Veal: 25% fat, breast riblet (lean and fat) | 1 oz (30 mL) | 28 | 89 | 0 | 4.7 | 7.7 |
| Vodka: see Liquor | | | | | | |
| Vinegar: cider | 1 cup (250 mL) | 240 | 34 | 14.2 | 0 | 0 |
| Waffle: made from mix, 7 x ⅝" (18 x 1.5 cm) | 1 waffle | 75 | 206 | 27.2 | 6.6 | 8.0 |
| Walnuts: English, chopped pieces | 1 tbsp (15 mL) | 8 | 49 | 1.2 | 1.1 | 4.8 |
| Water chestnuts | 4 nuts | 25 | 20 | 4.8 | 0.4 | 0.1 |
| Watermelon: diced pieces | 1 cup (250 mL) | 160 | 42 | 10.2 | 0.8 | 0.3 |
| Watermelon: 10 x 1" (25 x 2 cm) wedge | 1 slice | 926 | 111 | 27.3 | 2.1 | 0.9 |
| Whiskey: see Liquor | | | | | | |
| Weiner: 5 x ¾" (12 x 2 cm) | 1 whole | 45 | 139 | 0.8 | 5.6 | 12.4 |
| Wine: dessert (port, madeira, sweet sherry) | 1 oz (30 mL) | 30 | 41 | 2.3 | 0 | 0 |
| Wine: table (burgundy, rosé, white, dry sherry) | 1 oz (30 mL) | 29 | 25 | 1.2 | 0 | 0 |
| Worcestershire sauce | 1 tbsp (15 mL) | 15 | 6 | 1.4 | 0.1 | 0 |
| Yeast: bakers, dry package, scant tbsp | ¼ oz (10 mL) | 7 | 20 | 2.7 | 2.6 | 0.1 |
| Yogurt: skim, home recipe | 1 cup (250 mL) | 227 | 127 | 17.4 | 13.0 | 0.4 |
| Yogurt: plain, low fat | 1 cup (250 mL) | 227 | 114 | 16.0 | 11.9 | 3.5 |
| Yogurt: whole milk | 1 cup (250 mL) | 227 | 139 | 10.6 | 7.9 | 7.4 |
| Yogurt: with fruit (1-2% fat) | 1 cup (250 mL) | 227 | 225 | 42.3 | 9.0 | 2.6 |
| Yogurt: frozen (2% fat) | 1 cup (250 mL) | 227 | 244 | 48.0 | 6.0 | 3.0 |

This information is current as of this printing. Check the manufacturer's label for updated analysis.

A dash (—) indicates that data are not available. Trace (tr) indicates that a very small amount of the constituent is present.

Abbreviations used in this table are: tbsp = tablespoon; tsp = teaspoon; oz = pounce; lb = pound; g = gram; mg = milligrams; " = inches; Cal = calories; CHO = carbohydrate; Prot = protein.

# Index

Dr. Peter G. Hanson, M.D., may be reached at

Peak Performance Clinic
2535 S. Downing St., Suite 550
Denver, Colorado
80210
Tel.   (303) 733–2521
Fax   (303) 733–7682

For public speaking engagements:

Canada:   1–800–561–3591
USA:   1–800–323–9442